A LAW UNTO ITSELF

How the Ontario Municipal Board Has Developed
and Applied Land Use Planning Policy

The Institute of Public Administration of Canada
Series in Public Management and Governance

Editor: Peter Aucoin

This series is sponsored by the Institute of Public Administration of Canada as part of its commitment to encourage research on issues in Canadian public administration, public sector management, and public policy. It also seeks to foster wider knowledge and understanding among practitioners, academics, and the general public.

Networks of Knowledge: Collaborative Innovation in International Learning
Janice Stein, Richard Stren, Joy Fitzgibbon, and Melissa MacLean

The National Research Council in the Innovative Policy Era: Changing Hierarchies, Networks, and Markets
G. Bruce Doern and Richard Levesque

Beyond Service: State Workers, Public Policy, and the Prospects for Democratic Administration
Greg McElligott

A Law unto Itself: How the Ontario Municipal Board Has Developed and Applied Land Use Planning Policy
John G. Chipman

John G. Chipman

A LAW UNTO ITSELF

How the Ontario Municipal Board
Has Developed and Applied
Land Use Planning Policy

UNIVERSITY OF TORONTO PRESS
Toronto Buffalo London

© University of Toronto Press Incorporated 2002
Toronto Buffalo London
Printed in Canada

ISBN 0-8020-3625-2

Printed on acid-free paper

National Library of Canada Cataloguing in Publication

Chipman, John George, 1941–
    A law unto itself : how the Ontario Municipal Board has developed and applied land use planning policy / John G. Chipman.

(The Institute of Public Administration of Canada series in public management and governance)
Includes bibliographical references and index.

ISBN 0-8020-3625-2

1. Ontario Municipal Board.   2. Land use – Ontario – Planning.   I. Institute of Public Administration of Canada   II. Title.   III. Series: Institute of Public Administration of Canada series in public management and governance.

KEO872.C44 2002   346.71304'5   C2002-900800-X

This book has been published with the help of a grant from the Humanities and Social Sciences Federation of Canada, using funds provided by the Social Sciences and Humanities Research Council of Canada.

University of Toronto Press acknowledges the financial assistance to its publishing program of the Canada Council for the Arts and the Ontario Arts Council.

University of Toronto Press acknowledges the financial support for its publishing activities of the Government of Canada through the Book Publishing Industry Development Program (BPIDP).

To the memory of Joseph Aloysius Kennedy, Q.C., chairman of vision

Contents

LIST OF TABLES ix

PREFACE xi

Introduction 3

1 **The Genesis, Evolution, and Operation of the OMB** 10
   From Railway Regulator to Jack-of-All-Trades Tribunal 10
   The Structure and Operation of the OMB 12
   The Planning Appeal Role of the OMB 15
   The Emergence of the OMB as a Land Use Planning Tribunal 17
   The OMB as a Developer of Planning Policy 21

2 **The Evaluation of Interests** 26
   The Public Interest 28
   The Adverse Impact Test 36
   The Balancing of Public and Private Interests 45
   The Evaluation of Private Interests 49
   Has the OMB Been Captured? 51

3 **Policy Development in a Statutory/Judicial Context** 57
   The Adequacy of Approval Procedures 59
   Interference with Council Decisions 71
   The Adequacy of Decision Making 81
   Interim Control By-laws 91
   The Meaning of *Minor* 97

viii   Contents

4   Policy Development in a Public Policy Vacuum   103
    The Principles of Good Planning   104
    The Protection of Neighbourhood Character   112
    Commercial Competition   124
    The Provision of Social Housing   131
    Prematurity   136

5   The Treatment of Provincial Policy   145
    Sources of Provincial Policy   146
    The Pattern of OMB Involvement   150
    The OMB's General Approach   155
    Regional Planning Policy   160
    Urban Development and the Protection of Agricultural Lands   163
    Statements of Provincial Policy   172
    Matters of Provincial Interest   179
    Environmental Protection Policies   182
    Conclusions   184

6   A Tribunal Out of Time   191
    Theory v. Practice   192
    The OMB and the Province   193
    The Implications of Applying a Private Law Ideology   199
    A Forum for Sober Second Thought   202

APPENDIX: METHODOLOGY   209

NOTES   213

BIBLIOGRAPHY   241

INDEX OF CASES   249

GENERAL INDEX   251

Tables

I.1 General Decision Data   9
1.1 Planning and Non-planning Applications   21
2.1 Influence of Owners, Including Developers   53
2.2 Influence of Municipalities   54
2.3 Influence of Municipal Positions on Developers   55
3.1 Approval Procedures – Decision Data   60
3.2 Approval Procedures – Effect of Municipal Support   62
3.3 Interference – Decision Data   73
3.4 Decision Making – Decision Data   83
3.5 Decision Making – Municipal Support   85
3.6 Interim Control By-laws – Decision Data   92
3.7 Minor – Decision Data   99
4.1 Good Planning – Decision Data   105
4.2 Neighbourhood Character – Decision Data   115
4.3 Commercial Competition – Decision Data   125
4.4 Social Housing – Decision Data   133
4.5 Prematurity – Decision Data   138
5.1 Provincial Policies – Frequency of Consideration   151
5.2 Direct Provincial Participation   153
5.3 Approvals and Refusals   154
5.4 Food Land Guidelines Decisions   168
5.5 Provincial Policy Statement Decisions   174

Preface

The Ontario Municipal Board, established in 1906 as the Ontario Railway and Municipal Board, has been a fixture in the province for nearly a century, and has exercised a wide-ranging jurisdiction with respect to municipal and related matters. It has played a commanding role in the land use planning process in Ontario from the introduction of planning controls prior to the First World War to the present day. It was therefore a surprise to learn, when I began a study of the board several years ago, that its activities have received almost no attention in the literature of administrative law. That is not to say that the board has been ignored. The role it should play in the planning process, and the powers it should exercise, have been considered in studies undertaken by and for the province, but these have been focused on making recommendations as to what it should do, not on how it actually functions. Specific elements of the board's decision making have been regularly analysed by lawyers and other professionals who appear before it, but these have been papers written to assist practitioners in their day-to-day involvement with it. However, efforts to subject the board to more broadly based critical analyses of its decision making have been rare. This book endeavours to remedy this deficiency in part by examining one area of the board's operations: the manner in which it develops and applies planning policies, and in which it applies provincial planning policies, in making decisions on the matters brought before it.

The OMB is an administrative tribunal which, in the exercise of its planning jurisdiction, hears appeals from planning decisions made by municipal councils and local committees. Its job is to make decisions by evaluating the facts of each matter before it within a planning policy context. I undertook initially to examine that context to determine what planning policies the board has applied in its decision making, and the sources of those policies. As my study of these two areas progressed, I was drawn inescapably towards considering the implications of my findings as they pertain to the relationship between the province and the board, and to questioning the rationale for having the board continue to exercise a planning review mandate. The results of this study are contained herein.

I wish to thank Peter Silcox, Stanley Makuch, and John Bossons for their comments and advice. I must particularly thank Hudson Janisch for his ongoing support, guidance, and always positive criticism. The comments received from several unnamed reviewers have been of great value in identifying many shortcomings in the text, and I have endeavoured to respond to their concerns. Any remaining errors, discrepancies or ambiguities are mine alone. The Chair of the OMB, Douglas Colbourne, graciously allowed me access to some of the board's files, thereby providing an invaluable behind-the-scenes view of how a tribunal operates. The staff of the Ontario Provincial Archives were unfailingly helpful in locating and providing material. My thanks go most of all to my wife, Mary, whose constant support and encouragement made it possible for me to both undertake and complete this project.

A LAW UNTO ITSELF:

How the Ontario Municipal Board Has Developed and Applied Land Use Planning Policy

Introduction

This book is a study of the creation and application of land use planning policy by an important Canadian administrative tribunal, the Ontario Municipal Board. The board's most significant and time-consuming role is to consider appeals from the planning decisions of municipal councils and local boards. In carrying out this role, it has interpreted and applied provincial planning policies, and, of greater significance, it has developed and applied its own policies. The analysis herein of the board's decisions leads to the conclusion that, given the policies it has developed and applied, and the manner in which it has applied provincial planning policies, it has outlived its usefulness as a planning appeal tribunal.

There are several reasons, both of a general nature and specific to the OMB, for undertaking such a study:

The board plays a central role in the land use planning process in Ontario. It is therefore an important example of that unelected but omnipresent creation of the modern state, the *administrative agency*, a term which includes tribunals, boards, and commissions. As a former chief justice of the Supreme Court of Canada has said, the impact of such agencies on the lives of individual Canadians is great, and likely surpasses the direct impact of the judiciary.[1] While the manner in which they function has been the subject of a rich but often generalized and theoretical literature, there has been little published empirical scholarly analysis, from a legal perspective, of the manner in which they actually engage in their day-to-day activities. Court decisions are closely studied, but administrative decisions remain largely anonymous and unaddressed. This book is a partial redress of that imbalance.

The relationship between administrative agencies and the governments on whose behalf they are supposed to be acting and whose policies they are supposed to be implementing is a key feature of administrative law, and of public administration generally, because of the wide powers which these unelected entities can exercise within their areas of jurisdiction. It is thus important to understand the extent to which they act within the constraints of government policy, or, conversely, the extent to which they are able to develop and apply their own policies, based on their own perceptions of appropriateness, free of public accountability. A study of the manner in which the board deals with policy matters can therefore provide an instructive example of this relationship.

Another important consideration in administrative law and public administration is the manner in which agencies evaluate the interests of the parties affected by their decisions, and in which their decisions reflect the various interests of these parties. The board must take into consideration both the general public interest expressed in government policy statements and the very specific interests and concerns of the parties appearing before it: individuals, companies, community groups, business and professional associations, municipal and regional governments. An analysis of the policies upon which the board bases its decisions can provide a clear indication of the importance it accords to these various interests.

The OMB is unique in Canada in that it exercises a jurisdiction with respect to planning matters beyond that of similar tribunals in other provinces. It has for many years played a decisive role in overseeing planning in Ontario, as all land use planning decisions made by municipalities and local boards under the Planning Act[2] may be appealed to it, and it has the authority, generally speaking, to approve those decisions, refuse to approve them, or substitute its own decisions for them. Other provinces have boards which carry out some of these functions, but none exercises such an overarching degree of regulatory authority over planning activity as does this tribunal.

There is clearly a public interest in the role that the OMB plays in the planning process. Since the 1970s either it has been the direct object of study by the government[3] or its role has been considered in the context of studies directed towards changes in the planning process, and, more particularly, with respect to amendments to the Planning Act. These exercises have generally been normative in nature. Many observers have expressed widely varied views as to what jurisdiction the board should have and how it should carry out its duties. Many recommendations have been made, usually for procedural changes, but there has been little examination given to the matters it takes into account in arriving at its decisions. A study of the policies it has developed and applied in this respect will help fill this gap.

Summary of Organization and Findings

Chapter 1 provides a brief history of the Ontario Municipal Board, from its inception as a regulator of street railways to its present central role in the Ontario planning system, including an outline of its organization, membership, and manner of operation. Also introduced is the board's role as a developer of planning policy. Chapter 2 examines the manner in which the board has determined what it considers to be the public interest, and how it has balanced that with the interests of the various parties engaged in the planning process. It illustrates also how the board has developed an all-encompassing 'adverse impact' test based on the law of nuisance, and has applied this test in both balancing public and private interests and evaluating competing private interests. Chapters 3 and 4 consist of analyses of significant areas of the board's policy development. The former deals with policy development in several areas for which the board has received some statutory or judicial guidance, and shows how, in each instance, it has interpreted, applied, and occasionally extended its mandate in such a consistent manner that it can be said to have developed and applied planning policy. The latter includes similar analyses of several matters frequently addressed by the board, or referred to in its decisions, for which there are no expressions of public policy, but in which it is seen to have created and consistently applied its own policies. The importance of the adverse impact test to its decisions in these areas emerges as a central element of the analyses. Chapter 5 examines the manner in which the board interprets and applies provincial statements of planning policy, and shows how it has failed to accord priority to provincial policy and has often subordinated provincial policy to the application of its own policies. Chapter 6 presents conclusions arising from these analyses and questions the need to retain the board's planning review jurisdiction.

What this study reveals is that the OMB has developed and consistently applied policies which to a great extent invalidate the rationale for making local land use planning decisions subject to review by an appellate tribunal. Its policies have been focused on the impact of planning applications on those most immediately affected by them. Its major role has consequently been to substitute the opinions of its provincially appointed members for those of elected municipal councils, and, with respect to certain types of planning applications, of council-appointed committees. The board has most often had to make decisions without the benefit of guidance from provincial planning policies, but even where such policies have existed and been applicable, it has frequently accorded them no priority over municipal planning policy and has often subordinated them to the application of its own, internally generated policies.

There is another side to be sure. The board has, through its policies pertaining to municipal approval procedures and decision making, imposed standards of conduct that municipal councils ignore at their peril. Speaking more generally, the board's policy development has ensured an underlying consistency in its decision making, a matter of considerable importance to all parties engaged in the planning process. But this begs the question whether the appellate role played by a provincially appointed tribunal is required at all. My conclusion is that, with respect to its appellate planning jurisdiction, the OMB has become a 'tribunal out of time.' It bases its decisions largely on considerations of impact that can be equally well made by municipal councils, and, if planning is accepted as a political process, should be made by locally elected bodies. It largely fails to give priority to provincial planning policies. Its role is a vestige of Ontario's paternalistic regulation of municipal decision making. This may have been justified when municipalities were generally small and had little experience and expertise in planning matters, but it is no longer tenable in an era of larger municipalities whose councils and staff have considerable experience and expertise in dealing with planning matters.

The Use of Legal Ideology in the Analyses

The analyses herein are frequently placed within the context of legal ideology. The law is not neutral, but is an expression of the values and interests of dominant groups. A shared concept of what the law is, how it is supposed to operate, and who it is supposed to benefit may be termed an 'ideology' of law. Hutchinson states that ideology 'refers to the beliefs and assumptions which comprise a certain way of thinking about law at any given time.'[4] While ideology may be considered too strong a term, it does capture the idea that what is considered to be the most appropriate legal system is one reflecting shared beliefs in the proper distribution of power and influence in the larger society.

One line of analysis focusing on the ideology of law arises from critical legal studies, according to which, as Sossin states, 'laws and legal institutions operate as a form of ideology which, by obscuring the political quality of legal judgements, justify and legitimate existing arrangements of social, economic and political power.'[5] He suggests also that the application of this form of analysis leads to the conclusion that 'the role of administrative law in advanced capitalist society ... is thus to legitimate whatever administrative practice is deemed functionally necessary to perpetuate the status quo and at the same time suppress the emancipatory potential immanent in legal norms.'[6] McAuslan, another exponent of this approach, characterizes planning law in terms of three competing ideologies which provide a useful framework for analysing the board's decision making. He states that '[t]he law lacks objectivity and neutrality because it is based upon and is available to implement three distinct and competing philosophies or ideologies which dominate or conflict at different points of the system.'[7]

The private interest ideology is that 'the law exists and should be used to protect private property and its institutions.'[8] It is really the application of the nineteenth- and early twentieth-century common law, both by the courts and through the provisions of subsequent planning legislation, to protect landowners against actions taken by government or by other owners. The public interest ideology is one in which the law is seen as 'providing the backing and legitimacy for a programme of action to advance the public interest.'[9] Underlying this is a belief that the public interest can be determined and acted upon by government officials on the basis of their own views and assumptions. It results in laws designed for the benefit of these officials, laws which confer wide discretionary powers on them and either contain no provisions for appeal or provide for redress within the administrative system only. The third, which McAuslan terms the ideology of public participation, is that those who have an interest in a proposed planning application should have the right to participate in the making of a decision regarding it because they may be affected by it. He emphasizes, however, that substantive as well as procedural issues are involved here. The former would include not just input into the existing regulatory system, but also new government structures and processes which give more power to the governed and which ensure that greater attention is paid to social, community, and environmental matters and less to economic and technological ones.

McAuslan's categories of legal ideology, which he applies to the British planning system, are equally applicable to the Ontario planning system but with differing emphases. The public interest ideology plays a more limited role in this province, in that planning officials, particularly at the municipal level, have and are recognized as having an advisory rather than a decision-making role.[10] Public participation plays a greater role in the Ontario system to the extent that ensuring participation, public notice, and so on, appears to be the only explicitly recognized legal ideology. The analyses of the board's decision making, policies throughout this book reveal that it has supported this ideology, and, of even greater significance, that its decisions have to a great extent been based on policies of its own making, policies which reflect its strong commitment to the private interest ideology of property protection.

A Note on Methodology

The research methodology applied is described in the appendix. I note here only that three periods – 1971–78, 1987–94, and 1995–2000 – were chosen for review, and that 870 of the OMB's reported decisions for these periods were selected for analysis. Table I.1 provides a summary of the types of matters considered by the board, the positions of affected parties, and its disposition of them. The terms *supporter* and *opponent* refer respectively to parties either seeking or opposing approval of planning applications, whether they are technically appellants or respondents. The term *approval* means that an application was approved, either with or without modifications.

TABLE I.1
General Decision Data

	1971–1978		1987–1994		1995–2000	
	No.	%	No.	%	No.	%
Decision Total	348	100	321	100	201	100
Major application types						
Official plan	62	18	81	25	53	26
Zoning by-law	183	53	134	42	93	46
Interim control by-law	n.a.		19	6	9	4
Plan of subdivision	8	2	8	2	15	7
Severance	78	22	73	23	37	18
Minor variance	41	12	82	26	60	30
Major land use types						
Residential	224	64	208	65	118	59
Commercial	61	18	67	21	49	24
Industrial	20	6	12	4	8	4
Institutional	13	4	14	4	7	3
Agricultural	8	2	12	4	13	6
Recreational	13	4	11	3	8	4
Supporters						
Province	1	*	6	2	2	1
Municipalities	188	54	137	43	82	41
Owners	275	79	261	81	164	82
Neighbours	20	6	26	8	6	3
Opponents						
Province	16	5	43	13	7	3
Municipalities	131	39	122	38	75	37
Owners	30	9	50	16	29	14
Neighbours	240	69	179	56	111	55
Decisions[1]						
Approval	151	44[2]	151	47[2]	119	59
Refusal	193	56[2]	169	53[2]	82	41

1 Decision data is based on the analysis of 344 of the 1971–78 decisions and 320 of the 1987–94 decisions. The remainder were excluded because they either involved multiple applications and included both approvals and refusals, or they involved a motion, with neither approval nor refusal of the application itself.
2 Percentages based on 344 1987–78 and 320 1987–94 decisions.
* Less than 1%.

1

The Genesis, Evolution, and Operation of the OMB

From Railway Regulator to Jack-of-All-Trades Tribunal

The origins of the Ontario Municipal Board lie in the late nineteenth-century movement in the United States to regulate economic activities in which there was a strong public interest. The first fruit of this movement was the creation in 1885 of the Interstate Commerce Commission to regulate U.S. railways and other interstate carriers. The model established at that time was one of publicly appointed and funded commissioners given power to conduct hearings into the operation of the affected industry and to make binding decisions with respect to such matters as fares, freight rates, and standards of operation. This model was adopted in Canada in 1904 with the creation of the Board of Railway Commissioners to regulate federally incorporated railways. The commission model was adopted in both countries to meet political needs. In the United States, there were growing demands on Congress to regulate, as a matter of public interest, passenger fares, freight charges, and other elements of railway operations. Interprovincial railways in Canada were incorporated and regulated by federal statute, and such legislation was occupying ever greater amounts of Parliament's time and generating increasing political contention. It was believed that placing such matters in the hands of specialized agencies would serve to remove these time-consuming and contentious matters from the political arena, and that such agencies would develop expertise in their areas of jurisdiction, and would, as nonpartisan bodies, ensure that the interests of all affected parties were fairly addressed.

The same reasoning lay behind the creation in 1906 of the Ontario Railway and Municipal Board (ORMB), the predecessor to the OMB.

Provincial governments had jurisdiction under the British North America Act to incorporate intra-provincial railways, and, like Parliament, the Ontario legislature found itself devoting increasing amounts of time and political capital to railway legislation. As there was no general enabling legislation, each application for the incorporation of a provincial railway had to be dealt with by means of a specific bill. One area of particular concern was the incorporation and regulation of municipal street railways. Cities were growing rapidly during this period, and attempts to establish street railways to serve them were creating numerous technical, financial, and political problems. Once street railway companies were created and given generally monopolistic powers, disputes regularly arose between them, the public, and the councils of the municipalities they served with respect to such matters as the location of lines, fares, rental fees for the use of road rights of way, maintenance of roadbeds, and levels of service. It in fact became increasingly clear that the mere act of creating such companies was inadequate, and that there was an increasing public demand for some form of ongoing regulation. The provincial government concluded that the best method of dealing with both political and practical regulatory issues was to enact railway legislation that would have general application. Such legislation would preclude the need for individual bills and establish a tribunal that would have jurisdiction to regulate the ongoing operations of railways, particularly street railways, without the need to constantly bring matters before either the legislature or a committee of politicians. The Board of Railway Commissioners provided an obvious model for such regulation, and the legislature passed, in 1906, back-to-back legislation: the Ontario Railway Act, and the Ontario Railway and Municipal Board Act.

The latter act also gave the new ORMB other powers related to municipal utilities and financial management. In addition to the problems associated with urban transit needs, the provision of the newly emerging gas and electricity services was causing increasing political acrimony. As with the railways, the approach taken in Ontario was to incorporate private suppliers of these utilities. As a result there were frequent disputes between municipalities, the general public, and these suppliers relating to financing and provision of gas and electricity, which in turn led to increasing public demand for their ongoing regulation. Here too the commission model was seen as the answer. The use of the traditional private dispute-resolution methods was not considered appropriate because lawsuits were expensive and time-consuming, and because judges lacked the expertise to deal with the largely technical matters in dispute. Both provincial and municipal politicians thus concluded that '[t]he logical bodies to intercede between cities and companies seemed to be a provincially appointed panel of experts whose decisions would be appealable only on points of law.'[1] A close observer of these developments agreed, noting astringently that the new board would protect municipalities from 'the cupidity of railway and public utility corporations.'[2] In addition to these railway and utility issues, the province was becoming increasingly involved in approving such matters as municipal debt consolidation. These were all complex and time-consuming activities which lent further support to the idea of a tribunal separate from the legislature. It is thus clear that the prime reason for the board's creation was to remove from the shoulders of elected politicians and place on those of a tribunal composed of non-elected experts the time-consuming responsibility for decision making with respect to matters which were generally of a local nature and were often technically complex or politically contentious.

It is not clear how these various areas of regulatory activity came to be entrusted to a single tribunal. Humphries suggests that '[t]hese provisions for jurisdiction over municipal affairs appear to have been afterthoughts, possibly drawn into the legislation by the board's powers to direct municipalities on railway subjects.'[3] It is possible also that the proponents of provincial involvement in the regulation of other municipal matters saw the proposal to create an agency to deal directly with railway issues as an opportunity to piggy-back their issues onto the new agency. If so, they established an enduring precedent. The Ontario Railway and Municipal Board, which became the Ontario Municipal Board in 1932, was given responsibility for a changing yet increasingly wide range of regulatory matters. The ORMB's street railway regulatory responsibilities had largely atrophied by 1932. The financial collapse of many municipalities during the Depression years led to the OMB's being granted a wider jurisdiction over municipal affairs, particularly with respect to borrowing and other financial matters. For many years it regulated long distance trucking and municipal telephone systems. The board now exercises jurisdiction under more than 100 public and private statutes pertaining to municipal matters.

The Structure and Operation of the OMB

The structure of the OMB, and to a great extent its mode of operation, were established upon its creation as the ORMB in 1906 and have remained largely unchanged throughout the near century of its existence. It began life as a lean operation consisting of a chairman and two other members, and has grown gradually but considerably since then. In recent years the board has generally had between thirty and thirty-five members, including a chair and several vice-chairs. Lawyers have been most frequently appointed, with the majority of these having been in municipal or private practice and experienced in municipal or planning law. Other members have included accountants, engineers, planners, public administrators, citizen activists, and local politicians.

The members are all appointed by the provincial government. The selection of members has always been a political process, even though in recent years there has been an application and review procedure in place. Prior to 1988 they were appointed at pleasure, which effectively meant until retirement. Since then they have been appointed for three-year terms with a possibility, but no guarantee, of reappointment. Some of the short-term appointees have received more than one reappointment. On the other hand, members appointed by the New Democratic Party government during the early 1990s were not reappointed by the Progressive Conservative government that had come into power by the time their terms expired.

The board has from the date of its establishment as the ORMB operated in a court-like manner. While it has a general power under its enabling legislation, now the Ontario Municipal Board Act,[4] to make inquiries on its own initiative, it does not make use of this power and has dealt only with matters appealed or referred to it by interested parties. It employs panels of one to three members to conduct public, adversarial-style hearings throughout the province. The members base their decisions on the evidence, which is subject to cross-examination, and the arguments placed before them. Parties may be, and frequently are, represented by legal counsel. They may call witnesses as well as testify on their own behalf. The board has the authority to establish its own procedures, which it makes full use of. Decisions are made by the panel members who hear the evidence and argument. The board often conducts pre-hearing conferences for complex applications so as to gain some idea of the issues to be addressed and to determine the manner of conducting the hearings, but its decisions can be based only on evidence and argument submitted during the course of the hearings. It has also, in recent years, made increasing use of mediation to seek resolution of disputes without full hearings.

14 A Law unto Itself

The court-like nature of the board's mode of operation is reflected also in its staffing. The ORMB had a secretary, an engineer familiar with street railway operations who could advise members on matters before it. That has changed. The board now has a substantial staff, but these persons are engaged largely in administrative matters, such as scheduling and arranging for hearings and ensuring that the necessary preliminary documents are received, processed, and distributed. It does not have the equivalent of its original secretary, namely a staff member to review the substance of applications submitted to it or to provide members with advice, comments, or opinions with respect to the matters they are to hear and rule on. This function was partially met when the board received reports from the Ministry of Municipal Affairs concerning official plan amendments being referred to it by the minister, but the practice ended when referrals were abolished and replaced with appeals of official plans and amendments.

The OMB was created and continues to function as a quasi-judicial entity having jurisdiction to inquire into and make decisions regarding applications, appeals, and referrals; its decisions are final and not subject to judicial review except on questions of jurisdiction or law.[5] The board has played a dual role, depending on the nature of the jurisdiction being exercised. In dealing with such matters as property assessment appeals or appeals of compensation payable upon expropriation, it has acted in a judicial capacity and made its decisions on the basis of the evidence and the legal rights and liabilities of the affected parties. In dealing with land use planning matters it has played a more complex quasi-judicial role. As a planning tribunal it has been required to base its decision making on an evaluation of interests and the application of policy, however derived, rather than on the legal rights of individuals per se. Yet, as this analysis shows, the board has in fact based its decisions largely on policies derived closely from a legal, rights-orientated model. It is the study of this, and of the tension between the range of public and private interests it has been required to take into consideration, that forms much of this work.

It is ironic that, while one argument for using a tribunal rather than the courts is to avoid expensive and rule-ridden court hearings, the most frequent complaints about the OMB over many years have concerned the length, complexity, and cost of its hearings. This is partly a result of the nature of the planning process, as applications can often involve a wide range of planning issues and interests. But it reflects also the nature of the board's operation, which has been present since its

The Genesis, Evolution, and Operation of the OMB 15

inception, with its court-oriented focus on rules of procedure and on the formal presentation and testing of evidence by the parties.

The Planning Appeal Role of the OMB

The OMB exercises jurisdiction under more than 100 public and private statutes pertaining to municipal matters. For many years, however, its most time-consuming responsibility has been hearing appeals and referrals of local land use planning and planning-related decisions, made, with a few exceptions, under the Planning Act. This study is focused on this area of its decision making.

The board hears appeals or referrals from several types of planning decisions.[6] Official plans establish municipal policies for the use of land for private and public purposes, the provision of transportation facilities and water, sewage, and other services, as well as other matters considered important by municipal councils. To come into effect, they must be adopted by municipal councils and approved by either the Minister of Municipal Affairs and Housing or other municipalities given that authority. Until 1996, any person (using the term broadly to include incorporated entities and public bodies) could request that the approval authority refer to the OMB for its consideration all or part of an adopted official plan or amendment. Since 1996 the right to request a referral has been replaced with the right to appeal from the adoption of an official plan or amendment. A person requesting that council amend an official plan could, both before and after 1996, appeal to the board from council's refusal to do so. The board has wide powers. It may approve an official plan or amendment, refuse to approve it, or approve it with modifications it considers appropriate.

Zoning by-laws provide specific regulations for the use of land, governing matters such as the permitted uses, maximum densities, and building heights, as well as minimum lot sizes, lot frontages, and front, side, and rear yards. Any person can appeal to the board from the passing by council of a zoning by-law or amendment. As with official plans, a person requesting council to amend a zoning by-law can appeal to the board from council's refusal to do so. The board has the same powers of disposition as it does with respect to an official plan. It may also, on an appeal from the passing of a by-law, direct the council to repeal the by-law or amend it in accordance with the order of the board.

Interim control by-laws are a special variant of zoning by-laws. A council may within a defined area prohibit most types of development, otherwise permitted under the zoning by-law, for a period of one year, while it conducts studies and determines what the most appropriate development policies and zoning provisions for that area should be. The life of such by-laws may be extended for two additional one-year periods. Affected property owners may appeal to the board from the passing or the extension of an interim control by-law. The board has the same powers of disposition as it does with respect to a zoning by-law.

Minor variances from the provisions of zoning by-laws are changes that property owners may request, to enable them, for example, to build to a greater density, or build on a lot having a smaller frontage, than is permitted under a zoning by-law. Applications for minor variances are made to committees of adjustment – local boards established in each municipality and consisting of members appointed by the council. Any person having an interest in the variance may appeal to the board from the decision of a committee of adjustment, and the board may make any decision a committee could have made.

A plan of subdivision is a plan for the creation and servicing of lots, often a large number of lots, to permit the development of land. Plans of subdivision, and the conditions that must be met as part of their development, are subject to approval by approval authorities, either the Minister of Municipal Affairs and Housing or other municipalities given that authority. Until 1996, a person could request the approval authority to refer to the OMB for its consideration the plan of subdivision, if the authority refused to approve it, or any condition proposed by the authority. Since 1996 the right to request a referral has been replaced with the right to appeal either the refusal to approve or any proposed condition of approval. The board has the power to make any decision the approval authority could have made, and, when hearing an appeal of conditions, may determine the question as to the conditions appealed to it.

A severance, also known as a consent, is a division of a parcel of land into two or more parcels to permit the separate development of each. A severance may also be approved subject to certain conditions. Both the severance and the conditions require the approval of a committee of adjustment, or, in many areas, of a land division committee appointed by a county council. The referral and appeal provisions are substantially the same as for plans of subdivision. The board may make any decision that a committee could have made on the original application.

Other types of applications also appear in some of the decisions

The Genesis, Evolution, and Operation of the OMB 17

considered in this study. Municipal councils may have the authority to approve site plans governing design and other details of proposed developments, and the affected owners may appeal these decisions to the board. Other planning-related matters considered by the board – and occasionally referred to herein – are derived from legislative sources other than the Planning Act. A municipality must submit its proposed municipal debenture financing to the board for approval. Financing approval is occasionally sought for major public infrastructure projects, such as expressways, which raise significant planning issues. When these applications are appealed, the board must make what is essentially a planning decision as to whether the proposed projects should be permitted to proceed. The board also hears applications, made under the Aggregate Resources Act,[7] for the approval of licences to establish or expand gravel pits and other aggregate removal operations. These have a strong land use planning component, as the impact of these operations on their neighbours is an important consideration in deciding whether to give approval, and they often require official plan and zoning by-law amendments as well.

The Emergence of the OMB as a Land Use Planning Tribunal

Ontario did not regulate land development in 1906, and the Railway and Municipal Board was consequently given no responsibility in this area. This soon changed. It became apparent when the province first enacted rudimentary planning legislation shortly thereafter, that it intended municipal planning decisions to be subject to provincial review. The provincially appointed board, which was already developing experience and expertise in overseeing certain municipal matters, was the obvious vehicle for the conduct of this review.

Despite the great expansion and the numerous changes to the province's planning system over subsequent years, and the greatly increased scope and sophistication of municipal planning activity, the board's review role has remained a central feature of the planning process. This role developed gradually as successive provincial governments initiated and subsequently expanded the range of planning controls. When subdivision control within and adjacent to cities of 50,000 or more was introduced in 1912, plans of subdivision could not be registered until approved by the board, which could require any changes it considered proper to the number and location of streets and the size and shape of lots.[8] When cities, towns, and villages were given limited powers in 1917

18 A Law unto Itself

to prepare general municipal (official) plans, their adoption was made subject also to prior board approval, and the board could order any changes it considered necessary or proper.[9] Municipalities in 1921 were given limited authority to pass restricted area (zoning) by-laws, but these did not come into force until approved by the board in whole or in part.[10] Planning legislation remained largely unchanged from then until the first Planning Act was passed in 1946.[11] This established an entirely new planning system for the province, involving planning areas and planning boards, and created a process for the adoption and approval of official plans, with the now Ontario Municipal Board considering disputed plans referred to it by the Minister of Municipal Affairs. Restricted area by-laws, and the board's role in approving them, were brought into the Planning Act in 1959.[12] Since then the act has been amended on numerous occasions, to introduce new planning tools such as interim control by-laws, site plan control, and provincial planning policy statements, and to revise and expand approval, review, and appeal procedures. The requirement for prior board approval of official plans, zoning by-laws, and plans of subdivision has long been replaced by jurisdiction to hear appeals only, but local planning decisions remain subject to its review should anyone wish to challenge them. It appears that, despite concerns expressed at various times regarding aspects of the OMB's jurisdiction and manner of conducting hearings, there has been a general and ongoing acceptance that the board should be retained and should continue to carry out the role of overseeing local decision making that was assigned to it when the province first undertook land use regulation. As one significant interested organization has stated: 'The [Ontario Municipal] Association feels that the Ontario Municipal Board has served the Province and municipalities well, and is generally held in high regard throughout Ontario.'[13] A major government review of the board concluded that '[t]he OMB should continue as an independent appeal to review municipal legislation.'[14]

A salient feature of Ontario's planning legislation as it has evolved has been the limited guidance it has given to the parties engaged in the process – municipal councils and committees, owners, objectors, the board itself – with respect to anything other than procedural matters.[15] This was not the case under the initial planning legislation. The ORMB was directed as to the matters it was to consider in approving plans of subdivision, the items to be included in a general municipal plan, and the matters it was to consider in deciding whether to approve, repeal, or amend a restricted area by-law. With respect to the latter, the Municipal

The Genesis, Evolution, and Operation of the OMB 19

Amendment Act, 1921, stated that the board may approve the repeal or amendment of a restricted area by-law if satisfied that such is proper and expedient in view of 'the desirability of the proposed repeal or amendment in the interests of the owners of the land in the district affected and of the community as a whole.'[16] The latter criterion, while no longer found in the Planning Act, was significant because of its importance to the board's policy development activities. In an early decision, using language that would not be out of place today, the board refused to amend a restricted area by-law to permit a building in a residential area to be converted into apartments: 'There were, it is true, a number of duplex and semi-detached houses and quasi-public buildings within the area, but the great majority of the erections were high-priced detached private residences. The object of the legislation and original By-law was clearly to preserve the district and street as it was and to prevent their further deterioration ... the owners of the land in the district – who must be assumed best qualified to speak upon the matter – are overwhelmingly against the amendment.[17]

These words have captured what this study shows to have been the board's fundamental area of policy development: the evaluation of public and private interests, and, as part of this, the development and application of its adverse impact test. They show also that the genesis of the board's policy making may be found in its early history, and that the policy development analysed in the following chapters represents, not its beginning of such activity, but its continuing evolution in recent years as an activity central to the board's functioning. Even though the language of the 1921 act was eventually removed from planning legislation, its spirit remains a central directive in the board's thinking.

While the OMB may have been characterized overall as a quasi-judicial tribunal, its planning role has been administrative in nature. As the Ontario Court of Appeal stated in *Re Ashby* in 1934, 'The distinguishing mark of an administrative tribunal is that it possesses a complete, absolute and unfettered discretion and, having no fixed standard to follow, it is guided by its own ideas of policy and expediency.'[18] The Bureau of Municipal Research distinguished between its judicial and administrative functions: 'as an administrative agency the board decides according to public policy and expediency, whereas judicially these decisions are made according to legal rights and liability.'[19] Yet as the analysis of the board's decision making in the following chapters shows, it has to a great extent applied its own policy as opposed to externally derived public policy, and it has blurred the division between these two roles through the development of policies which are derived from legal concepts of 'rights' and 'liability.'

The board's history probably made the latter inevitable. As stated earlier, it was created as a judicially oriented tribunal, and has never departed from that model. Its initial role was primarily one of adjudicating disputes and giving formal approvals to by-laws and agreements with respect to the matters under its jurisdiction. However, it quickly established the trappings of a court, with adversarial hearings, the formal determination of parties, the application of rules of procedure, and rules of evidence, the examination and cross-examination of witnesses, and the issuance of legally enforceable orders. Its three initial members were lawyers and six of its seven chairs between 1906 and 1972 were lawyers. While only one of the six chairs since 1972 has been a lawyer, the board's legalistically oriented mode of operation has become firmly established. As noted above, the legal profession has been its largest single source of members. The history of the board's increasing involvement with planning matters has thus been an example of grafting what is recognized as an administrative, policy-oriented function onto a judicial, legally oriented tribunal without any corresponding changes to its mode of operation. It should therefore come as no surprise that its own planning policy development has been governed largely by this legal model, and has been directed primarily to the protection of private rights and interests as determined through its adversarial hearing process, rather than the exploration and development of public policy options. It is likely that the preponderance of lawyers throughout the board's history has had a significant bearing on the nature of its policy development. Legal training and practice have traditionally focused on the rights of and harms to individuals rather than on matters of public policy, and, as the following chapters illustrate, this has been to a great degree the focus of its policy development also.

Table 1.1 shows the number of planning and non-planning applications received by the ORMB and the OMB in selected years. It illustrates the emerging predominance of the former, yet greatly understates the amount of the board's time and the number of its resources devoted to planning matters. Planning applications constitute the great majority of applications for which public hearings are eventually required. The largest number of non-planning applications have been for the approval of municipal debenture financing, for which approval has been largely automatic and public hearings are rarely required. An ostensibly *municipal* tribunal has thus evolved into a

TABLE 1.1
Planning and Non-planning Applications

	1907	1925	1940	1959	1989–1990
Planning applications	–	76	116	1169	3346
Other applications	191	564	1057	3199	2409
Total applications	191	640	1173	4368	5755
Planning applications as % of total applications	0	12	10	27	58

N.B. 1989–90 is a 12-month period including portions of two calendar years.

predominantly *planning* tribunal, but in doing so this particular administrative leopard has not changed its spots. The process it follows in dealing with policy-focused planning matters is the same as it uses in exercising its judicially related functions.

The OMB as a Developer of Planning Policy

As the references to early planning legislation indicated, the Ontario Municipal Board has been given some policy direction from the beginning of its planning mandate. Legislation is itself an expression of policy, and a tribunal acting under legislative jurisdiction must be expected to follow it. But matters are not that straightforward. There is an extensive literature dealing with government regulatory activity. The early 'public interest' view was that regulation is imposed to protect the interests of the public generally, or at least the interests of identified public groups.[20] This was largely superceded by the 'private interest' view that, whatever the intended results, regulation serves primarily to benefit the industries being regulated.[21] Other writers have argued that the fundamental determinant of regulatory behaviour is the political context within which agencies operate.[22] Canadian writers have often taken the position that regulation is imposed to achieve certain public policy goals. This notion was central in early Canadian work on the subject.[23] Later writers have examined this theme more critically and have addressed the economic rationales for regulation, but have generally retained at least a partial public interest rationale.[24] It is implicit in this writing that there will be public policy for tribunals to follow, but two important questions arise. What if there is no public policy with respect to much of the work tribunals do? How are tribunals to apply public policy, which is of necessity expressed in general terms, to the many and varied factual situations they encounter in their day-to-day decision making?

It is inevitable that tribunals are involved to some degree in policy development, whether or not they acknowledge doing so. They receive varying amounts of direction through their legislative mandates and other expressions of public policy. Yet if they are not to engage in ad hoc decision making, they must develop and apply, in a reasonably consistent manner, policies which provide guidance to both their members and the participants in their hearings. The OMB has, since its inception, received little policy direction from the province. The limited substantive policy directions found in the early planning legislation were soon removed. The extensive development and application of land use regulation in Ontario in the past half-century has occurred within the context of legislation focused almost exclusively on the procedures to be followed in preparing, approving, and appealing official plans, zoning by-laws, plans of subdivision, and other land use control tools, and providing minimal substantive policy direction. The board has received only limited direction from provincial planning policy statements or the guidelines and internal policies of provincial ministries. It has made up for this lack of direction by actively engaging in developing and applying its own policies, yet has long exhibited an ambivalent attitude towards policy development. It has long recognized that it is responsible for the application of policy: 'The distinguishing character of these [administrative] powers is that the board is required and expected to make decisions based on upon policy and expediency within certain limits laid down in the legislature.'[25] The anticipated source of this policy is not often made clear, however. The board has at the same time recognized a need to show some consistency in its decision making. It has regularly stated that it is required to decide each case on the facts placed before it, but has also, at least by implication, recognized that it cannot make its numerous decisions on a purely ad hoc basis. In this, the board has trodden a fine line between recognizing the need for consistent decision making through the application of certain general principles or standards, while at the same time ensuring that these are not formally espoused as policy. As it stated in *IPCF Properties* v. *City of Windsor*: 'The board ... has often ... articulated "principles" that have proven helpful in addressing similar planning matters. The board, though, has always stood on the understanding that board decisions are not precedent-setting so as to bind later panels as does the rule of *stare decisis* in the courts.'[26] The position expressed here is accurate as to the very specific examples referred to, but it begs the question of the board's articulation and application of more general underlying principles such as policy.

There has been no question among participants in the planning process nor among knowledgeable observers that the OMB engages in policy development. There has been disagreement, however, as to the nature of that activity, its relationship with provincial policy, and, most importantly, the extent to which it should engage in policy development at all. As its then chairman, J.A. Kennedy, stated in his appearance before the Select Committee of the Legislature on the Ontario Municipal Board (the MacBeth Committee): 'I do not deny that we are making policy frequently because what we do is we apply government policy ... when there is no government policy on that particular subject we make our own.'[27] After hearing Mr Kennedy and other interested parties, the committee concluded that '[i]ts decisions are based on government policy, where known, but otherwise on its own policy formulated according to its interpretation of the facts and sentiments of people.'[28] In the following year, the Ontario Economic Council gave strong expression to a similar view, stating that 'over time, and in the critical areas where pre-established provincial policy is lacking (e.g., high-density residential development), the board's decisions have served to become provincial policy, rather than to elaborate such policy.'[29] The Planning Act Review Committee (PARC), engaged in a major review which led to the Planning Act, 1983, later gave a more circumspect expression of this position: 'It is clear that the board does attempt to establish criteria that can be employed in a consistent way throughout the Province and with respect to particular kinds of applications.'[30] Jaffary and Makuch, writing at the same time, put the matter more strongly, stating that '[t]he role of the board in protecting individual rights and making planning policy is indeed important.'[31] As we will see, however, the board has accorded less importance to provincial policy and more to its own than any of these comments might lead one to believe.

The OMB's right to develop and apply policies, or general principles by which to govern its exercise of discretion, is influenced by the statutory jurisdiction granted to it. The Planning Act, under which it has exercised its appellate jurisdiction, is and always has been primarily a procedural statute. Other than the limited direction provided by provincial land use policy statements and ministry guidelines, it must therefore be concluded that the legislature has left the determination of planning policies in the hands of municipalities, and, by extension, in the hands of those individuals and corporations seeking or opposed to changes in planning policies and land use designations. The legislature has similarly given no direction to the board as to what policy it is to bring to bear on these local decisions which come before it for review, again subject to the limited policy direction noted above. In dealing with official plan referrals, for example, the board's policy development scope is very broad. As an approving authority it is standing in the shoes of the minister. The Court of Appeal has held, in *Re Cloverdale and Township of Etobicoke*, that in this instance the board must decide whether a proposed change to a municipal plan is not only good for certain parties before it but is sound planning in the public interest.[32]

This language leaves unanswered, however, the question as to the source of such a policy, but if the board is to fulfil this mandate it must, in the absence of external sources of policy direction, formulate its own policies so as to ensure some consistency in its decision making. Its right to establish policy in hearing zoning appeals was articulated in *Hopedale Developments Ltd.* v. *Town of Oakville*. The Court of Appeal stated that '[t]he right of an administrative tribunal to formulate general principles by which it is to be guided is undoubted and has been considered upon many occasions in the Courts,' but it went on to say also that the board 'must not fetter its hands and fail, because a guide has been declared, to give the fullest hearing and consideration to the whole of the problem before it.'[33] *Hopedale* prevented the board from stating in advance the policies it was to apply, but did not prevent it from developing policies which, if not explicitly expressed as such, it has in fact applied with a substantial degree of consistency. As MacFarlane has noted: 'The *Planning Act* does not contain any policy statement on the purposes of zoning; however, the decisions of the Ontario Municipal Board, on zoning appeals or hearings on objections to municipal rezonings, have played a leading role in setting broad administrative policy guidelines for the approval of zoning or the ordering of a council to enact zoning by-laws which it has refused to pass.'[34]

The approach taken by the OMB in considering plans of subdivision, severances, and minor variance applications has a more substantial statutory basis. With respect to plans of subdivision, subsection 51(3) [now subsection 51(24)] of the Planning Act required it, and the minister or municipality having approval authority, to have regard to the matters specified therein. With respect to severances, subsection 53(1.1) [now subsection 53(12)] required it on an appeal to have regard to the matters listed in subsection 51(4). The Divisional Court established in *Re 251555 Projects Ltd. and Morrison* that the board, when considering a minor variance application under subsection 42(1) [now subsection 45(1)] of the Planning Act, must satisfy itself that the variance is minor and is desirable for the appropriate development or use of the property and that the general intent and purpose of the official plan and zoning by-law are maintained.[35] While the board is thus provided with a statutory framework for the consideration of these types of applications, there remain broad areas within which it can exercise a policy-making discretion.

As the following chapters show, the OMB has developed policies extending beyond these largely procedural statutory directives. Most importantly, it has developed policies, primarily substantive in nature, in many areas in which planning legislation is silent.

2

The Evaluation of Interests

Land use planning exhibits a tension between two often incompatible goals, the development of policy reflecting the interests of a substantial portion of the general public and the protection of the interests of private property owners. As a reviewer of the Planning Act Review Committee Report stated: 'Planning is not an independent operation: it seeks to adapt the decisions of private interests (which seek their own benefit) to the decisions of public interests (which seek public benefits). To a considerable extent these interests and benefits are in opposition, and though the public sector provides a framework for private decisions, it is limited to the extent which it can override them.'[1] The Ontario Municipal Board has had to seek the resolution of these opposites in carrying out its function as a planning appeal tribunal. It was given this role initially because provincial politicians believed that municipal decision making required provincial oversight, and they saw the board as a useful tool to enable them to avoid becoming directly involved in this. The board has retained this role for almost a century because successive provincial governments, whatever their political persuasion, have seen it as adding something to the planning process which they believed to be lacking at the municipal level. These 'value-added' arguments have included:

1 A concern that local decision making may be too political, in that certain groups and positions can be favoured for political reasons. A review process allows for the reconsideration of these decisions in a forum free of local political pressures.
2 The fact that negative impacts of planning decisions are often felt beyond municipal boundaries, but local decision makers may approve

development applications without giving consideration to their extramunicipal aspects. A review process allows other municipalities and their residents to have their positions and concerns regarding these proposals considered by a body whose viewpoint extends beyond municipal boundaries.
3 A belief that, while the policies of senior levels of government are often important in assessing planning proposals, municipal councils will vary greatly in the degree to which they consider such policies. A review process allows both the senior level of government and other interested parties to ensure that these policies are placed before an agency which will give them full consideration.
4 A belief that municipalities will be unable to give proper consideration to the views of various interests because they vary greatly in the expertise they can bring to bear in dealing with often complex planning matters, and because municipal councils often cannot devote the time required to consider policy and technical issues in detail. A review procedure allows for detailed consideration of such issues by a body possessing a degree of expertise and having sufficient time to consider them.

The argument is, in summary, that a review tribunal is able to evaluate the full range of public and private interests represented in the planning process more fairly, professionally, and comprehensively than municipal councils can be expected to.

The OMB's evaluation of the interests of the parties appearing before it and its balancing of these interests within the context of a larger public interest are central to the exercise of its planning review function. It has noted that 'Although the *Planning Act* does not explicitly address the matter of hierarchy of rights, the core idea that informs the Act throughout is a concern for the balancing of the different interests and therefore different rights.'[2] The board is engaged primarily in adjudicating disputes between parties supporting or opposing specific development proposals, but its role is not limited to evaluating, as in a matter before the courts, the interests of each of the parties. It recognizes that there is a public interest element to its deliberations; that as a provincially established review agency it has a duty to apply public policy considerations to its evaluation of these private interests. We consider in this chapter how the board has engaged in this balancing act, the matters it has considered important in doing so, and, by extension, the legal ideology that lies at the heart of its decision making.

28 A Law unto Itself

The Public Interest

A major reason for establishing a tribunal such as the OMB is to ensure that the public interest and public policy concerns are adequately addressed in the making of land use planning decisions, the implication being that local decision makers may not do so. The board has endorsed this view by regularly stating that it bases its decisions on whether or not applications are in the public interest. Yet matters are not that simple, and our analyses show that the board has accorded less importance to the public interest than its stated position would suggest.

The Application of the Group Public Interest Theory

Students of regulation have long recognized the existence of the public interest but have expressed disparate views as to what it consists of and how it is to be determined.[3] The OMB's manner of identifying this interest has reflected this discussion. Early writers on regulatory activity believed that there was an objective public interest that encompassed the entire body politic. Later recognition of problems with this notion led to the formulation of the 'interest representation' or 'group public interest' theory, which postulates that an understanding of the various parties having an interest in a regulatory matter, and an understanding of their interests and of the environment in which they operate, is critical to an understanding of regulation. There is not a general public interest; it is only the interests of different groups, which, if sufficiently influential in the context of the issues under regulatory consideration, come to be considered as the public interest.[4] This view was certainly accepted by the province's Planning Act Review Committee, which concluded that, while there might have in the past been commonly shared views which constituted a public interest, '[t]here is equally little doubt that in many places there is today a wide disparity in the values held by different groups in the community, and by different public agencies dealing with common situations.'[5]

The OMB has not hesitated to invoke the public interest in a wide range of situations, and to attribute great significance to the concept. It has stated that '[a]t the core of the board's decision-making in planning cases is, at all times, the determination of the public interest'[6] and that '[t]he board is obliged, when considering an application for consent, to have regard for whether the proposal is in the public interest ... this determination is at the heart of decision-making in planning cases.'[7]

The Evaluation of Interests 29

There can be little doubt that, in speaking of the public interest, the board has espoused the group public interest theory. It has not always been clear, however, which groups it has had in mind when deciding whether the approval of a matter before it is or is not in the public interest. As the following shows, its predominant public has been that represented by municipal councils, yet it has also treated more local, restricted groups as being those whose interests must be served. In doing this it has often blurred the distinction between public and private interests.

The Equation of the Public Interest with Municipal Interests

Given the nature of the matters before it, the board has frequently identified the decisions of municipal councils as the most authentic expression of the public interest. It has treated the residents of a municipality, as represented by its locally elected council, as the single most important interest group. More specifically, this has meant that it has generally accepted approved official plans, council decisions with respect to zoning by-laws, and the approval of plans of subdivision as the truest expressions of the public interest. The evidence from the review periods and the lack of deviation in its views throughout strongly suggests that this approach was well established prior to 1971 and has been followed consistently since then.

The board's community-oriented view of the public interest has been particularly evident in its treatment of official plans. These represent an amalgam of local and provincial interests. The Minister of Municipal Affairs or the upper tier municipality having authority to approve official plans must ensure that the policy statements based on the local interests contained in them are in general conformity with broader provincial policies and interests. During the period under study the board was at first required to consider an official plan referred to it by the minister, and, when so doing, it had the same powers as the minister to approve or refuse to approve the plan in whole or in part. The referral of official plans was later replaced with an appeal process, but the board's powers remained unchanged. Thus, when it is dealing with a referral or appeal of an official plan it is not determining a *lis inter partes*, but is standing in the shoes of the minister and addressing the same policy issues that he or she is required to consider. As it stated in *Maxine*: 'The Board's function in dealing with an Official Plan upon reference is much different than its function in determining other matters.

It goes without saying that the public interest is of paramount importance.'[8] The distinction drawn between official plans and other planning tools is noteworthy because, as we shall see, other interests come to the fore in the latter. Moreover, the board has generally looked to official plans, not to some objective standard beyond them, for substantive expressions of the public interest. It has shown a willingness to weigh expressions of provincial policy against community interests as expressed in official plan policies, and has often favoured the latter. It has stated, either directly or by implication, that the public interest is to be equated with the policies adopted by municipalities in their approved official plans.[9] It has held in shopping centre decisions, for example, that the public interest lies in protecting the existing planned commercial structure of municipalities, as set out in their official plans.[10] It has refused to approve the use of apartments in cellars to create additional affordable housing – although this use complied with the provincial Housing Policy Statement – because it contravened the city's official plan policy of prohibiting such accommodation.[11]

The OMB has given similar consideration to what constitutes the public interest in dealing with referrals of draft plans of subdivision. During the review periods the minister, and, upon referral, the board, have been required under the Planning Act to consider, inter alia, 'whether the proposed subdivision is premature or in the public interest.'[12] The implications of this requirement have rarely been addressed in subdivision referrals, but the board did give a clear statement of its position in *Caledon East*: 'The fact of approval from time to time by council and by agencies charged with the responsibility of expertly considering subdivisions is an important element in considering what is or is not in the public interest.'[13] The result, once again, was that a particularistic, contextual concept of the public interest prevailed.

Zoning appeals have been the type of application most frequently before the board, but its position with respect to the public interest has depended on the source of these appeals. Where they have arisen from the enactment of zoning by-laws, its position has been to treat the by-laws as being expressions of the public interest. Where, on the other hand, an appeal has arisen from the refusal or neglect of council to pass a requested zoning by-law, the board has tended to treat the appeal as a *lis inter partes*, and to direct its efforts towards balancing the public interests of the refusing municipality and the private interests of the proponent without giving special consideration to the former.

One might conclude from this constant invocation of the public inter-

The Evaluation of Interests 31

est, often without further explanation and in such differing contexts, that the OMB has held no consistent view of what constitutes it. I do not believe this to be so. The board has certainly found there to be a public interest in a wide range of planning-related matters, such as protecting the environment and good farmland, providing various forms of social housing, obtaining an orderly pattern of development, meeting pressures for urban growth, developing land rather than keeping it undeveloped for the benefit of neighbouring residents, retaining the character of established single-family residential areas, and protecting historic elements of the urban fabric. Through all this, however, it is evident that the board has regularly relied on the decisions and policies of elected councils as being the most valid expression of the public interest. To the extent that it has done so, it has given credence to a particularistic concept of the public interest.

The Limited Identification between the Public Interest and Provincial Planning Policies

In contrast to the above – a contrast made even more striking by the OMB's ostensible provincial role – the board has accorded limited priority to provincial policy interests. In the minority of its decisions in which it has had to address provincial policies it has generally given them no priority over the public interest as expressed in approved official plans or the interests of private property owners. It has noted the importance of the public interest as expressed through statements of provincial policy, but this has not prevented it from refusing in specific instances to approve applications supportive of such a policy, most frequently the province's affordable housing policy, where such approval would adversely affect the private interests of neighbouring property owners.

Provincial policy is expressed primarily through the enactment of legislation and the promulgation of policies relating to specific matters that the government considers of significant interest. The province has, through the Planning Act, created a system for the regulation of land use. This act is so fundamental to the OMB's exercise of jurisdiction that the board does not need to refer to its application of the act as being a matter of public interest. The board has nevertheless spoken of the public interest inherent in the carrying out of certain planning functions which take place under the act, such as ensuring that development occurs and that pressures for urban growth are met in an orderly fashion.[14]

One would expect a provincial tribunal to treat provincial policy as an important element of the public interest. What we find, however, is that the OMB has only occasionally addressed specific statements of provincial planning policy as being expressions of that interest. This has been to some extent a matter of circumstance, as the board has received through expressions of provincial policy only limited direction as to what the broader public interest might encompass. Yet it has occasionally addressed the application of such provincial policy as does exist. It refused, for example, to approve the redesignation in an official plan of one large area from industrial to residential. It established instead a direct link between local planning, provincial policy, and the public interest in stating that the municipality's official plan and zoning by-law were 'in the best public interest in view of the role that Barrie will be expected to assume under the general provisions of the [province's] Toronto-Centred Region Plan,'[15] and in determining that the existing official plan designation was best suited to the achievement of the goals of the provincial plan. It has frequently affirmed the primacy of the public interest in refusing to approve farm severances that were not in accordance with the province's Food Land Guidelines or the agricultural land protection policies of the more recently adopted Provincial Policy Statement. Its position in these instances has been that the public interest is to be found in both provincial policy and local policy as expressed in duly approved official plans, and it has given equal weight to both. Other than this, the board has occasionally indicated that achieving certain general goals, which may or may not have been expressed in provincial policies, was in the public interest. It has spoken of the public interest in the preservation of good agricultural land, as embodied in provincial policy, and in the provision of low-cost and senior citizens' housing. During the 1987–94 review period it occasionally noted that it was in the public interest to have regard to statements of provincial interest, and that it was not in the public interest to contravene provincial policies, but these comments were generally obiter and its decisions were based on other grounds.

The OMB has occasionally treated local council decisions as expressions of the public interest because there were no provincial expressions of policy for it to apply. The *Spadina Expressway* decision, while not a planning decision, provides an example of this. The proposed expressway for which borrowing approval was being sought was clearly a matter of great importance to the public at large, but at the time of the hearing there had been no statement of a provincial position as to its desirability.

The province took a position only when the board's decision to approve the funding was petitioned to the cabinet, at which time cabinet members concluded that proceeding with the scheme was not in the public interest. In another decision the board complained about a lack of provincial or regional policy directives, which forced it to make a decision about the proposed designation of large areas for commercial-industrial development with no indication of the planning rationale for such development. In both of these instances the board was faced with the problem that provincial policy, at least after the demise of the Toronto-Centred Region Plan, was of such a general nature as to be of little assistance in dealing with the specific matters before it.

The Public Interest and Good Planning

The OMB has been consistent in recognizing that a close relationship exists between the public interest and good planning. It has frequently spoken of these conjunctively, stating after reviewing evidence and arguments that a proposed development either is not in the public interest and does not represent sound and good planning, or the opposite. Yet it is unclear whether it has meant that the public interest and good planning are two ways of expressing the same concept; that is, that it is in the public interest that the principles of good planning be respected, or that good planning contributes to but is not the totality of the public interest. Despite the variability of the board's statements in this regard, the latter appears to be a better expression of its position. This was clearly stated in the *Ottawa-Carleton* decision in which it approved a comprehensive regional official plan: 'it is necessary to discuss and clarify the board's interpretation of the planning process and of good planning generally that have developed from the use of the *Planning Act* over many years and must be recognized as being in the interests of the public as a whole.'[16]

The board's partial equation of the public interest and good planning has led it to look beyond council decisions for an articulation of the public interest. It is regularly exposed to the opinions of another of its 'publics' – one that might be broadly identified as the planning community – as to what constitutes good planning. This is a very amorphous community, consisting as it does of public officials, planners, and other experts, lawyers, and other parties regularly engaged in the planning process. These persons regularly appear in support of or opposition to individual applications, and they are influential players in the approval process whose evidence and opinions with respect to good planning cannot but help influence the board's thinking.

The Uncertain and Shifting Distinction between Public and Private Interests

The belief that the public consists of all residents of a municipality, who speak collectively through their elected councillors, is implicit in the OMB's adoption of council decisions as best expressing the public interest. Yet it has been obvious in many situations that the group interest approach reveals other publics, and that the board has often identified the public interest on a less than municipal-wide scale. The ambiguity inherent in this approach has only been increased by its attempts to distinguish between what it is prepared to characterize as public and as private. At what point, for example, do the interests of a community within a municipality, whose interests the board tends to characterize as public, metamorphose into the interests of neighbouring property owners, which are clearly private? The point at which the public becomes private must be a matter of judgment. The board has adopted different positions in making such a judgment and in balancing these interests, which reflect its ambiguity in defining the public interest.

In the majority of the OMB's decisions the effect of development proposals on owners and residents in the immediate community has been in dispute, and the board has distinguished between the immediate interests of those identifiable persons and the broader interests of the larger community, as variously defined. Its concept of the public interest has thus included, at one end of a continuum, those matters it believes to be of general benefit to society as a whole, such as the protection of good agricultural land and of the environment generally, and the provision of social housing. At a step below this level of generality, the OMB has considered the public interest as being the interest of a broad but geographically defined community, such as the residents of a municipality. Occasionally this has been clearly enunciated. In *1099184 Ontario Ltd.* v. *London*, for example, the board approved the sale for development purposes of a redundant separate school site that was used informally as a neighbourhood open space. It held that the interests of the larger community, the tax paying separate school supporters, in obtaining the financial benefit of the sale outweighed the interest of the neighbourhood in having the property remain available for recreational use.[17] In most instances, however, what the board has meant by *community* has not been clearly stated. The relativistic nature of the board's general approach was clearly expressed in *Malahide*: 'Of even greater importance is the effect on the properties which make up the neighbourhood and the uses to which they are entitled because the interests of the individual ... may have to give way to the interests of the neighbourhood. Similarly, a major planning change may require that the special interests of an individual neighbourhood be sacrificed for the common good of the municipality as a whole.'[18]

In this instance the board determined that the community was the low-density single-family neighbourhood within which an apartment development was proposed and refused. However, which is the larger and which the smaller community has depended on the facts in each application. Moreover, as the board has been required to address the interests of ever smaller and more geographically circumscribed communities, on the scale of the neighbourhood or an individual street, it has found it increasingly difficult to distinguish between the public interest of a given socio-spatial association and the private interests of its individual members. It has not been able to resolve this matter in a consistent fashion. For example, in *Price Club* it referred to the benefits of a proposed major shopping centre to the citizens of Metropolitan Toronto, the City of Scarborough, and the Wexford community near which the development was to be located.[19] In other decisions the board has set the interests of the larger community in the provision of such public facilities as a hospital, hospital residence, bridge, police communications tower, and are active sports facility against the interests of the more immediate community, or neighbourhood, in which that facility was to be located.

At the other end of the public-private continuum are those decisions in which public and private interests have become indistinguishable. The board has held that there is a public interest in maintaining the character of neighbourhoods, particularly single-family neighbourhoods. It has, for example, refused to approve severances to create lots smaller than those generally found in the neighbourhood, even where such severances would meet the requirements of the zoning by-law, on the ground that such lots 'would not be compatible in aesthetic terms with the existing development and thus would not be in the public interest or the interests of good planning.'[20]

Given that the larger public interest has been, in such instances, expressed through the enactment of the zoning by-law, the only public which has clearly benefited from such a decision has been the property owners and residents adjacent to the subject properties. In other decisions, interests of this nature – the protection of neighbourhoods and the expectations of property owners residing in them that only certain types of development should be permitted in their community – have been treated as private interests. The board has rarely gone to the extreme of equating the public interest with the interests of private property owners. There is, however, a strong but implicit sense underlying many of its decisions, not that protecting the rights of landowners is in the public interest, but that one aspect of the public interest is protecting the rights of private property owners to the extent that this can be done without unduly compromising or failing to have adequate regard for those various other sources of the public interest, as reviewed above.

The only consistency shown by the OMB in this regard appears to have been geographical. As noted, it has tended to identify the larger community in a given situation as the public, even if this community is only an individual neighbourhood, and to identify the private interest with a smaller group within that community. The difficulty inherent in this approach, however, is that the normative distinction between public and private has tended to disappear, particularly as the board has identified ever smaller groups as the public. Yet it has regularly followed this empirical, uncritical approach, most noticeably in developing its policy for the protection of neighbourhood character.

The Adverse Impact Test

The Ontario Municipal Board's manner of carrying out its planning review function provides a clear example of how the structure and mode of operation of a tribunal affects the nature of its decision making. As we noted in chapter 1, the Ontario Railway and Municipal Board was modelled on the courts – formal hearings, a focus on procedure, decisions based on the evidence introduced by the parties, as filtered through cross-examination, emphasis on the recognition and protection of the legal rights of the parties – and this model has remained unchanged for almost a century. Given these elements, it is hardly surprising that the board has leaned heavily towards one element of planning – the protection of private property interests – to the detriment of the broader, public policy-related element. The fact that a high percentage of the planning appeals heard by the board pertain to disputes between limited groups of property owners has reinforced its tendency, which is inherent in its structure, to focus on private rights and interests.

The result has been the development by the board of a rationale for the protection of property interests, which I refer to as nuisance in a new guise. The driving force behind much of its decision making has been the protection of the right to enjoy the use of one's property without suffering adverse impacts. It is the imposition of an adverse impact on another person's property that constitutes the tort of nuisance, and that enables that person to claim damages from the offending party. The board cannot order the payment of damages, but it can prevent adverse impacts from occurring in the first place by refusing to approve development proposals.

A planning appeal tribunal might be expected to fully address both the public policy and private property protection elements of planning, and to seek to achieve an appropriate balance between them. While it must be mindful of the rights of property owners, it must evaluate those rights within the context of planning policies adopted by local and senior levels of government. Such is the theory, but my analysis of the OMB's decision making reveals that it has failed to achieve that balance. It has instead devoted itself largely to a private law-oriented approach by giving precedence to the property protection aspect of planning, even in the face of express statements of public policy. Yet in so doing it has demonstrated the ability of tribunals to expand the application of legal tests that enable them to adequately respond to matters within their jurisdiction. The board has thus adopted and transmuted the common law tort of nuisance, which is based on *measurable harm* to private property, into a remedy based on both *measurable and potential harm* to property, and, moving into the psychological realm, on the *perceived concerns* of property owners.

Common Law Remedies: Pros and Cons

Before we look more closely at the board's private law-based approach to resolving planning issues we should consider the utility and limitations of reliance on legal tools for this purpose. The common law remedies for the torts of private nuisance, trespass, strict liability, and negligence have long been available to property owners to enable them to prohibit, mitigate, or obtain compensation for adverse impacts imposed on them by the actions of other owners or occupants of land. Nor has the application of these legal tools been static. The law of nuisance, for example, has had a long and varied history, and new grounds for obtaining damages are constantly being accepted by the courts.

Whereas such grounds were originally limited to tangible physical harm to property, they have been expanded to include other kinds of interference, such as fumes, smoke, noise, and vibration, whose harm is imposed as much or more on the occupant as on the property itself. These legal remedies have some advantages over the administrative remedies. The courts have established certain standards of protection. The test 'in nuisance' is one of substantial interference with the use and enjoyment of land. Where a plaintiff can satisfy a judge that he has suffered harm, he is entitled to receive damages from the defendant, and occasionally to obtain an injunction to prohibit the continuance of the activity causing the nuisance. Where the defendant can show, however, that he is acting within a regulatory standard, as where factory emissions are within a limit permitted by a regulation, that is a sufficient defence, and a plaintiff will not be entitled to redress. Moreover, a property owner can act on his own to deal with adverse impacts by commencing legal action, and need not rely on a regulatory agency taking action to protect his interests.

These advantages are accompanied by significant drawbacks. As Lane notes,

> Private enforcement also leads to uncertainty and inconsistency. Each individual will seek to use the law to his own purpose. If the courts can only hear privately-initiated complaints, and must limit their action to the facts offered and remedies asked for, the ultimate application of the law by the courts will be based upon a distorted image of economic reality. It will develop in response to the random order in which individual cases reach final judgement, and by the innate selecting factor of litigation: ability to afford it.[21]

Even persons able to defend their interests might be dissuaded from engaging in a costly process having an uncertain payoff arising from the major uncertainties associated with invoking any legal remedy. While the courts have developed general tests for determining whether a compensable harm has occurred, it is difficult to foresee how these tests will be applied in any given situation. It is unlikely also that a set of agreed-upon judicial standards could be sufficiently well established and disseminated to avoid problems. This is compounded by the difficulties and costs that can be incurred in establishing proof that the harm has been sufficient to meet a legal test and thereby trigger a remedy. Under the current system of land use regulation, for example, a developer relies on expert planning and legal advice as to whether his proposal meets planning and zoning requirements. This can be complex and uncertain enough. Under a common law remedies approach, the developer might require in addition a legal opinion as to his degree of exposure to damages, but even thus armed a degree of uncertainty would remain pending the outcome of litigation. Such uncertainties are major cost elements in land development, and, given the nature of the activity, are likely to act as disincentives to development.

Another disadvantage of common law remedies is their reactive nature. They can be used only to redistribute costs by providing compensation for harms after they have come into being,[22] thus failing to meet a major goal of positive land use controls: preventing the establishment in the first place of land uses having potentially adverse impacts. These remedies are reductive because they can provide a (sometimes high) degree of protection from measurable physical harms, but are of little value in providing protection from the perceived or psychological impacts of private land use decisions. It is extremely unlikely, for example, that the residents of a neighbourhood of single-family homes could successfully bring an action in nuisance to obtain damages arising from the construction of apartment buildings in their neighbourhood, or to require their removal. Moreover, these remedies can provide no assistance to positive planning, to influencing the nature or distribution of land uses to achieve broader planning goals such as directing new urban development to areas where it can be most efficiently serviced and have the least adverse impact on other valued social goals – goals such as farmland or environmental protection, or encouraging land use and density changes in older built-up areas so that changes take place in a manner least disruptive to existing social and economic patterns.

The Adoption of a Common Law Test by an Administrative Tribunal

While the OMB's prime concern has been the protection of private property interests, the adverse impact test it has used to achieve this has proved, in its hands, to be most adaptable: the test is equally applicable in balancing both public and private interests and competing private interests, and in providing an underlying rationale for the more specific substantive planning policies reviewed below.

The private interest addressed by the board has been, at its most fundamental level, the right to enjoy one's property, a right which lies at the heart of the tort of private nuisance. There is a certain irony in this. The board has played a significant role in using public regulatory tools, zoning and other direct land use controls, to correct the deficiencies of private regulation as exercised through the courts. It has applied the central tenet of the law of nuisance: the protection of property from harmful impacts. In adopting this approach it could be said to have come full circle, but it has in fact gone beyond what the courts can accomplish. Because the board is a tribunal whose role is to apply policy, it has not been bound by the court-determined actionable causes of nuisance. It has acted firmly in the tradition of planning, epitomized by zoning and other similar direct land use controls, as being a means of public regulation to correct the deficiencies of private regulation as exercised through the courts. In so doing it has, by implication, adopted the concept of nuisance and applied it in its regulatory activities, but it has also had far more freedom than have the courts to develop and apply grounds of impact to meet the wide range of concerns which have arisen in the context of the planning approval process.

The OMB has regularly referred to such impacts as *shadowing, noise, traffic volume,* and *air, water,* or *soil pollution*. These are objectively measurable, for the most part, and underlie both the law of nuisance and land use controls. The one vitally important difference between the treatment of these impacts by the board and by the courts is that the latter are limited to addressing actual impact while the former has the jurisdiction, and the need as a planning review tribunal, to consider prospective impacts. In considering them, the board has addressed the following elements of impact that have extended its consideration of nuisance beyond that contemplated by the courts.

Credible Perception of Harm by Neighbours

In a private nuisance action a plaintiff can obtain damages or other relief only if he can prove that he has suffered harm. If the parties opposing a development application satisfy the board that they have reason to fear it will have an adverse impact on their properties, the onus for proving that such an impact will not occur shifts to the proponent.[23] The board has regularly accepted expressions of concern from neighbours regarding impacts, particularly where the latter are able to demonstrate that there are existing problems they claim will be exacerbated by the proposed developments. Common examples of such problems include traffic and parking concerns, the adequacy of public services to meet current needs, the adequacy of groundwater supplies, and the ability of soils to handle additional sewage from septic systems. The board has recognized that 'it is a valid function of planning ... to recognize the objectors' perception of harm.'[24] It has noted also, however, that the concern must relate to specific feared impacts: that its obligation 'is to decide on the evidence as to impacts, and not to provide a referendum.'[25] Objectors must give reasons why a proposal is unacceptable, not just assert that it is.

The interests the board has recognized have covered a wide spectrum. They have frequently been tangible, thus corresponding closely to the types of harm required to support nuisance actions. Beyond these, interests considered worthy of protection have depended on the type of land uses affected. Where such uses have been residential, the board has addressed more subtle interests. These may be termed perceptual interests, such as the effect of shadowing, or of a building being considered out of scale because it looms over its neighbours, or, on a larger scale, traffic congestion affecting a larger area than the immediate vicinity. Impacts of this nature can often be measured. Shadows that would be cast at different times of day and in different seasons can be precisely measured. Vehicle trips likely to be generated by a proposed development can be calculated with a reasonable degree of accuracy. Yet these impacts can be subjective also. One person may consider the shadowing of her property by a new building a matter of real concern, while another might respond with indifference.

These interests merge into what might best be described as psychological interests, which combine varying elements of a desire to preserve the environment, amenities, and lifestyle one has achieved with an underlying fear of psychological and economic loss, the latter expressed through loss of property value, if these 'goods' are threatened by proposed development. These interests and concerns may be highly subjective, but they can be real enough to those holding them, even if they are not actionable in the courts. Where neighbouring uses have been commercial, industrial, or agricultural, the affected interests have been more directly economic. Commercial neighbours have been concerned about competition from proposed shopping facilities. Industrial and agricultural neighbours have been concerned that permitting new residential development adjacent to them may lead to pressure from the new residents to curtail their operations. While the board does not deal with these economic interests specifically, it does so in the context of making what it considers appropriate planning decisions.

The Expectations Principle

The OMB has responded to these various interests largely through the application of its adverse impact test: a determination of whether the impact of a proposed development on neighbouring properties is so adverse as to outweigh its benefits. Proof of impact has not been required; credible perception has been enough. In dealing with tangible interests, this determination can be a relatively straightforward matter of assessing the evidence. The evaluation of perceptual interests is similar, at least to the extent that impacts affecting these interests can be measured. Where they cannot be measured, and where the psychological interests of neighbours are an issue, the board has been faced with the more difficult task of establishing a rationale for its evaluation of such interests. What harm will arise, for example, as a result of permitting a lot or dwelling within a residential area that will be smaller than that of its neighbours, or by permitting townhouses that will be no higher than adjacent single-family homes?

The board's answer has been the development and application of the expectations principle. The underlying rationale has been that persons who have purchased property in an area where certain uses are permitted and standards imposed have a right to expect that these uses and standards will be maintained – except where the board is satisfied that a proposed change is desirable in its own right and will not impose an unacceptably adverse impact on existing uses. This principle is expressed in widely varying contexts, and, because it involves a balancing of interests, whether a decision favours proponents or opponents will depend on the facts and the quality of the evidence presented in each case. While it is infrequently given explicit expression, it is, in my view, a principle which is implicit in many of the board's decisions, a principle arising from its private law orientation, which enables it to apply the double-onus test described below even where objective indicators of harm are lacking.

The expectations principle and the limits of its application were addressed in *Chedoke*. The board stated that the fulfillment of expectations required that

1 The circumstances and interests of the different publics originally involved and currently involved remains essentially the same after the present designation and zoning came into effect ...
2 The character of the existing built and natural environments remains essentially the same after the designation and zoning came into effect.

If any one of the above two conditions change, then the expectation is unlikely to be fulfilled.[26] Yet the board ensures that such expectations

The Evaluation of Interests 43

will be fulfilled by often refusing to approve development proposals which will have the effect of changing the character of the existing environments, particularly where an environment is one of single-family homes.

The Majority v. Minority Rights Test

During and for a short period after the tenure of J.A. Kennedy as chairman (1960–72), the board sought to balance the rights of the majority, as represented by council decisions, with the rights of a minority, those persons adversely affected by such decisions. This appeared to be a public law-oriented test of interest evaluation, but it was essentially a variant of the board's private law orientation. Its 1969 annual report asserted that

> The function of the board in this area, which consists of reviewing decisions by local elected representatives, is to protect the rights of individuals and minorities. Democracy is by definition the rule of the majority, but if democracy is to promote justice it must have a built-in mechanism to protect the rights of the individual, the minority. This is basically the role of the board under The Planning Act.[27]

The role here being articulated for the board was that of 'ombudsman,' the protector of the individual or minority against arbitrary or harmful decisions of public authorities. This approach was addressed in a number of important decisions during the 1971–78 review period, although never adopted in a pure form. In the *Spadina Expressway* decision the board considered the matter of majority versus minority interests but sought to achieve a more even balance between the two: 'There is, of course, a duty on this board to protect minority rights, but not at the expense of majority interests. Surely it is axiomatic that when there is a conflict between minority and majority interests, the plan which favours the common weal is paramount.'[28] In the *Toronto-Metro Centre* decision the board distinguished between dealing with zoning and official plan matters:

> In exercising this jurisdiction under the *Planning Act* with respect to the approval of land use (zoning) by-laws this board has conceived its duty primarily to be to protect the rights of individuals and minorities, if they are being overlooked in measures intended to serve the greatest common

good. In Official Plan matters such as these, however, the function of the board is somewhat different. The Court has ruled, as must be evident from the statute, that in Official Plan matters this board 'stands in the shoes' of the Minister. The function of the Minister is not only to protect the rights of individuals and minorities but also to see that the provisions of these plans follow sound planning principles and are for the benefit of the community.[29]

In another decision the board held that ratepayer organizations had too much influence over the council, stating that '[w]hile public participation in planning debates is not to be discouraged, it is wrong in our view that decisions finally made be based on narrow interests and not the wider objectives as expressed in an Official Plan.'[30]

The test expressed in these comments appears to be the recognition of an obligation to address the public interest. Yet, when examined more closely, it emerges as a variant of the OMB's dominant, private law-oriented approach to balancing public and private interests. It was articulated in cases involving major public decisions in Toronto: the approval of funding for an urban expressway, a huge redevelopment project involving lands adjacent to the central business district, and the approval of restrictive planning policies affecting the entire central area of the city. There was clearly a general public interest in the outcome and there were broadly based 'minorities' in opposition. Yet these minorities were not opposed solely for the public good. They also had direct interests as property owners, either in the protection of their neighbourhoods, protection from what they considered to be unacceptable impacts that the proposed redevelopment would impose upon them, or the preservation of their existing development rights. The rationale for protecting the individual and minorities was that the protection of these parties from undue harm resulting from a decision was intended to benefit the majority. Yet the board was really protecting the rights of private-property owners against the encroachment of planning proposals approved by those elected councils, which, in other circumstances, it recognized as the repository of the public interest. It is not difficult to conclude, as the Ontario Economic Council noted in 1973, that there was 'an apparent danger of the Board becoming recognized as a sort of ombudsman for property owners.'[31] This private law focus alluded to by the council has been more clearly evident in those decisions, the great majority, in which the board was addressing the public interest in the context of decisions pertaining to specific development applications having more limited, if any, public policy considerations or impacts.

The Balancing of Public and Private Interests

The adverse impact test has lain at the heart of the Ontario Municipal Board's decision making throughout the review period. Where both public and private interests have been at issue, the board has acknowledged the public interest in the approval of applications but has refused to approve them if satisfied that the impact of the proposed developments on neighbouring property owners would outweigh the public interest.

The Subordination of the Public Interest to the Adverse Impact Test

The board has clearly recognized the existence of a public interest but has subjected the furtherance of this interest to the application of its adverse impact test. This has been largely but not entirely its own doing. It has recognized the existence of a range of public and private interests and the need to achieve a balance among them, but has received little policy direction with respect to achieving such a balance. As it stated in *Chedoke*: '[A]lthough the Planning Act does not explicitly address the matter of the hierarchy of rights, the core idea that informs the act throughout is a concern for the balancing of the different interests and therefore different rights.'[32] This recognition is not new. The zoning provisions of the Municipal Amendment Act, as passed in 1921, required the board to consider '[t]he desirability of the proposed repeal or amendment [of a zoning by-law] in the interests of the owners of the land in the district affected and of the community as a whole.'[33] This language encapsulating the balancing act the board was required to perform was dropped in 1959 when zoning was transferred to the Planning Act. Other than the references to the public interest in sections 2 and 3 (provincial policy) and 51 (subdivision plans), the act no longer provides guidance as to how decision makers are to achieve such a balance.

As the balancing of interests is inherent in land use decision making, it is no surprise that the board's decisions exhibited a well-developed policy from 1971 on. These matters had clearly received substantial consideration prior to 1971, and the review of post-1971 decisions reveals an underlying approach to dealing with them which changed little throughout the period. This may be summarized as follows: While there may be a public interest in a development proposal, there is certainly a private interest that must be taken into consideration, and, if the impact of the proposed development on a private interest is considered by the board to outweigh the public interest, it will not approve the proposal.

The relative weight the OMB has given to public and private interests has varied throughout the review period. In more recent years it has given vigorous expression to the need to accord protection to private property interests, particularly where the interests in dispute would be limited by the application under consideration. Thus, in refusing to apply official plan-mandated limits to the range of permitted commercial uses on a property, it stated that '[t]he owner of the land should be able to obtain as much economic gain as possible so long as it does not override, to any significant degree, the public interest.'[34] It has held, when considering a by-law to curtail existing development rights, that 'when a zoning by-law amendment removes a right previously held, the community good or public good occasioned by the amendment must outweigh the individual rights of the person(s) affected by the amendment.'[35] It has stated more recently that it was not prepared to take away existing property rights unless there were good planning grounds for doing so,[36] and that the legitimate private aspirations of property owners should be overridden only when it is clear that there are no viable options for achieving the public interest.[37]

The OMB has elevated one element of this balancing act to the status of a policy, its only explicitly stated policy (although it has spoken of this as a principle, not a policy). This principle is, in a nutshell, that the board will not approve a rezoning for a matter of public benefit (most often for parks or conservation purposes), which will have the effect of dramatically limiting or sterilizing development rights, unless the municipality or other public agency involved undertakes within a limited period of time to purchase the property. This position was clearly expressed in what has been referred to, unusually, as a leading case in this area: the 1978 *Nepean* decision, after which the board stated: 'We do not wish or intend to depart from that general principle.'[38] There have been other decisions, both before and after that date, in which the board has given expression to this principle.[39] In a recent aberration from this policy the board approved an interim control by-law and a subsequent downzoning to protect the environment, although it had the effect of prohibiting the development of a property, on the ground that it prevented speculation.[40] The board soon recovered itself, however. It granted a request made under section 43 of the Ontario Municipal

Board Act for a review of that decision, itself an infrequent occurrence, and, citing *Nepean,* reversed the original decision on the oft-repeated ground stated in my nutshell summary, above.[41]

The board has consistently refused to extinguish or substantially reduce the proprietary interests of property owners in order to achieve a public benefit, but has recognized that it is required to balance public and private interests. However, the threshold for giving precedence to the former, as it stated in *Dickinson,* is high: 'Where the health and safety of existing and future inhabitants are involved, where there are patent and imminent hazards to the well being of the community, the municipality should have the unfettered discretion to sterilize the use of lands, without the additional burden of compensation.'[42] The implication is clear: anything less and the municipality should not have this discretion. Given this hurdle, it is not surprising that there is little evidence of the taking away or radical diminution of development rights in the public interest. There is evidence, however, that the board is prepared to accord more weight to the public interest where there is clearly such an interest, and where an owner's rights would not, in its opinion, be seriously affected. It has thus refused to approve the severance of a lakefront lot in the face of Ministry of Natural Resources opposition, taking the position that 'all things being equal, the protection of the public good carries a heavier weight than the recognition of an individual's interest in a matter.'[43] It has noted that the public interest in preserving the integrity of planning controls outweighs the impact on a private owner of refusing to give minor variance approval to an illegally constructed residential addition.[44] On the whole, however, it is safe to conclude that the board's decisions have tended to focus on the protection of private rights, with the public interest being cited in limited circumstances.

The most revealing example of this policy of leaning towards the protection of private rather than public interests is found in the decisions dealing with applications to build affordable housing for households unable to afford normal market prices, and social housing for persons having specific needs, such as group homes for the disabled. Affordable housing applications frequently involved consideration of the province's housing policy statement, thus requiring the board to address stated provincial interests as well. It recognized in these decisions a public interest in the production of such housing, both to meet demonstrated needs and to comply with the requirements of public policy. It regularly balanced this need, however, with the interest of neighbouring private property owners in being protected against adverse impacts arising from such developments. The board evaluated affordable housing applications no differently than it did normal market residential proposals, despite the recognized public interest attached to the former. It stated in *Von Zuben*, a decision in which it refused to approve an affordable housing project, that it must show tolerance in applying zoning standards to assist in the creation of affordable housing, but '[s]uch tolerance must be underlaid with respect for the rights and reasonable expectations of the immediate neighbours.'[45]

The board has been consistent. Where it has been satisfied that there would be no adverse impacts on neighbouring properties, it has approved the applications. Where it has been satisfied that adverse impacts could be alleviated by design modifications, it has approved them subject to such modifications. Where it has concluded that the impact on neighbouring properties outweighed the public interest in providing affordable housing, it has refused to approve them.

In zoning hearings, whether dealing with a municipal by-law or a private request for a rezoning, the board has seen its primary role as that of protecting private interests. Even in official plan hearings, where the public interest was clearly to be addressed, the protection of private interests remained important. Yet in both types of applications the onus has appeared to be on the proponents of the public interest, not of private interests, to make their case.

The one exception has been the board's treatment of the public interest when it hears appeals against interim control by-laws, under which private development rights are temporarily frozen, while municipalities engage in planning studies to determine the best development policies for the areas covered by them. The enactment of these by-laws engenders a clear and specific conflict between public and private interests. The board has concluded in hearing most such appeals that the public interest in proper land use, environmental planning, and public safety outweighs the temporary restriction of private rights.'[46] The ascendancy of the public interest was not unlimited, however. The need to balance the two elements was stated in *Oshawa*, where it noted that its major role was to ensure that municipalities acted in a timely fashion to ensure that the added cost to the individuals was kept to a minimum.[47] The board has refused to approve such by-laws in the few instances where no planning (i.e., public interest) rationale has been established for imposing such by-laws on some properties, or where it has concluded that the hardships to affected owners outweigh the benefit to the general public of keeping their development rights frozen.

Implications of the Board's Approach

The OMB's regular use of the adverse impact test has provided consistency in its decision making, but a reliance on this test has diminished its ability to address broader, more diffuse impacts which may impinge on public policy concerns. The board has focused on impacts on the parties before it, has generally considered each application on its own merits, and has rarely addressed the question of the cumulative impact of similar applications. Also, by addressing almost solely the concerns of parties to its hearings, it has failed to consider the interests of non-represented persons or groups, or aspects of the public interest which are not raised by parties. Its approach has, for example, made for difficulty in acknowledging, much less evaluating, the impact of refusing to approve affordable housing developments on those persons who are not represented before it, but who would benefit from such housing. This has not mattered where actual or perceived impacts have fallen only on directly affected private property owners. It is, however, an approach that has severely limited the board's ability to consider the impacts, on broader public policy, of approving or refusing to approve the applications before it.

The board's application of this approach is not surprising given the generally property-rights-protective thrust of the planning process in Ontario, but it does represent a lost opportunity. Because it is a policy tribunal, the board has not been bound by the common law-determined, actionable causes of nuisance relating to physical impacts, such as pollution impacts, but has been able to develop a concept of impact based on perceived harm and expectations of protection from change. Yet, for the same reason, it has been free to address and give predominance to public policy considerations which lie beyond the purview of the courts. It has done this to a limited degree, but its focus has nevertheless remained, as in the courts, on the protection of private property interests.

The Evaluation of Private Interests

As we have seen, the main theme running through the OMB's decisions has been a need to balance the rights of owners wishing to develop their property with the rights of their neighbours who might be adversely affected by such development.[48] The impact test which it has regularly applied can be considered from the perspective of developers or neighbouring property owners, but the result is the same: If the impact of a proposed development on neighbouring properties is sufficiently adverse, the right of an owner to develop will be overridden by the right of neighbouring owners to be protected from such impact. The qualification is important. The board has recognized that any change will have some impact, and that neighbours cannot be protected from any and all impacts. It has thus effectively applied a *de minimus* rule to avoid wasting its and the parties' time and resources dealing with trivial impacts. Conversely, it has held that the right of an owner to continue a land use will not be overridden unless there is clear evidence that the use is creating an adverse impact on other uses.[49] The policy developed by the board may be characterized as a double-onus test. Starting from the proposition that an owner has a right to develop, the onus is on her neighbours to establish at least a credible perception of harm. If they do so to the board's satisfaction, the onus shifts to the proponent to show that her development proposal will not have an unduly adverse impact on her neighbours. Where she fails to do this, or fails to respond to their concerns, the proposal will most likely be refused. These concerns must be real and legitimate, but these words can encompass the wide range of objective and perceived impacts discussed above.

While this test may be simply stated, it has been subject to variable interpretation by the board, and it can be difficult to trace a consistent thread through the widely varying range of factual situations considered in appeals. The question of balancing these disparate private interests arises regularly in zoning, severance, and minor variance decisions, but infrequently in official plan referrals or appeals. This reflects the differing nature of these applications, as the focus in official plan referrals or appeals is generally on the policy issues dealt with in the plan, while in the other application types the focus is on the uses, density, building height, and so on, proposed for specific properties. In keeping with this distinction, the board has stated that it 'is of the opinion that a zoning by-law for a developed area is intended to protect the existing development from development that will have an adverse effect,' and that it 'agrees that the impact of a proposal on neighbours and the area should be of prime concern in any decision to grant a variance.'[50]

Keep in mind that it is generally the interests of the existing owners and neighbours which the board takes into account. This is particularly apparent in decisions involving affordable or social housing, where the inchoate interests of those who need such housing have rarely been addressed except in the broad public interest terms discussed above, and have certainly not been accorded any weight against the interest of existing owners in not suffering adverse impacts. There have been occasional exceptions in which the board has recognized the interests of those who are not parties before it, such as its statement that the provincial housing policy statement requires a supply of housing 'not just [for] people who would like to have comfortable homes, but for people who, because of financial straits, have to do with things that are perhaps less than they would eventually hope for. In particular, small basement apartments.'[51] Such comments are, however, notable for their infrequency.

There is evidence that in recent years the board has been taking a broader look at the costs and benefits to the various affected parties. In *Price Club* it stated that 'Today's economic realities require the board not only to protect residents from abuse from developers, but also to look critically at the price of neighbourhood opposition. This is a reasonable project with significant community benefits.'[52] This does not suggest, however, that its policies of evaluating impacts on the different affected parties and of imposing a double-onus test in the evaluation of such impacts are undergoing any significant change.

I am not suggesting, in the discussions with respect to balancing interests, that the OMB should not address impacts. A major reason for using public land use regulation has been to avoid the costs and inadequacies of private legal action to forestall the imposition of adverse impacts on property by land development activity, and the board has a role to play in giving this protection. My purpose has been to show that the OMB has developed and consistently applied a policy that is fundamental to its decision making, and to explore here and in the following chapters the manner in which it has balanced the protection of private property with broader public policy concerns. This analysis enables us to discover the tensions between its role as a tribunal responsible for the interpretation and application of public policy and its role as a body responsible for protecting individual property interests from land use initiatives, whether public or private, which may be objectively or subjectively harmful to them.

Has the OMB Been Captured?

The capture theory emerged early in the study of regulatory activity as an attempt to illustrate and explain a relationship that was seen by observers to develop between a tribunal and the economic actors it was required to regulate.[53] The essence of the capture theory is that organized interest groups which are subject to regulation by a tribunal are able, through constant contact and the regular, well-financed, and professional presentation of their arguments, to persuade it to adopt their views as the norm that should be upheld. The standard capture model is not applicable to the OMB because it does not, as the theory supposes, regulate a single industry, but oversees a process in which both private and public organizations play important roles. Nevertheless, the influence of two major and regularly appearing interest groups, the development industry and municipalities, can be determined to some extent by noting the frequency with which the board accepts or rejects the positions taken by them in support or opposition to matters before it. Because of methodological limitations, the following analysis can be suggestive only. The patterns of support and opposition can vary considerably, and it is not possible to know what factors, or interests, influenced the outcome of each hearing. The determination of which of the named parties are members of the development industry cannot be certain in all instances.[54] With these limitations in mind, data pertaining to the frequency with which the board has approved or rejected applications supported or opposed by municipalities or developers, or a combination of the two, provide a general indication of their ability to persuade the tribunal to accept their views.

Another way of evaluating the influence of the development industry is to compare the frequency with which it achieves approval of its positions with the frequency with which non-developer property owners achieve the same result. The latter are owners who wish to build on or make use of their property for various business, residential, or institutional purposes, but who are not engaged in the business of land development per se.

Developers and Non-developer Owners

The group of owners who constitute what is loosely defined as the development industry is most comparable to a regulated industry in the classic capture theory. They are relatively few in number. Their activities, while not invariably subject to board hearings, are potentially exposed to consideration by the tribunal whenever they require, or are affected by, various types of planning changes. They use organizations such as the Housing and Urban Development Institute of Canada and the Ontario Home Builders' Association to represent their interests, not on

TABLE 2.1
Influence of Owners, Including Developers

	1971–78		1987–94		1995–2000	
	No.	%	No.	%	No.	%
Total decisions[1]						
All	344	100	320	100	201	100
Approved	151	44	151	47	119	59
Owner support						
All	289	100	260	100	164	100
Approved	121	42	115	44	97	59
Developer support						
All	132	100	90	100	47	100
Approved	67	51	51	57	27	57
Non-developer owner support						
All	157	100	170	100	117	100
Approved	54	34	64	38	70	60

1 From Table I.1.

individual applications, but with respect to general planning policy discussions at the provincial level, including consideration of the role to be accorded to the board in the planning process.[55] It is evident from table 2.1 that, during the 1971–78 and 1987–94 review periods, applications supported by developers were more likely to be approved than were applications overall, 51 to 44 per cent and 57 to 47 per cent, respectively. Their success rate, moreover, was considerably better than that of non-developer owners during the two periods, as the rates for the latter were only 34 and 38 per cent, respectively. This could be attributed to the fact that developers were regularly able to retain counsel and expert witnesses and thus to effectively make their case and respond to concerns raised by opponents. Yet a significant shift occurred during the 1995–2000 period. Applications supported by developers were slightly less likely to be successful that those supported by non-developer owners, whose success rate increased dramatically from those of previous periods. The board's increased rate of approvals during this period did not translate into higher approval rates for developer-supported applications. The possible reasons for this change and for the overall

TABLE 2.2
Influence of Municipalities

	1971–78		1987–94		1995–2000	
	No.	%	No.	%	No.	%
Total decisions						
All	344	100	320	100	201	100
Approved	151	44	151	47	119	59
Municipal support						
All	192	100	137	100	82	100
Approved	109	57	84	61	56	68
Municipal opposition						
All	139	100	124	100	75	100
Approved	44	32	48	39	34	45

increase in approval rates during the 1995–2000 period are considered elsewhere, but the changes certainly support the contention that the board has not been taken over by the development industry, and that, while it has proved more disposed overall to give approvals, it has not shown any favouritism towards that interest group.

Municipalities

Municipalities do not constitute an organized, regulated interest group, but they do share a general and substantial common interest in persuading the board to uphold their decisions. The board could therefore be said to have been captured by municipalities if it consistently upheld their decisions to approve or refuse to approve planning applications. The evidence suggests that municipalities have achieved a significant degree of influence with the OMB. As table 2.2 shows, approval rates during all approval periods have been substantially higher where municipalities supported applications than where they were opposed. This reflects the board's policies, discussed in this chapter and in chapter 3, of treating the decisions of municipal councils as being the best expression of local public interest, and of being reluctant to interfere with council decisions unless satisfied that they were based on inadequate approval procedures or information.

TABLE 2.3
Influence of Municipal Positions on Developers

	1971–78		1987–94		1995–2000	
	No.	%	No.	%	No.	%
Developer-support decisions						
All	132	100	90	100	164	100
Approved	67	51	51	57	97	59
Developer support and municipal support						
All	76	100	38	100	20	100
Approved	49	64	30	79	16	80
Developer support and municipal opposition						
All	57	100	40	100	21	100
Approved	23	41	16	40	6	29

Municipalities and Developers

Municipal positions have also influenced the success rates of developers. As table 2.3 shows, municipal support or opposition has meant considerable difference to the success rate of developers. The 79 and 80 per cent approval rates during the most recent review periods for applications having both municipal and developer support suggests that these two interest groups acting in concert have been able to achieve levels of success tantamount to capture. The table shows also, however, that these two interest groups have as frequently been opposed to each other. In this circumstance the influence of municipalities on the board appears to be the stronger, as developers opposed by municipalities have had increasingly lower rates of success.

The results are mixed, but they do not suggest that the board has been captured by any interest group. The increased rate of approvals certainly suggests that the board has been increasingly willing to give overall support to property owners seeking development approvals. Yet an increased approval rate, from 44 to 59 per cent, while substantial for contiguous review periods, is not great enough to suggest capture. Developers were, during the earlier review periods, more successful than non-developer owners, but they remained at the same level of approvals during the post-1994 period, whereas the latter experienced a far higher approval rate during this period than previously. It has only been when the two most concentrated interest groups – municipalities and developers – have combined to support applications, that their rates of success, at least since 1987, have been tantamount to capture.

It is difficult to say that these results reflect a policy on the part of the board to favour one interest group or combination of groups over others. Rather, they have arisen from the board's application of its policies, as discussed in this and other chapters. They do suggest, however, that research into areas beyond the scope of this work, such as an examination of the board's hearing procedures and their impact on different parties and interest groups, might prove fruitful.[56]

3

Policy Development in a Statutory/Judicial Context

This chapter demonstrates how a regulatory tribunal has built on the limited policy directives embodied in its governing legislation to create and apply its own policies in several procedural and substantive policy areas. While it is a truism to state that a tribunal must apply the relevant law in exercising its authority, what is of real interest is how it works with and moulds the statutory language, how it applies the necessarily general statutory provisions to the facts of each application before it. Does it stick to the letter of the statute, or does it use this as a springboard to the achievement of other goals? If the latter, what are these goals? How did the tribunal come to select them? To put these questions in the language of regulatory studies, what degree of interpretative independence does the tribunal exercise in applying the laws within which it must operate?

It has long been recognized that the Ontario Municipal Board has developed policies with respect to matters governed by the Planning Act. In 1972 the Select Committee on the Ontario Municipal Board (the Macbeth Committee) concluded that it makes policy when it 'has only a generalized government policy to guide it and feels obliged to make detailed policy applicable to the issues before it.'[1] Statutory provisions are certainly a form of generalized government policy. The committee's statement is correct, but it falls far short of encompassing the range of the board's policy development activities. It suggests that the board has limited itself to refining the general policy expressions 'within the four corners' of the act, to ensuring that the act's provisions have been complied with in the context of widely varying sets of facts. We show here that the board has not limited itself to a technical interpretation and the application of statutory language, but has gone well beyond this to ensure that matters it considers important are taken into consideration. It has done so mostly with respect to procedural matters, as the act deals primarily with these, but has shown a similar latitude with respect to those matters of substantive planning for which the act gives some direction.

This chapter consists of studies of several areas of the OMB's decision making in which it is required to apply and interpret statutory provisions in considering either procedural or substantive planning matters. In each instance the language gives expression to policy enacted by the legislature which may take different forms. It may be proscriptive, setting out procedural steps that must be followed, as in the requirement that a municipal council may not pass a zoning by-law until it has given notice of and held a public meeting at which certain information is made available. Such a provision gives the review tribunal limited discretion, as it may challenge only the adequacy with which council has followed the procedure. A policy may, on the other hand, provide general direction to decision makers but leave its application to their discretion in individual situations. For example, the board may not approve a minor variance unless satisfied that it is minor, and in this instance the tribunal is given significant discretion in making that judgment call.

Our examination of each of these areas shows how the OMB has interpreted, applied, or extended its statutory mandate, and reveals a consistent pattern of decision making that may be described as a policy. In dealing with the adequacy of approval procedures under the Planning Act, the board has exceeded its statutory mandate in order to ensure what it considers to be adequate consideration by the affected public of the policy issues inherent in planning applications, and, by extension, to ensure public confidence in the planning approval process. It has regularly overruled council decisions, as it might be expected to do in exercising its statutory jurisdiction as a review agency, and has consistently done so where such decisions have run counter to its own policies pertaining to impact and good planning. It has engaged in extra-statutory procedural policy development by deciding whether councils and committees have given adequate consideration to the matters before them, even though they may have met the statutory notice and meeting requirements. The board's treatment of interim control by-laws shows how it quickly developed a policy for evaluating appeals pertaining to a newly introduced land use control tool. Its interpretation of the term *minor*, as applied to minor variances, provides a clear and specific example of how a tribunal has applied its own policy to assist in its interpretation and application of a statutory provision.

The Adequacy of Approval Procedures

The Planning Act requirements for giving notice and holding public meetings at various stages in the local planning process are directed to providing opportunities for public involvement in this process. The adequacy of the approval procedures followed by municipalities is not an issue in most hearings, but when it does become an issue the OMB must interpret and apply the relevant statutory provisions. Our analysis shows both that it has not limited itself to a strict interpretation of the act and that its position has evolved over time. It has introduced considerations which extend beyond statutory interpretation, and, in these areas as well as in the carrying out of its interpretive role, it has developed its own policies. During the 1971–78 review period the board was generally satisfied if statutory requirements were met. By the 1987–94 period, however, it was subjecting compliance with these requirements to the test of its own standard for the provision of opportunity for public participation in the approval process, and it was applying this test in a wide range of procedural situations. It had to be satisfied that both the content of the notices given and the circumstances of the public meetings were such as to ensure adequate consideration by the affected public of the policy issues inherent in planning applications, and, by extension, to ensure public confidence in the planning approval process. The board's position has not changed during the post-1994 period, although it has been more explicit in linking the value of public participation with the determination of impact on parties who may be affected by proposed schemes.

Table 3.1 summarizes OMB decisions in which the adequacy of approval procedures was specifically addressed. The number of decisions in each review period has varied considerably. There was some consistency during the two earlier review periods as to the types of applications in which it dealt with this issue. Zoning by-law applications were by far the most frequently considered, followed by official plans. The pattern of interest group involvement is similar to the overall pattern for the two periods, as shown in table I.1, but it differs significantly in one respect. The 79 per cent municipal support rate in both periods was well in excess of the 54 per cent overall rate in 1971–78 and the 43 per cent overall rate in 1987–94. This reflects the fact that it was most frequently the process followed by municipalities in approving official plans and zoning by-laws which was at issue in these decisions. The level of owner opposition, 29 and 33 per cent, was also well in excess of the

TABLE 3.1
Approval Procedures – Decision Data

	1971–78		1987–94		1995–2001	
	No.	%	No.	%	No.	%
Total decisions	14	100	33	100	7	100
Application types						
Official plan[1]	4	29	8	24	1	14
Types Zoning by-law[2]	7	50	20	61	1	14
Interim control by-law	n.a.		3	9	1	14
Severance	2	14	2	6	–	–
Minor variance	2	14	3	9	4	57
Supporters						
Province	–	–	–	–	–	–
Municipality	11	79	26	79	3	43
Owner	9	64	19	58	5	71
Neighbour	–	–	2	6	–	–
Opponents						
Province	1	7	–	–	–	–
Municipality	3	21	6	18	4	57
Owner	4	29	11	33	2	29
Neighbour[3]	11	79	16	48	2	29
Other board policy areas						
Interest evaluation	7	50	14	42	4	57
Decision making	3	21	8	24	–	–
Interference	3	21	1	3	–	–
Prematurity	2	14	4	12	–	–
Good planning	4	29	6	18	–	–
Neighbourhood character	1	7	4	12	2	29
Social housing	–	–	4	12	–	–
Minor	2	14	–	–	2	29
Decision[4]						
Approve	4	29	14	42	2	29
Refuse to approve	9	64	18	55	5	71

1 Includes both comprehensive official plan and official plan amendment referrals.
2 Includes both comprehensive by-law and by-law amendment appeals.
3 Includes both commercial and residential neighbours.
4 One decision excluded from each review period. One 1971–78 decision, involving competing applications, including both approval and refusal. One 1987–94 decision involving motion for dismissal only.

Policy Development in a Statutory/Judicial Context 61

overall owner opposition rate of 9 and 16 per cent, respectively. This suggests that it was frequently property owners, unhappy with council decisions, who raised the issue of the adequacy of the approval procedures followed. The seven decisions during the 1995–2000 period are insufficient for numerical analysis, but they suggest that patterns of board involvement have been very different during this period. Procedural inadequacy has been addressed most frequently in minor variance appeals in which municipalities have opposed the proposed minor variances on the ground that the development they would permit should be subject to the more extensive analysis that takes place under the rezoning process. Unlike during the earlier review periods, the hearings have only rarely involved neighbours. The approval rate shows that the board has been even less willing than it was during earlier review periods to give approvals where approval procedures are in issue.

The province has played no part in dealing with this matter at any time. Its sole appearance in any of these decisions was to oppose a severance application on substantive planning grounds. This is consistent with its emphasis, in its planning policy directives, on specific substantive matters related to planning and development. It is suggestive also of the province's willingness to allow the board to play an unfettered role, subject only to the possibility of judicial review, in dealing with the procedural provisions of the Planning Act.

The 'success' rate of municipalities in these decisions, as seen in Table 3.2, shows that the board was often ready to find inadequacies in the approval process followed by them. Although there was a very high degree of municipal support where approval procedures were at issue, the approval rate was only 40 per cent in the 1971–78 review period and 50 per cent in 1987–94, as compared with the overall approval rates for municipal-supported decisions, at 57 and 61 per cent, respectively. Municipal support was clearly of no benefit during the most recent period, as the board approved none of the applications supported by the municipality.

Notice and Hearing Requirements

The evolution of the OMB's policy over the review period reflected to some degree the revision and expansion of notice and hearing requirements that occurred with the enactment of the Planning Act, 1983. The pre-1983 act required only that planning boards, as part of their duties, hold meetings 'for the purpose of obtaining the participation and co-

TABLE 3.2
Approval Procedures – Effect of Municipal Support

	1971–78		1987–94		1995–2000	
	No.	%	No.	%	No.	%
All decisions	13[1]	100	32[2]	100	7	100
Approved decisions	4	31	14	44	2	29
Municipal support						
Total	10[1]	100	26	100	3	100
Approve	4	40	13	50	–	–
Municipal support						
Overall	192	100	137	100	82	100
Approve	109	57	84	61	56	68

1 One decision excluded because involving both approval and refusal of competing applications.
2 One decision excluded because involving motion for dismissal only.

operation of the inhabitants of the planning area' in dealing with planning matters generally (s. 12(1)(b)). The act imposed no notice or public hearing requirements on municipal councils with respect to their adoption of official plans or enactment of zoning by-laws. The only notice requirement arose after the enactment of a zoning by-law. As a by-law did not at that time come into force without board approval, the council was required to give notice of its application for its approval 'in such manner and to such persons as the board may direct' (s. 35(1)). The 1983 act stated, with respect to notice, public meetings, and dissemination of information pertaining to the adoption of official plans, that

> The council shall ensure that in the course of the preparation of the plan *adequate information* shall be made available to the public, and for this purpose shall hold at least one public meeting, notice of which shall be given in the manner and to the persons prescribed [emphasis mine]. (s. 17(2))

The act instituted the same meeting and notice requirements prior to the passing of a zoning by-law (s. 35(12)). Because under the act a zoning by-law now came into force on the day it was passed if no appeal was filed, the act ensured provision for public input by replacing the post-enactment with a pre-enactment notice requirement. This language was amended in 1989 to clarify the purpose of the public meeting, but its effect appears to have been the adoption of the general position that had already been taken by the board, as noted below:

> Before passing a by-law under this section ... the council shall ensure that *sufficient information* is made available *to enable the public to generally understand the zoning proposed* that is being considered by council, and for this purpose ... [emphasis mine].[2]

Apart from the applicable Planning Act provisions noted above, the underlying due process requirements were established by the Statutory Powers Procedure Act, passed in 1971.[3] The act deemed municipalities to be tribunals exercising statutory powers of decision to which the minimum rules of procedure applied. These included the requirement that '[t]he parties to any proceedings shall be given reasonable notice of the hearing by the tribunal' (s. 6(1)). Applicable law during the 1971–78 review period was largely defined by the *Wiswell* and *Zadravec* decisions. In *Wiswell* v. *Metropolitan Corporation of Greater Winnipeg* the Supreme Court of Canada held that a municipality, in enacting a zoning by-law, was engaged in a quasi-judicial matter and was therefore required to act fairly and impartially by acting in good faith and listening to both sides.[4] The by-law was held to be void because the municipal council had not afforded known opponents an opportunity to be heard before passing it. But the Ontario Court of Appeal subsequently held in 1973, in *Zadravec* v. *Town of Brampton,* that a municipal council was exercising only a legislative function because the Planning Act as it then was provided that neither an official plan, if a hearing was requested, nor a zoning by-law, come into force until approved by the board. The judicial requirements of giving notice and giving parties a fair hearing were thus transferred to the board.[5] Throughout the 1971–78 period, therefore, neither the Planning Act nor the courts required that the board impose any procedural requirement other than the general requirement, under then clause 12(1)(b) of the act, that the planning board hold public meetings.

The OMB's position in the few 1971–78 decisions in which it addressed this matter was generally that municipalities need not go beyond the statutory requirements in providing notice of and opportunity for public participation, but that those limited requirements must be complied with. At the same time the Ontario Divisional Court confirmed that the board's obligation when hearing an appeal was no higher. The court held in *Re Pugliese and Borough of North York* that, while section 35(12) of the Planning Act required that the board hold a public hearing for the purpose of inquiring into the merits of an application, it was not required to make an independent investigation beyond those issues that were raised before it.[6] The board thus held, in dealing with an official plan amendment, that the failure of an owner, who had been heard at the meeting called by the planning board, to receive notice of council's intention to consider the amendment was not a failure of natural justice.[7] In another official plan decision, it noted the failure of a planning board to hold a public meeting until requested to do so by the Department of Municipal Affairs, but it did not refuse to approve the official plan on that ground.[8] In a zoning decision, where there were no statutory notice or hearing requirements, it noted that 'when applications are submitted to the board, adherence to or avoidance of the locally voluntary process of public meetings is not a defect in the application such as to prevent the board from considering the matter nor is it necessarily a ground for rejecting same.'[9] Similarly, it rejected an argument in a development control by-law application, for which no notice was required, that objectors would not be entitled to notice of future specific decisions, but noted also that there was nothing in the legislation to prevent the council from inviting public participation if it chose to do so.[10]

Even during this period, however, the board recognized that there was a rationale for requiring public participation even though there was no statutory or, following *Zadravec*, no legal requirement for municipalities to do so. It held that a municipality was bound to act fairly and in good faith and give all interested parties an opportunity to be heard.[11] It refused to approve a zoning by-law on the ground that the municipality had failed to make full use of its powers under section 35 of the Planning Act to resolve objections, thereby stating by implication that it should have engaged more fully in public participation, notwithstanding the lack of any requirement in section 35 that it do so.[12] But it was only by the 1987–94 review period that its policy had developed fully in this regard. The context had changed considerably by then. In addition to the statutory amendments described above, the courts had dealt further with notice requirements. In *Re Central Ontario Coalition Concerning Hydro Transmission Systems and Ontario Hydro* the High Court quashed a decision of a joint board established to select electricity transmission corridors in southwestern Ontario on the ground of the inadequacy of

Policy Development in a Statutory/Judicial Context 65

notice given by the provincial government to review the board's powers and mandate.[13] The hearing notices, given under section 3 of the Consolidated Hearings Act, 1981, had referred only to 'south-western Ontario' without describing the area meant by that term and without indicating the location of the alternate transmission routes which were to be considered. The court stated that, even though there was no express statutory requirement as to the content of the notice, such notice must meet the requirements of the Statutory Powers Procedure Act in that 'a notice given must be reasonable in the circumstances.'[14] As to the test to be applied: '[I]t is well established that where the form or content of notice is not laid down it must be reasonable in the sense that it conveys the real intentions of the giver and enables the person to whom it is directed to know what he must meet.'[15] In *Re Joint Board and Regional Municipality of Ottawa-Carleton*, another decision involving notice, the Court of Appeal refused to quash a joint board hearing regarding the locating of electricity transmission facilities in eastern Ontario because it was satisfied that notice was adequate. It gave a clear description of the undertaking, including its location, and made reference to the availability of a report containing all the particulars of the proposal that anyone could reasonably require.[16]

In the only post-1994 decisions dealing with notice and hearing requirements the board's policy was not in issue. It refused to approve official plan and zoning by-law amendments on the ground that statutory requirements for the holding of public meetings had not been met.[17]

Ensuring Public Confidence in the Planning Approval Process

On the surface, the OMB's policy during the 1987–94 period was similar to that in the earlier period. It frequently took the position in dealing with zoning applications that the notice provisions of subsection 34(12) must be strictly complied with, but that it was not necessary to go beyond these requirements. As long as municipalities held the statutory public meetings and gave adequate notice of these meetings and of the passing of a by-law, objectors could not claim to have had insufficient opportunity to be involved in the planning process.[18] Similarly, there was no need to go beyond the statutory public meeting requirement and deal individually with each of many objections to designation under comprehensive official plans and zoning by-laws.[19] Underlying this apparently unexceptional approach to interpretation, however, was what by this time might be described as the board's real policy on this issue, namely that there was a need to ensure public confidence in the planning approval process even if the statutory requirements had been technically complied with, and that this confidence must be based on a full opportunity for public participation. This policy was manifested in the following contexts.

Adequacy of Notice and Public Meetings
The OMB was not required to consider adequacy during the 1971–78 review period because there were no statutory notice or meeting requirements in place then. These were introduced in the Planning Act, 1983, and by the later review period the board was applying its 'public participation' test to these requirements.

While the 1983 act required the giving of notice, it provided no guidance as to the adequacy of such notice. The board was thus obliged to develop and apply its own tests of adequacy. It sought to ensure that notice was sufficiently clear to enable members of the public to understand the nature of the development being proposed, and its location; without this understanding the ability of the public to participate in the appeal process would be compromised. Its position regarding the linkage between notice and public participation was well stated in *Thornbury*: 'Notice is a cornerstone of the planning process and the *Planning Act, 1983* was amended in the 1980s to ensure that public input be given an important place in council's "planning issues" consideration.'[20] The board has consequently refused to approve a zoning by-law where it was impossible to locate the site from the notice,[21] where the notice referred to only one area while the by-law applied to the entire municipality,[22] and where it was not clear from the notice that the meeting was being held to obtain the input of the public with respect to a proposed by-law.[23] In an unusual situation, where the tenants of buildings to be converted into condominiums were mostly university students, it held that the notice was inadequate because it was given in the summer months when the students were not in residence to receive it.[24] Where, on the other hand, a notice referred to department store-type uses, but did not specify the exact commercial use proposed (i.e., a 'big box' or warehouse outlet), the board refused to find that the notice was misleading, stating that the nature of the proposal was never in doubt and that the public was given enough information to know its basic nature.[25] Similarly, it has balanced a strict application of notice and meeting requirements with its recognized need to ensure adequate public participation, and, following *Zadravec*, has relied on participation in its own hearing as correcting the deficiencies in the statutory meeting requirements. The board thus took the position, where a council had complied with legal notice requirements but residents were not aware of a public meeting until it was to late to attend, that it should not on this ground reject the by-law, as it was its hearing of the appeal that provided the opportunity for objectors to state their concerns.[26]

The Planning Act, 1983, stated that the purpose of a public meeting is to provide the public with adequate information. As we have noted, this was amended in 1989 to require that sufficient information be provided to enable the public to understand generally the zoning proposal. In keeping with this language, the OMB's policy has been to require that a sufficient level of information be made available to enable the public to participate knowledgeably in the approval process. A municipal claim that subsection 34(15) – which states that councils are to forward information on zoning proposals to agencies having an interest in them – gives the board total discretion in deciding what information to present at a public hearing, was overridden on the ground that members of the public must have sufficient information before them at the time of a public hearing to enable them to assess the true impact of a proposal.[27] The board has refused to dispense with a public hearing on the ground that environmental reports should have been part of the public hearing process that was held for a zoning by-law involving wetlands.[28] On the other hand, it has found notice to be sufficient where the public was given enough information to understand the basic nature of the proposed development.[29]

Selecting an Application Type to Ensure Participation and Policy Consideration

The OMB's application of its public participation policy has been illustrated in its selection of application types to ensure the greatest degree of public participation and policy consideration, and its rejection of applications it has considered inadequate in these areas.

A property owner has, in some circumstances, a choice in the type of application required for his proposed development. Changes pertaining to height, density, bulk, setbacks, and, to a limited extent, land use, may be made by way of either a zoning amendment or a minor variance. The former requires a public meeting and a policy determination by council, and generally involves a planning study. The latter requires only a hearing of the applicant and his immediate neighbours by a committee of adjustment, and may involve little or no planning review. The board's position through the review periods has been that the use of zoning amendments is preferable to minor variances where the changes being proposed are such as to require broader policy consideration. During the 1971–78 period it refused, for example, to approve a minor variance permitting significant reductions in residential lot frontage on the ground that such reductions should be made only after the studies required in connection with a zoning application have been undertaken.[30] During this period it dealt similarly with severance applications, holding that the development that would follow proposed severances would constitute strip development and should most appropriately be subject to the planning studies required for official plan and zoning applications.[31] During both the 1987–94 and 1995–2000 periods the board has dealt similarly with a number of minor variance applications. It refused the use of minor variances to change the use of existing buildings from industrial to high-density residential because the minor variance process did not allow for the formulation of standards, and, in the absence of such standards, objectors would be acting in a policy vacuum and would not be properly able to address their concerns.[32] It has refused to approve minor variances reducing lot frontage, depth, and area in order to provide affordable housing, taking the position that this matter should be dealt with in the context of an area-wide zoning change requiring study and public review rather than through the granting of individual variances.[33]

While the approval of zoning by-laws requires public notice and public meetings, the approval of site plan agreements dealing with many of the details of a development proposal involves only the municipality and the landowner. Only the latter may appeal to the OMB. Neighbours have no right of appeal, even though they may be directly affected by the design details of the proposal. The board's policy of ensuring that public participation should be provided for, even where there is no statutory requirement for it, is illustrated in the earlier review periods by its treatment of the situation where site-specific, but very general zoning by-laws were proposed, with the design details to be dealt with in subsequent site plan agreements. During the 1971–78 period it refused to approve such a zoning by-law because 'it would permit an apartment building and any conditions and siting would be left to be determined between Council and owner without any right in potential objectors to bring their objections before the Board.'[34] During the 1987–94 period it refused to approve a by-law that contained only a range of commercial

Policy Development in a Statutory/Judicial Context 69

land uses, and no design details, stating that the zoning appeal was the appropriate forum for reviewing the concerns of the appellants, who would have no right of appeal from the subsequent site plan decision.[35] Similarly, it has stated that '[t]he board finds itself in a position that is becoming more and more frequent. Land-use impacts at the zoning by-law stage are pushed aside on the vague hope that the site plan process will resolve everything,'[36] and has given approval subject to a by-law being revised to provide protection against adverse impacts on adjacent properties.

The procedures for the approval of an interim control by-law, applicable only during the post-1986 period, are very different from those required for zoning by-laws. No notice or public hearings prior to its enactment are required, although notice of passing of the by-law must be given subsequently, and an appeal to the OMB is provided for (s. 38(1), (3), (4)). The board has developed a clear policy towards dealing with such by-laws on appeal, based on a four-part test discussed later in this chapter (see Interim Control By-laws, p. 93). One element of that test is consistent with its policy of requiring participation in the planning review process. In order to approve such a by-law, the board must be satisfied that the authorized review, which is the reason for imposing interim control, is being carried out fairly and expeditiously. It is only through this review process, in which affected members of the public are able to comment on the planning studies that the municipality must undertake, and to put forward their views, that public participation at the standard discussed above can occur.[37]

The Enhancement of Approval Procedures

The primarily procedural nature of the province's land use planning system as embodied in the Planning Act is a reflection of the predominantly private law ideology upon which planning in Ontario is largely based. The protection of private property, particularly residential property, from adverse impacts and from uncertainty regarding the same, is seen most directly in the use of zoning by-laws, minor variances, and site plan control, but also more generally through the adoption of policies in official plans. Such protection is to be achieved through the formal consideration of changes to land use controls, a process involving public notification, public hearings, and rights of appeal. This belief in the efficacy of procedure in the planning process is fully in keeping with what has been a dominant element in the prevailing public law ideology in the province, the necessity for notice and full participation in a judicially oriented decision-making process. The OMB has been an enthusiastic proponent of this ideology throughout the entire review period, but its policy with respect to public participation has evolved over time. There was limited evidence during the 1971–78 review period that it was looking beyond the minimal statutory requirements of the time to require a higher degree of participation. Evidence from the 1987–94 period, however, strongly suggests that it was by then imposing its own standard. It was not enough that notice be given and public meetings be held. The board had to be satisfied that both the content of the notice and the circumstances of the meetings were such as to ensure adequate consideration by the affected public of the policy issues inherent in planning applications, and, by extension, to ensure public confidence in the planning approval process.

The OMB's application of this policy resulted also in its refusal to accept, in certain circumstances, the adequacy of the statutory approval procedures for minor variance, site plan, and interim control by-law applications. It often expressed the view that these procedures did not, by their very nature, provide sufficient opportunity for the public consideration of planning policy in those situations where it believed that public policy considerations, and not just the particulars of the applications, should be addressed. Minor variance applications were thus refused on the ground that they warranted the full study and public consideration possible only under the zoning review process. During the most recent review period the board has, more explicitly than previously, equated adequacy with impact. Where it has found no evidence of adverse impact, or is satisfied that the issue of impact has been adequately addressed through the minor variance approval process, it has given approvals without a need for a full rezoning process.[38] Where it has concluded that a development proposal has potentially adverse impacts, it has refused to approve minor variances and has required the full scrutiny of a zoning application.[39]

A Legislative Springboard to Policy Development

In dealing with the adequacy of approval procedures the OMB has, as a matter of policy, established standards for public participation beyond those required by the Planning Act. Public participation has played such a significant role in the Ontario planning system that the ensuring of participation and public notice appears to be, as we noted in the introduction, the only explicitly recognized legal ideology. It is probably more correct to say that the provision of participation and notice in a judicially oriented decision-making process is a dominant element in the prevailing legal ideology in the province, and has been so particularly since the McRuer Report was released in 1968.[40] The board has been an enthusiastic proponent of this ideology throughout the entire review period. Its policy with respect to public participation has evolved over time. There was limited evidence during the 1971–78 review period that it was looking beyond the minimal statutory requirements of the time to require a higher degree of participation. Evidence from 1987 and after strongly suggests that it was by then imposing its own standard. It was not enough that notice be given and public meetings held. The board had to be satisfied that both the content of the notice and the circumstances of the meetings were such as to ensure adequate consideration by the affected public of the policy issues inherent in planning applications, and, by extension, to ensure public confidence in the planning approval process. The board similarly refused to accept, in certain circumstances, the adequacy of the statutory approval procedures for minor variance, site plan, and interim control by-law applications on the ground that they did not provide sufficient opportunity for the public consideration of planning policy in those situations where such consideration was required.

Interference with Council Decisions

The OMB has, as a matter of ritual, expressed deference for council decision-making, yet has not hesitated to use the application of its own policies as grounds for overriding council decisions. Much of its time is devoted to reviewing the decisions of municipal councils, primarily with respect to official plan and zoning by-law applications. It cannot choose but to interfere, short of abdicating its role by rubber-stamping council decisions, and the data show that it has done so. The board's decisions pertaining to interference have highlighted a tension between different elements of its own interest evaluation policies. It has generally regarded decisions of municipal councils as being the best expression of local public interest, which should be interfered with only when there are cogent and serious reasons for doing so. Yet it has regularly found such reasons through the application of its own policies, particularly those pertaining to impact and good planning. It has found a higher private interest in the avoidance of adverse impacts which must overrule the public interest when the two are in conflict. As the following analysis shows, it is generally when such conflict has arisen that the board has not hesitated to interfere with and overrule council decisions.

There is little doubt that the OMB has for many years had a policy in place regarding interference in council decisions with respect to zoning matters. There is clear evidence of such a policy in its annual reports from the early 1960s.[41] The 1961 annual report stated that 'The duty of the board is to review what the council has done under authority reposed in the council by the Legislature. Under that authority the council is given a discretion and the board should interfere only if it is shown that the council has not made a proper exercise of that discretion.'[42] The fact that this was the only policy matter addressed in these annual reports is indicative of its importance to the board at that time. However, this and similar statements leave open the question as to what constitutes the 'proper exercise of discretion.' It is in addressing this matter more closely, both here and under other headings of analysis of the board's policy-making activities, that its policy development becomes most apparent.

The decision data for the review periods show a significant lessening in the degree of emphasis the OMB has accorded to interference with council decisions. As table 3.3 shows, this matter was specifically addressed during the 1971–78 period in 62, or 18 per cent, of the total number of decisions analysed for that period. During the 1987–94 period the comparable figures were 11 or 3 per cent. The matter was addressed on only one of the 1995–2000 decisions reviewed. This change in emphasis reflects a maturation of the planning process over time. The frequent consideration of this issue during the earlier period indicates a general uncertainty as to the appropriate degree of interference with council decisions, and the consequent desire of the parties to test the limits of the board's position in this regard. It reflects also the board's desire to make clear the circumstances under which it would interfere or refuse to interfere with council decisions. The infrequency with which this issue was addressed from 1987 on can be read as reflecting a stable situation, one in which the 'rules of interference' have been generally established and accepted by the parties and need not be constantly reiterated by the board. It must not be forgotten, however, that while the board has seen less occasion over time to address the matter of council decision making, it has continued to subject council decisions to its review. As table 2.2 has shown, during the three review periods the board has approved only 57, 61, and 68 per cent, respectively, of the

TABLE 3.3
Interference – Decision Data[1]

	1971–78		1987–94	
	No.	%	No.	%
Total decisions	62	100	11	100
Application types				
Official plan[2]	17	27	4	36
Zoning by-law[3]	49	79	8	73
Interim control by-law	n.a.		1	9
Plan of subdivision	2	3	–	–
Severance	3	5	2	18
Minor variance	–	–	–	–
Supporters				
Province	–	–	–	–
Municipality	38	61	5	45
Owner	44	71	9	82
Neighbour	8	13	1	9
Opponents				
Province	2	3	–	–
Municipality	28	45	7	64
Owner	10	16	2	18
Neighbour	46	74	7	64
Other board policy areas				
Adequacy of decision	15	24	3	27
Prematurity	9	15	1	9
Interest evaluation	27	44	7	64
Good planning	19	31	5	45
Neighbourhood character	9	15	3	27
Social housing	2	3	4	36
Decision[4]				
Approve	34	55	7	64
Refuse to approve	26	42	4	36

1 As there was only one decision during 1995–2000, it is not included.
2 Includes both comprehensive official plan and official plan amendment referrals.
3 Includes both comprehensive by-law and by-law amendment appeals.
4 Excludes 2 multiple application decisions in 1971–78 involving both approval and refusal.

74 A Law unto Itself

applications which were supported by municipalities, and it approved 32, 39, and 45 per cent in the face of municipal opposition. These figures make it evident that municipal support or opposition did have some bearing on the board's decision making, but was not the only factor it considered.

Table 3.3 shows that interference has been an explicit issue mostly in the context of official plan and/or zoning by-law applications. Such applications were considered, either singly or in combination, in 92 per cent of the 1971–78 decisions, and in 82 per cent of the 1987–94 decisions. The single 1995–2000 decision also involved an official plan amendment. This reflects the fact that official plans and zoning by-laws are the major planning tools to which councils must direct their attention and give significant policy consideration. Applications involving plans of subdivision, severances, and minor variances tend to lead to disputes between neighbours and not to require policy-based decision making by councils, although the latter may intervene to uphold their official plan policies. The board has made only a moderate link between the issues of interference and the adequacy of municipal decision making, as the latter is addressed in only one-quarter of the decisions involving the former. Once again, a notable feature illustrated by the breakdown of supporting and opposing parties is the almost total lack of involvement of the province. This is clearly an issue that the province is willing to leave to the board.

Municipal Applications for Approval of Official Plans and Zoning By-laws

The position that the OMB stated in its annual reports during the 1960s with respect to interference was exhibited in its decisions during the later review periods. While it expressed deference for council decision making, it did not hesitate to use the application of its own policies as grounds for overruling council decisions. Moreover, while it was making its decisions within an established statutory and judicial context, the necessarily generalized nature of this context had little bearing on its reasons for approving or refusing to approve such decisions.

The effect of the Planning Act provisions pertaining to referrals and appeals of official plans is that the board is standing in the shoes of the Minister of Municipal Affairs when hearing them. The act stated during the 1971–78 period that when a plan was referred to the board: 'the approval of the Municipal Board has the same force and effect as if it were the approval of the Minister' (s. 15(1)), and, during the 1987–2000 period, '[t]he Municipal Board may make any decision that the Minister could have made' (s. 17(18)). The board has therefore had a clear statutory directive throughout the entire review period to approve official plans and amendments, refuse to approve them, or approve them with whatever modifications it considered appropriate.

The board's role in the approval of zoning by-laws was very different, and was one that changed considerably over time. During the 1971–78 period, a zoning by-law did not come into force without the board's approval, and its jurisdiction was limited to approving all or part of the by-law (s. 35(9), (19)). The act provided it with limited guidelines, stating that 'the Municipal Board may have regard to the restrictions on any land adjacent to such land, area or highway' (s. 35(19)). By 1987 the requirement of board approval had been replaced with an appeal process, with a zoning by-law automatically coming into force if not appealed within thirty-five days of its enactment (s. 34(18), (19)). The board had essentially the same jurisdiction on such an appeal as it had on the referral of an official plan or amendment, namely to dismiss the appeal, approve the by-law in whole or in part, or, an additional power, to 'amend the by-law in such manner as the Board may determine,' or direct council to do so (s. 34(27)). The 'have regard to' provision was no longer in the Act, however, and it was thus no longer subject to any statutory direction with respect to the exercise of its discretion in this area.

The OMB's consideration of municipal applications has, during both review periods, taken place within an established judicial context. In the *Highbury* decision, the Supreme Court of Canada held that the minister or the board, in considering a subdivision application under section 26 [now section 51] of the Planning Act, was granted a wide discretion, but also 'that the discretion, wide though it is, must be exercised judicially and that it is not a judicial exercise of discretion to impose upon the applicant, as a condition of the giving of approval, an obligation the imposition of which is not authorized by the Act.'[43] As a result, the board could not withhold approval of a plan of subdivision until the applicant agreed to sell the indicated school sites to the board of education for a price fixed by that board. This decision set limits to the board's exercise of its discretion, but neither it nor the act gave any guidance as to how it was to engage in that exercise. It was therefore left on its own to decide how it should do so, and it has filled this legislative and judicial vacuum with its own policies.

The OMB expressed its general position throughout the review period. It stated in the 1971 *Spadina Expressway* decision that it 'should not presume to interfere with the exercise of discretion by local elected representatives within the limits of power conferred upon them by the Legislature without some serious reasons for so doing.'[44] In *Pembroke* it stated, as a principle, a presumption that 'a decision made by a municipal council was so made in the interest and for the welfare, benefit, safety and health of the inhabitants.'[45] The board has repeated statements of this nature throughout the review period.[46] They may, however, be taken as ritualistic expressions of a general position which assumes substance only when its application is observed in detail in differing circumstances. When we consider how the board determines what reasons are significant, it is evident that it applies its impact test and its planning policies considered here and in other chapters.

Our examination of a number of decisions during which interference with council decisions was explicitly addressed reveals that the OMB refused to interfere with council decisions in a wide range of circumstances, including where a zoning by-law to permit a retail shopping centre did not grossly exceed the development standards established by the council in its official plan,[47] where proposed apartments near a single-family residential area were held not to be incompatible with the latter,[48] where proposed developments were in accordance with good planning principles,[49] where council had decided that a parcel of land should remain privately owned, and thus available for development, rather than being acquired as public open space,[50] where it was satisfied that the council had considered the risk of over-zoning lands for shopping centre purposes,[51] where it was satisfied that a development control by-law properly implemented the legislation and was not implemented in an unfair manner,[52] and where it was satisfied that permitting second suites in single-family and semi-detached dwellings would not have an adverse impact on neighbourhood character.[53] While the individual sets of facts differ greatly, the decisions to which they pertain reveal a common thread of interference with council decisions on the basis of the board's own, often unstated, policy considerations. It noted, for example, in approving the expansion of industrial use into an agricultural area in accordance with an official plan staging scheme that '[t]he matter of minimizing any possible impact that might occur is, in the opinion of the board, a matter of planning which is the prerogative of Council.'[54] While minimizing impact was thus a planning matter, which the board recognized as a prerogative of council, it did not bow

Policy Development in a Statutory/Judicial Context 77

to council's decision in this or other matters. When it was not satisfied that its tests regarding impact had been met it did not hesitate to refuse to uphold council's approval. It refused to approve municipal applications in an equally wide range of circumstances, including failure to consider alternative locations for a police communications tower located too close to single-family residences,[55] giving conforming status to a nonconforming paint factory in a residential area,[56] approving a residential development in an agricultural area without considering the long-term effects,[57] downzoning from residential to agricultural when services would soon be available,[58] not having council follow its established planning process in approving residential lots in an extraction area,[59] and approving a performance standards by-law which was of benefit to private interests, but was not in the public interest.[60] Again, these decisions were grounded largely on the board's application of its substantive planning policies.

Private Applications for Amendments to Official Plans and Zoning By-laws

One-third of the decisions in both review periods in which the OMB explicitly addressed interference involved appeals resulting from the refusal of councils to approve rezoning applications made by property owners. Its jurisdiction differed from that which it exercised in hearing applications by municipalities for approval of their own zoning by-laws, and it claimed a different responsibility in dealing with each type of application; yet in each instance it based its decisions largely on its own policies pertaining to impact and good planning.

The Planning Act has contained since 1959 provisions under which a person could request an amendment to an official plan or zoning by-law, and, if refused by council, could request that the minister refer the former or appeal the latter to the board.[61] The board's application of these provisions was therefore well established by 1971. When dealing with either an official plan referral or a zoning appeal, it could reject the proposed amendment or direct the council to make an amendment in accordance with its order (s. 17(5), 35(22)). By 1987, the board's jurisdiction with respect to both official plan and zoning amendments had been expanded by the re-enactment of the Planning Act in 1983. The board's authority in dealing with either an official plan referral or a zoning appeal was expanded to enable it to amend the plan or the by-law 'in such a manner as it may determine' (s. 34(11)).[62]

The OMB has exercised its discretion in this area within a judicial context, well established before 1971, in which the courts specifically addressed the board's policy-making role. The Ontario Court of Appeal in *Re Mississauga Golf & Country Club Ltd.*, in which it considered a rezoning application to permit apartments in an area zoned for low-density residential use, noted that

> On the appeal to the board [under (then) subsection 30(19) of the *Planning Act*], the board is exercising an original jurisdiction and may direct the council to do anything a council could have done in dealing with the application to it, even if this departs from the strict terms of the relief requested in the application.[63]

The court held that the board was therefore required to exercise its independent judgment upon the merits of the application. The courts further developed their consideration of the board's jurisdiction on these applications in *Hopedale*, which also involved a rezoning to permit an apartment building in a low-density residential area. In the appealed decision, the board had relied on its policy of not interfering with a decision of council unless it concluded on the evidence that the latter's action was not for the greatest common good, created an undue hardship, unduly interfered with or denied a private right, or was an action taken arbitrarily or on incorrect information or advice.[64] The court rejected this approach:

> Although it is proper for the board in an appeal under s. 30(19) of the *Planning Act* to consider certain principles in deciding an appeal, it is not proper for the board to limit its consideration to the application of these principles ... to say that the appellant *must* comply with them before the board will allow the application is clearly wrong and the board, if it so fettered its jurisdiction, would be in error.[65]

The court concluded, after making this general statement as to the manner in which the board must consider an application, that it had not in this instance fettered itself and that it had considered all matters that it should have.

The OMB addressed the distinction between its role in considering council applications and in considering council refusals in *Tollefson*, in which it stated that it should overturn a council refusal 'only when the board is satisfied that the municipality has not acted in a reasonable fashion in its consideration of the application.' It should, however,

Policy Development in a Statutory/Judicial Context 79

make this decision on the evidence: 'It is not a question of second guessing or acting on one's own sense of priorities.'[66] It is difficult to see how the board differed in its treatment of municipal and private applications, despite the different statutory contexts within which it was treating each type of application. The key to its dealing with both appears to lie in the statement in *Tollefson* that the board is to seek to justify council's decision, 'taking into account the evidence and argument of opposing interests.'[67] The analysis of its decisions strongly suggests that it has not been doing this in a vacuum, but has regularly filtered the evidence and argument in each hearing through the sieve of its own procedural and substantive planning policies, and has subjected them to its 'own sense of priorities.'

During the 1971–78 review period the OMB clearly recognized the judicially determined scope of its jurisdiction in dealing with these appeals. As it stated in refusing to approve a spot rezoning for higher-density residential use, '[t]he power vested in the board in such matters where it is being requested to set aside the decision of an elected council is one which should be proceeded upon with all judicial caution.'[68] It stated its position even more strongly in *Claverley*: 'If there is ever a situation where "judicial self-restraint" should be exercised, it is when this Government-appointed board is asked to overrule the considered decision of a democratically-elected Council and compel them to pass a by-law.'[69] In other decisions, it spelled out circumstances under which it would be prepared to overrule a decision of council, such as the failure of council to follow its usual procedures before refusing an application,[70] or an error in judgment on the part of council,[71] but it refused to overrule because there was no evidence of these failings. The major substantive planning ground for refusing to interfere was the likely impact on neighbouring properties of proposed developments.[72]

Despite this, the OMB recognized its authority and obligation to interfere by overruling council decisions in some circumstances. It stated in *Crofton*, after citing *Claverley* to the effect that it should overrule council decisions only with extreme caution: 'On the other hand, the Legislature in its wisdom has vested this power in the board and when the board feels the circumstances warrant it, it should not shrink from fulfilling its obligations, particularly so in these days of housing shortages and rising rents.'[73] In this instance the board was satisfied that the need for apartments for senior citizens overrode council's reasons for refusing to approve the required zoning. It similarly overruled the decision of council to refuse approval where it might have 'acted arbitrarily

80 A Law unto Itself

on improper information' by being unduly influenced by incorrect opinions of residents as to the impact of a proposed home for mentally hadicapped adults,[74] where council had relied on a technical report that later appeared to be of doubtful validity,[75] and where evidence of likely flooding had not been adequately addressed by council.[76]

The OMB's position had changed to some degree by 1987. Its amended position was clearly expressed in *Nicholson*, in which it stated that 'there is no greater onus in considering the validity of a by-law already refused by council than one approved by it.'[77] It further developed this position in *Maiocco*, stating that being asked to interfere with a council decision was only one of the matters it must consider.[78] It was still prepared to interfere with council decisions where warranted, but was now treating the act of decision making as the only consideration, and was no longer prepared to give greater weight to a council refusal than to a council approval. In any event, the number of decisions following 1986 in which private zoning applications were specifically addressed was too small to provide any indication of a policy trend.

What the Board Says and What It Does

The OMB has clearly adhered to the 'group public interest' theory of interest determination. As a result, it has spoken of the decisions of locally elected municipal councils with respect to official plan and zoning matters as being the most legitimate expression of this local public interest, which should be interfered with only with caution. Yet the evidence shows it has not followed the logic of its frequently stated position. The manner in which it has actually interfered with council decisions, rather than its statements in this regard, is the better indicator of its understanding of its role as a review agency. Its decisions reveal two aspects of this understanding: what it has said and what it has done. The board vigorously expressed the view throughout both review periods that it should interfere with the decisions of elected councils only with caution, only when there were cogent and serious reasons for doing so. In adopting this position, it was saying that it was prepared to accept the decisions taken by a council as being higher or more inclusive expressions of the public interest than the interests of those who were opposed to those decisions.

The ritualistic nature of these statements must, however, be considered in the context of its pattern of decision making. The board frequently refused to approve municipal applications, or to support

Policy Development in a Statutory/Judicial Context 81

municipal opposition to private applications. The sheer volume of these decisions is evidence that its openly stated policy of deference to council decisions was frequently subordinated to other considerations. A second indicator is found in examining the circumstances under which the board has chosen to support or refuse to support council decisions. It is evident that this choice is based, not on any abstract notion as to the pre-eminence to be accorded to such decisions, but rather on the application of its own policies, particularly those pertaining to the evaluation of interests and good planning. It is in these areas that the board has not hesitated, on the basis of the evidence placed before it, to interfere with and overrule decisions of councils.

These conclusions are illustrated in the pattern of the OMB's interference with council decision making. The data with respect to this suggests a maturation of the planning process between the first and second review periods. The frequent consideration of this matter during the earlier period suggests an uncertainty at that time as to the appropriate degree of interference with council decisions, and the consequent desire of the parties to test the limits of its position. It reflects also the board's desire to make clear the circumstances under which it would interfere or refuse to interfere with council decisions. The infrequency with which this issue was addressed during the 1987–94 period can therefore be read as reflecting a stable situation, one in which the rules of interference have been generally established and accepted by the parties and thus raised with less frequency at hearings. This conclusion is reinforced by the almost total lack of consideration of this issue after 1994.

The Adequacy of Decision Making

The Ontario Municipal Board's treatment of this matter provides an excellent example of using a limited statutory provision as a springboard for further policy development. The Planning Act has delineated the procedures that councils and committees of adjustment must follow prior to making decisions, but has given them little guidance in how to do this. The act has always, for example, included a definition of *official plan*, which in the Planning Act, 1983, was 'a document ... containing objectives and policies established primarily to provide guidance for the physical development of a municipality ... while having regard to relevant social, economic, and environmental matters' (s. 1(h)). Despite that, the act has never stated what municipalities, or persons seeking amendments to official plans, were required to do in order to have adequate regard to the elements of the definition. Similarly, the act has provided no indication as to what should be addressed in considering a zoning application. It has included a listing of those matters to which an approval authority, and, on appeal, the board, must have regard in considering a proposed plan of subdivision or a severance – such as 'whether the proposed subdivision is premature or in the public interest' (s. 50(4) cl. (b)) and 'the adequacy of public services' (cl. (i)) – but has given no direction as to what constitutes adequate consideration of these matters.

Faced with this situation, the OMB could have adopted a reactive position by choosing not to address the adequacy of the decision made by the council or committee of adjustment, and to make its decision on the basis of whatever evidence the parties chose to introduce. Alternatively, it could have undertaken a more proactive role by considering the adequacy of studies and other evidence supporting applications placed before it, and, furthermore, giving consideration to the adequacy of the application process itself. The board has done the latter. It has filled this statutory gap with its own test, a test relying heavily on the adequacy with which impacts have been addressed in the decision-making process. The questions it has addressed have been (1) did the decision maker have adequate information and analysis available to it to enable it to make an informed decision? and (2) given the type of application, was the required approval process one that would elicit adequate information and analysis to enable a properly informed decision to be made? The former question pertains to the material upon which municipal councils have based their decisions, and the latter to whether the process followed was adequate to ensure proper consideration of the relevant planning considerations. As a result, the board has established standards of study and analysis that municipalities must meet in preparing official plans and zoning by-laws, and committees of adjustment must apply in considering applications for severances and minor variances. This board has sought to ensure that councils and committees, when making planning decisions, have available to them adequate studies on which to base their decisions, and in doing so it has established a benchmark which active participants in the planning process cannot help but be aware of.

Data summarized in table 3.4 suggest that the board has chosen, as a matter of policy, to adopt a proactive stance where the adequacy of local decision making has been called into question, and that it has

TABLE 3.4
Decision Making – Decision Data[1]

	1971–78		1987–94	
	No.	%	No.	%
Total decisions	52	100	30	100
Application types				
Official plan[2]	15	29	10	33
Zoning by-law[3]	29	56	16	53
Interim control by-law	n.a.		7	23
Plan of subdivision	–	–	2	7
Severance	9	17	2	7
Minor variance	4	8	3	10
Other	4	8	–	–
Supporters				
Province	–	–	2	7
Municipality	35	67	23	77
Owner	35	67	19	63
Neighbour	7	13	8	27
Opponents				
Province	3	6	4	13
Municipality	19	37	4	13
Owner	8	15	10	33
Neighbour	33	63	16	53
Other board policy areas				
Interest Evaluation	20	38	21	70
Approval procedures	3	6	8	27
Interference	15	29	3	10
Prematurity	17	33	5	17
Good planning	11	21	12	40
Neighbourhood character	9	17	3	10
Interim control by-law	n.a.		7	23
Social housing	3	6	4	13
Decision				
Approve	8	15	11	37
Refuse to approve	44	85	19	63

1 As there were only four decisions during the 1995–2000 period, they are not included.
2 Includes both comprehensive official plan and official plan amendment referrals.
3 Includes both comprehensive by-law and by-law amendment appeals.

frequently done so in respect of those applications for which it has received neither statutory nor other policy guidance. Sixty-seven per cent of the fifty-two decisions considered during 1971–78 involved applications for approval of official plan and/or zoning by-law amendments, planning applications for which there were no statutory directives at all as to adequacy. The comparable figure for 1987–94 was 57 per cent. Conversely, only 17 per cent of these decisions in 1971–78 and 14 per cent in 1987–94 involved subdivision or severance appeals, for which there was limited statutory guidance. It is of interest to note that the adequacy of council decision making has almost ceased to be an issue in recent years. This matter was addressed in only four decisions during the 1995–2000 period, a number too small for them to be included in the analyses.

The approval rate reveals a significant difference between the two periods. In 1971–78, 85 per cent of the hearings in which this matter was addressed resulted in a refusal, well in excess of the overall refusal rate of 56 per cent, while in 1987–94 the refusal rate fell to 63 per cent, albeit a figure well above the overall rate of 53 per cent. These figures strongly suggest that, where the adequacy of local decision making did become an issue, the board was prepared to impose a high standard, a standard arising from its own policy position. A similar conclusion arises from examining the subset of these decisions in which municipalities were supporting what were generally their own official plan and zoning amendments. As table 3.5 shows, during the earlier review period, 80 per cent of these applications were refused, as opposed to a refusal rate of only 43 per cent for all applications supported by municipalities. During the later period, 52 per cent of these applications were refused, still well above the overall comparable refusal rate for the period, of 39 per cent. This data shows that the board's willingness to approve municipally supported applications declined considerably where the adequacy of the local decision-making process was called into question and it was given an opportunity to apply its own policy to this issue.

Table 3.4 shows that the province appeared infrequently as a party in hearings wherein this matter was addressed. This fact, plus the paucity of statutory guidance noted above, strongly suggests that the province had little interest in overseeing the adequacy of local decision making and was content to leave this to be determined at the municipal level, and, on referral or appeal, by the OMB. The province did play a somewhat greater indirect role, however. During both review periods municipalities submitted official plans and amendments to the Minister of

TABLE 3.5
Decision Making – Municipal Support

	1971–78		1987–94	
	No.	%	No.	%
Adequacy of decision making				
Total	35	100	23	100
Approve	7	20	11	48
Refuse to approve	28	80	12	52
Overall municipal support				
Total	184[1]	100	136	100
Approve	105	57	83	61
Refuse to approve	79	43	53	39

1 Excludes 4 decisions in which there were multiple applications and results.

Municipal Affairs for review and approval. If they were subsequently referred to the board, ministry reports on them were forwarded to it. While the board was making independent decisions on these referrals, it would also have received and given consideration, generally not acknowledged in the decisions, to the views of the ministry regarding them.

Informed Decisions

As we have noted, the OMB has been reluctant to interfere with council decision making where it believes the councils have properly exercised their discretion. Despite this, it has often been called upon to consider whether councils had sufficient material before them to be able to do so. The policy it has developed is that councils are unable to properly exercise their discretion if they have inadequate data and analysis before them on which to base informed decisions,[79] or if they make decisions solely because they are desired by residents in the face of inadequate information or contrary recommendations.[80]

The board's position has more frequently been stated where it has had to rule on the adequacy of studies supporting applications. The level of adequacy expected has depended on the scale and nature of the changes being proposed, and the criteria it has applied in determining adequacy have been as discussed below. The board has regularly refused to approve applications, whether or not there were substantive planning grounds for approval, because in its opinion they were based on insufficient study. In most cases this has meant insufficient study of the potential impact of proposed developments. It stated its position in *Lavigne* when dealing with appeals from refusals to pass privately initiated official plan and zoning applications: 'Before a change in land use from residential to commercial is made which may have a substantial impact on the amenities of a nearby residential area, careful planning studies should be carried out which would support the proposed change.'[81] Its position was no different when dealing with appeals of municipally initiated zoning by-laws: '... there is an obligation upon the municipality to satisfy the board that there should be a change in zoning. I am satisfied that the Planning Board did not have before it sufficient information upon which to make its decision.'[82] The board was not saying in these instances that the proposals were necessarily flawed, but that matters which it believed should have been addressed were either inadequately considered or not addressed at all. These matters were, in brief, *impact* and *comprehensiveness.*

A major element in determining adequacy appears to have been the degree to which the planning studies undertaken have addressed the issue of impact on potentially affected persons and properties. This was implicit in *Lavigne*, in which the board spoke of the need for studies where a change 'may have a substantial impact' upon existing uses in its vicinity.[83] In a rare reference to the definition of *official plan* in the Planning Act, for example, it stated that a municipality did not have regard to social, economic, and environmental matters as it failed to address the impact on social and recreational services of permitting higher-density residential development than had originally been intended within the area.[84] The board has refused to approve municipal official plans and zoning by-laws and private development proposals largely on the ground that the municipalities had failed to adequately consider these impacts in their decision making.[85] It refused approvals where it was not satisfied that the potential impacts on neighbours, or the concerns of neighbours, had been adequately addressed.[86] It even refused to approve amendments required for a municipal sewage treatment plan which had received Environmental Assessment Board approval, on the ground that there had been inadequate study of the impact of the proposal on the water supply of its neighbours.[87] It refused to give approval where the source of recognized impacts had been incorrectly identified and the wrong property downzoned.[88] While these decisions focused primarily on municipal planning activity, the board took a similar position with private appeals arising from the refusal of municipalities to approve official plan or zoning amendments, refusing to give approval where proponents had not presented planning justification to support their requests.[89]

The board has refused to approve applications also on the grounds that either the planning analyses upon which the applications were based had not been sufficiently comprehensive, or that piecemeal, site-specific changes should not be undertaken without overall study of the areas for which they were being proposed. In refusing the extension of commercial use into a residential area, it stated that 'consideration should be given based upon sound planning principles as to whether or not this street in the vicinity of the subject property should be studied with a possibility of arriving at a land use more consistent with a busy thoroughfare.'[90] In approving an official plan and zoning by-law to permit substantial high-density commercial and residential redevelopment, it stated that 'the application as a major change in planning policies for the area should not be decided in isolation without a comprehensive analysis of the area.'[91]

The OMB has treated interim control by-laws as a special case when considering the adequacy of initial preparation. These by-laws are intended to give municipalities time to undertake studies and put new planning policies into effect by placing a temporary freeze on some or all development within defined areas. They are a form of protective and pre-emptive planning control, and the Planning Act allows municipalities to pass them without prior public discussion or notice. Because of the circumstances of their enactment, the board has accepted that 'the level of information that exists at the time that an interim control by-law is passed will almost certainly be less than that normally expected as the basis for passage of a more permanent limiting regulation.'[92] As this language suggests, it has required that there be some planning justification for imposing interim control; a purely political decision to appease ratepayers is insufficient.[93] This position does not represent a derogation from its general position regarding the adequacy of decision making, but is a specific exception justified by the circumstances in which interim control by-laws are imposed. Moreover, the need for municipalities to provide adequate supportive studies is only deferred, as once the by-law has been passed the municipality must substantiate the planning rationale behind the by-law by undertaking planning studies in a fair and expeditious manner.[94]

Correcting Deficiencies Occurring at the Municipal Level

The OMB has occasionally taken the position that, while a municipal council had less than adequate studies upon which to base its decision, it was satisfied that the evidence placed before it on review was sufficient to remedy that deficiency and provide it with enough information on which to base its approval. In *Oshawa*, for example, it 'filled the gap in the process'[95] by hearing evidence regarding issues which were not raised when an official plan was adopted, but which became issues when a concrete development proposal led to a zoning amendment. In a more significant decision of this nature, the *Ottawa-Carleton* decision, the board was clearly troubled at being asked to approve a major arena within an agricultural area in the face of what it clearly believed to be an inadequate level of study when the matter was being considered at the municipal level. Yet despite stating that councils should never bow to public pressure to give approvals when faced with evidence of insufficient planning, it approved the arena at a slightly reduced size.[96] It accepted during the hearing evidence that the arena could be accommodated in the proposed location without undue adverse impact, but clearly did so under pressure to give an approval that was a prerequisite to 'a matter of major public and provincial interest,' the granting of a National Hockey League franchise to Ottawa.

The danger in adopting this position, which the board has admittedly done rarely, is the impact it can have on its policy of requiring an adequate standard of planning analysis as a part of the municipal decision making process. Where the parties expect that an application will likely be appealed, they may be tempted to undertake less than adequate planning analyses at the municipal level and to provide comprehensive studies only at the board hearing. This can have the effect of downgrading the municipal decision making process from its prime role in the planning system to that of a preliminary hearing, thus reversing the position accorded to municipalities and to the board by the Planning Act. This concern is not hypothetical, as the author is aware that parties anticipating appeals of council decisions will often 'save their ammunition' for the appeal by presenting limited information to the council and a more comprehensive case to the board.

The Adequacy of the Decision-Making Process

In addition to addressing the adequacy of the planning studies undertaken, or the lack of such studies, the OMB has considered whether

Policy Development in a Statutory/Judicial Context   89

the process followed has, by its nature, enabled decision making to be based on adequate information. The focus here has not been on the formal processes but on whether, in specific situations, an application has been adequately considered before a decision has been made regarding it.

The board has found the decision-making process to be flawed in a number of situations. In one early and unusual decision, that in which the locating of a police communications tower in a park was strongly opposed by ratepayers, it refused approval because there had not been an adequate search for alternate sites.[97] It has held that a lack of consultation with the public,[98] or consultation limited to only one segment of the public,[99] meant that council decisions were inadequately based. It has also stressed the importance of consultation with public agencies as part of the decision making process in deciding that proposed multiple severances should be processed as subdivision applications.[100] The board has expressed concerns about approving development proposals in a planning vacuum; that is, where there is no official plan or zoning by-law in place,[101] or where it has recognized a need for comprehensive planning to establish the proper planning context in which to evaluate individual applications.[102] It has refused to approve minor variances on the ground that the more comprehensive study and analysis required for a zoning amendment should be undertaken before an approval is given. While it has normally confined its considerations to the matter before it, it has taken the unusual step of finding the overall approach taken by a council in dealing with rural residential applications to be at fault.[103] These decisions have covered a wide range of factual situations. They have, however, given expression to the board's view of the 'ideal' planning process which underlies the policies discussed in this chapter, a process in which municipal councils play an active role, development decisions are made within the context of local planning policies embodied in official plans and zoning by-laws, and the public is fully involved.

The Establishment of Standards for Local Decision Making

The OMB could have chosen to accept council decisions as givens, not look behind them, and decide each application before it solely on its substantive merits. This approach would have been consistent with its stated deference to and reluctance to interfere with council decision making. As with the issue of interference, however, the evidence regarding its treatment of the adequacy of council decision making shows that it has, on its own initiative, developed standards which local councils ignore at their peril.

The board's main role in this area has been to establish, as a matter of policy, standards of study and analysis which municipalities must meet in preparing official plans and zoning by-laws, and which committees of adjustment must apply in considering severances and minor variances. The policy has been focused on the adequacy, comprehensiveness, and timing of the planning studies that councils have relied on. These standards have sometimes been applied to the consideration of planning policy, but they appear most often to have been related to the adequate consideration of impacts on affected properties. The board's decisions have also reflected another consistent element in its approach. While public participation has been considered important, it has been necessary also that councils and committees, when making planning decisions, have available to them adequate studies on which to base their decisions. This is not to say, of course, that councils and committees have not themselves required adequate levels of supporting documentation, but that the board has established a benchmark which active participants in the planning process cannot help but be aware of.

The OMB's decision to treat the adequacy of municipal decision making as an issue has given it a considerable 'power of reservation' over such decision making. It has often chosen to uphold or reject municipal decisions on the basis of the planning process followed by the council or committee, regardless of the substantive merits of the decision itself. The data, particularly for those decisions in which applications were refused because the board concluded that the standard had not been met, are indicative of the influence that it can exercise over municipal planning practices. Its decisions, particularly if they are seen to follow a consistent pattern, have come to provide benchmarks that municipalities recognize they must meet if their planning decisions are not to be overturned.

We cannot prove that, in the absence of these board policies, municipalities would have subjected their planning applications to lower standards of scrutiny by councillors, officials or the public, or established better groundwork for their decision making. Nevertheless, it seems highly likely that as municipalities have become aware that the board has been applying these procedural policies, they have sought to ensure that the standards being set by it were met. Otherwise, they would have run the risk of having their applications dismissed on procedural grounds alone, without consideration of their substantive merit.

Interim Control By-laws

The OMB's treatment of interim control by-laws provides a particularly instructive illustration of how it has developed policy to guide it in the interpretation and application of new law. It provides an example also of how a test developed to assist in the application of this policy can, while outwardly unchanged, be applied to achieve very different results.

Unlike the other matters reviewed herein, the power to enact interim control by-laws was not introduced until 1983, and the board considered the first appeals involving them only in 1986. It was therefore required to start from scratch in determining how it was to deal with appeals of these by-laws. It did so, partly by developing policy specific to them, and partly by applying its interest evaluation policy in a novel way crafted to fit the circumstances of interim control, in order to subject public and private interests to a different balance than it applied when dealing with other types of applications. The board quickly took a sketchy statutory direction, elaborated a four-part test that had to be met before it would consider approving such a by-law, and developed a refinement of its interest evaluation policy to enable it to decide whether an interim control by-law should be upheld even where the four-part test was met.

The Planning Act, 1983, stated that where the council of a local municipality has 'by by-law or resolution, directed that a review or study be undertaken in respect of land use planning policies in the municipality or any defined area or areas thereof, the council of the municipality may pass a by-law ... prohibiting the use of land, buildings or structures within the municipality or within the defined area or areas thereof for, or except for, such purposes as are set out in the by-law' (s. 37(1)). Such a by-law would be in effect for only one year from the date of its passing, but could be extended for up to two additional years (s. 37(2)). Unlike a zoning by-law, no prior notice of the passing of an interim control by-law was required, but any person could appeal its enactment to the board (s. 37(3), (4)). A second such by-law could not be imposed on an area for a minimum of three years after the first ceased to be in effect, so as to prevent interim control from being used to impose a permanent fetter on development (s. 37(7)). These provisions have remained essentially unchanged.

Interim control by-laws were considered in only eighteen reported decisions during the 1987–94 review period and nine during the 1995–2000 period.[104] As table 3.6 shows, these hearings were primarily disputes between the municipalities which had enacted the by-laws and

TABLE 3.6
Interim Control By-laws – Decision Data

	1987–94		1995–2000	
	No.	%	No.	%
Total decisions	18	100	9	100
Supporters				
Province	1	6	–	–
Municipality	18	100	9	100
Owner	–	–	–	–
Neighbour	6	33	2	22
Opponents				
Province	–	–	–	–
Municipality	–	–	–	–
Owner	18	100	8	89
Neighbour	2	11	1	11
Board policy areas				
Approval procedures	3	17	1	11
Adequacy of decisions	7	39	1	11
Interest evaluation	15	83	9	100
Good planning	4	22	–	–
Decision				
Approve	11	61	2	22
Refuse to approve	7	39	7	78

property owners within the areas subject to them who sought either their repeal or to have their properties exempted from their application. The board approved the by-laws in the majority of the 1987–94 decisions, but refused to approve the majority during the 1995–2000 period. The reasons for its approving or refusing to approve were found in its application of its interest evaluation policy as applied through the filter of the interim control legislative provisions.

The only statutory guidance available to the board in considering the appeal of an interim control by-law was found in the words of section 37(1), quoted above. Despite this, the board quickly began to formulate a policy with respect to the evaluation and approval of such by-laws. In *Gilbert*, its first reported decision it stated, in refusing to approve a by-law, that there were few guidelines as to what issues should be consid-

Policy Development in a Statutory/Judicial Context   93

ered in determining the appropriateness of enacting an interim control by-law, but that, at the very least, a municipality should apply the planning standards it would apply in enacting a zoning by-law.[105] This decision was cited with approval in a number of subsequent interim control by-law decisions, although the board has not normally admitted reliance on precedent, thereby reinforcing the fact that it quickly and consciously adopted a policy with respect to such by-laws. It was the extraordinary nature of an interim control by-law that provided the clue to the board's policy development. Municipalities had to be held to exacting standards because they were here given authority to severely limit or even freeze development activity without any prior public input. Moreover, such by-laws were tools to be wielded by local councils in the public interest, and it was thus necessary to give consideration to the balancing of public and private interests in this particular statutory context.

The main elements of the board's policy were the development and application of a test establishing conditions precedent to the approval of an interim control by-law, the brief application of a double-onus test derived from its adverse impact test, and its unusual balancing of public and private interests.

The Conditions Precedent Test

The OMB soon moved beyond *Gilbert* to formulate a four-part test, loosely derived from the language of the statute, which had to be met as a condition precedent to the approval of interim control by-laws. The elements of this test were that

– section 37 must be interpreted strictly in view of the fact that it permits a municipality to negate development rights;
– the municipality must substantiate the planning rationale behind the authorizing resolution and interim control by-law;
– the by-law must conform with the official plan; and
– the authorized review must be carried out fairly and expeditiously.[106]

This test constituted the threshold element of the board's policy, and all four parts had to be complied with if a by-law was to be approved. Every subsequent instance of refusal to approve arose from what the board perceived to be a municipal failure to meet one or more of these requirements. The board refused approval most often where the planning rationale had not been substantiated, generally because the council had passed a by-law in response to a public outcry against a particular development proposal rather than for reasons of good planning.[107] It refused approval also where the municipality had not conducted its planning review in an expeditious manner.[108] If the four parts of the test were complied with, the board subjected the by-law to its interest evaluation policy, modified to fit into the context of the interim control by-law policy expressed through the legislation. It is likely that this test followed the spirit of the legislation, but there was certainly no policy directive for it.

The Modified Application of the Impact Test

The OMB briefly attempted to apply its adverse impact test, but quickly recognized that it must attach greater importance to public policy considerations than it did when dealing with other types of applications. This led to a fairly rapid evolution of policy. It initially applied a double-onus test in *Gilbert*: once an appellant had demonstrated the potential or actual adverse impact of an interim control by-law upon his property the onus shifted to the municipality to justify its course of conduct.[109] This test was shortly thereafter applied in other decisions.[110] In the *Archipelago* decision, however, the board repudiated this element of the policy, and reduced the importance to be attached to allegations of adverse impact. It recognized that it must modify the application of its impact-based interest evaluation to reflect the public policy interests inherent in the statutory grant of authority to pass interim control by-laws, and it developed a modified test placing greater emphasis on other elements of the policy formulation, the establishment of a proper balance between public and private interests, and the need to encourage good planning.[111] Nevertheless, this represented a shift in emphasis, not a real policy change. The board continued to treat the four-part test as the threshold test, thereby leaving the municipality with the onus of showing that it had satisfied all conditions. At the same time, however, it reiterated its policy, expressed in its consideration of public policies generally, that the matters brought before it, however justified by these policies, must also be supported by proper planning principles if they are to be approved.

The double-onus test, long abandoned by the board, was recently repudiated by the Court of Appeal for Ontario in *Re Equity Management of Canada and Corporation of the Town of Halton Hills*. The court held that a lower court judge had erred in law in placing the onus on a municipality to justify an interim control by-law where an adverse impact had been shown.[112]

1987–1994: The Subordination of Private to Public Interests

The OMB's treatment of interim control by-laws provides a unique example of deviation from its commonly applied policies to meet the demands of dealing with an unusual type of planning application. Once the board accepted that interim control by-laws were by their nature bound to have some adverse impact on property owners, it started to examine more closely the relationship of the public interest and the interests of property owners in the context of the policy expressed in section 37 of the act. As a result, it came to treat the public interest in imposing interim control by-laws as paramount. It held that the public interest in determining the impact of additional dock construction and commercial uses on resort lakes,[113] reviewing development policies in a central commercial area,[114] preparing development policies for riverfront lands,[115] and developing wetland protection policies,[116] all outweighed the temporary impact of restrictions on private property owners.

The board quickly recognized that the creation of adverse impacts in the implementation of interim control by-laws was inevitable, and that a strict application of its own adverse impact test would negate the purpose of interim control. It therefore developed a variant of its policy for dealing with objections to interim control by-laws. Under this approach, the allegations of adverse impact by objecting property owners were not subject to the board's normal impact test, but were weighed against the impact on the interests of other property owners within the area subject to the by-law. Where it concluded that all owners were being treated equally, even though their development rights were being fettered, the board refused to either repeal the by-law or exempt the properties of objecting owners from it.[117]

The public interest orientation of the board's policy received judicial approval. In *Re 715113 Ontario Inc. and City of Ottawa* the Ontario High Court stated, in upholding the enactment of an interim control by-law, that such a by-law was authorized for the purpose of protecting the public interest in the suitable development of the area covered by it, and that 'it takes precedence over the right of affected landowners to use their lands freely.'[118] The position expressed in this decision was recently repeated with approval in the *Equity Waste Management* decision.[119] Despite these judicial statements, however, the board appears to have taken a different approach in recent years.

1995–2000: Same Policy, Different Application

The OMB's treatment of interim control by-laws after 1994 was, at least on the surface, a remarkable change from earlier years. Of the two approvals during this period, one was of an extension to a by-law already in force and the second was quickly reversed on a review under section 43 of the Ontario Municipal Board Act.[120] The refusals were based on extreme prejudice to the rights of owners to develop their property if the by-laws were approved, and, most frequently, on failures on the part of municipalities – overreaction to proposed developments, lack of or inadequate planning rationales for the by-laws, and undue delay in conducting the follow-up planning studies.[121]

These decisions did not, at least on the surface, represent a change in policy. In each case the approval of an interim control by-law was refused because, in the opinion of the board, the municipality failed to meet one of the four tests it had developed in previous years. The focus was almost entirely on the fault of the municipality, and the consideration of the public interest found in earlier decisions was almost nonexistent here. Moreover, the board no longer considered whether the property interests of those opposing the by-laws were more adversely affected than those of other owners to whom the by-law applied.

It is difficult to understand why such a shift occurred. It is possible that municipalities were in fact acting in an overbearing manner and without proper justification in enacting the by-laws. It is also possible, particularly as the board made so little reference to the public interest in this context, that these decisions do represent a change of thinking by it, with a greater focus being placed on the possible impacts of interim control by-laws on property interests, a lesser focus being placed on the public interest justification for such by-laws, and a higher threshold being applied to municipal decisions to enact them. In any event, the board does not appear to have addressed, as it did previously, the underlying rationale for interim control by-laws as expressed in the *715113 Ontario Inc.* and *Equity Waste Management* decisions. Whatever the reasons, there is little doubt that the likelihood of obtaining the board's approval of an interim control by-law has diminished in recent years.

Policy Development in a Statutory/Judicial Context   97

A Clear and Specific Example of Policy Development

The Planning Act states only that a municipality that intends to undertake a study of planning policies for a given area may pass a by-law limiting development within that area to defined uses for one to three years. The OMB quickly took that sketchy direction and elaborated a four-part test that a municipality had to meet if its by-law was to be upheld. It did not stop there, but developed refinements of its interest evaluation policies to enable it to decide whether an interim control by-law should be upheld even where the four-part test was met. In doing this it demonstrated an unusual shift of emphasis, at least until recent years, from private interests to the public interest, with increasing emphasis being attached over time to achieving a balance between the public interest in undertaking planning studies and the private interest in not having one's development rights fettered. The board came to accept, in dealing with these by-laws, that the public interest was paramount and that the temporary limitation of development rights was justified as long as the rights of all owners within the area subject to a by-law were equally affected. Under this unique variant of its interest evaluation policy it did not consider the effect of the by-law on the interests of the objectors per se, but whether the by-law affected their interests more adversely than those of other property owners within the by-law area. Since 1994, however, while the four tests have remained unchanged, the board's treatment of interim control by-laws has moved closer to its treatment of other types of planning tools, with greater emphasis being given to impacts on the property rights of affected owners and less on the public interest in imposing such by-laws.

The Meaning of *Minor*

The OMB's interpretation of the term *minor*, when dealing with minor variance appeals, provides a clear and specific example of how a tribunal has applied its own policy to assist in its interpretation and application of a statutory provision. Also, unlike the active policy development which the board engaged in when dealing with interim control by-laws, its policy with respect to the meaning of *minor* is an example of stasis. The policy it has applied in this area appears to have been established by the beginning of the review period, and it has not changed since then.

In 1952 the Planning Act was amended to give committees of adjustment – local boards whose members are appointed by municipal councils – the authority to grant minor variances from the standards set out in zoning by-laws and from the uses permitted under such by-laws. The board was at the same time given the authority to hear appeals from the decisions of these committees. It has been judicially determined that one of the matters the board must address on such appeals is whether the proposed variances are in fact minor, but the act has given no indication as to how it is to make this determination, and the courts have given only minimal direction. What we consequently find here is a clear example of how, when faced with statutory provisions, a tribunal has interpreted and applied them in the context of its own policies. Our analysis of the board's decisions in which it has addressed the meaning of minor shows that it has throughout the entire review period relied largely on its adverse impact test to provide consistency in making this determination.

The board's decisions in this area, summarized in table 3.7, exhibit in many respects a consistent pattern during the three review periods. These decisions were prime examples of local, micro-planning. Each one involved, of course, a minor variance application, which was on occasion accompanied by a severance application. Except for the latter, the applications pertained to individual lots only. While it is not evident from table 3.7, the variances sought were almost entirely in respect of by-law standards, not use changes. In almost every instance the owner of the property supported the variance, and was generally the sole party in support. Neighbours were the most frequent opponents, but there was considerable municipal opposition also. The only significant differences are found in the approval patterns. In 1971–78 the board was much more likely to refuse to approve minor variance applications than it was in the later review periods. In the earlier period it gave approvals in only 27 per cent of its decisions, while in the later periods its approval rate was 52 and 56 per cent, respectively. Since the following analysis shows that the board applied the same policy considerations in both periods, it is likely that the remaining difference in approval patterns turned largely on individual sets of facts.

The Application of a Judicial Test

In dealing with minor variances the OMB has been required to make its decisions in accordance with both a statutory and a judicially deter-

TABLE 3.7
Minor – Decision Data

	1971–78		1987–94		1995–2000	
	No.	%	No.	%	No.	%
Total decisions	26	100	42	100	18	100
Application types						
Official plan	–	–	–	–	–	–
Zoning by-law	–	–	–	–	–	–
Severance	3	12	2	5	–	–
Minor variance	26	100	42	100	18	100
Supporters						
Province	–	–	–	–	–	–
Municipality	3	12	2	5	3	17
Owner	26	100	42	100	17	94
Neighbour	2	8	–	–	–	–
Opponents						
Province	–	–	–	–	–	–
Municipality	11	42	18	43	7	39
Owner	–	–	–	–	1	6
Neighbour	18	69	33	79	10	56
Other board policy areas						
Interest evaluation	5	19	16	38	4	22
Good planning	1	4	6	14	–	–
Neighbourhood character	6	23	11	26	3	17
Decision						
Approve	7	27	22	52	10	56
Refuse to approve	19	73	20	48	8	44

mined test. Section 45 of the Planning Act permits a committee of adjustment, and, on appeal, the board, to grant minor variances from such zoning by-law standards as maximum building height or density, or minimum lot frontages, lot areas, front or side yard requirements, or parking requirements. The statutory provisions pertaining to minor variances have remained essentially unchanged throughout the entire period. While the section gives the board only the authority to hear appeals, the Ontario Divisional Court has held, in *McNamara Corporation Ltd. and Colekin Investments Ltd.*, that it exercises the same powers and is required to apply the same tests as a committee of adjustment when it is hearing appeals from decisions of the latter.[122]

The courts have given some consideration to the meaning of minor. In *Re Perry and Taggart* the Ontario High Court stated that 'the phrase "minor variations" [the term used by counsel for the applicants] is a relative expression and must be interpreted with regard to the particular circumstance involved.'[123] In *Re 251555 Projects Ltd. and Morrison* the Ontario Divisional Court established a four-part test which a committee of adjustment, and, by extension on appeal, the board, must apply in deciding whether to grant a minor variance. It must be satisfied, as one part of the test, that '[t]he variance must be a minor variance from the provisions of the by-law,'[124] but the court gave no guidance as to what minor might mean. The only guidance, and that not very helpful, was provided in *McNamara*, where the court said of the term *minor variance* that '[t]he term is a relative one and should be flexibly applied ... No hard and fast criteria can be laid down, the question whether a variance is minor must in each case be determined in the light of the particular facts and circumstances of the case.'[125] This served only to give a judicial imprimatur to what had been and continued to be the board's own policy, which has been that '[t]he board is of the view that its discretion is not restricted in any way and that the determination of what is minor is dependent solely on the facts.'[126] This decision has been echoed in other decisions throughout the review periods.[127]

Applying the Impact Test to Statutory Interpretation

The OMB's determination of what *minor* means provides a clear illustration of how its interest evaluation policies have been central to its interpretation and application of section 45 of the Planning Act. Because of their site-specific nature and the generally small scale of the development proposals under review, minor variance hearings are focused more on competing private interests than on public interest considerations. As we have noted, the heart of the board's interest evaluation policy is the determination of impact: If the impact of a proposed development on neighbouring properties is sufficiently adverse, the right of an owner to develop will be overridden by the right of neighbouring owners to be protected from such impact. Throughout the review period it has been this test which has most often provided the thread of consistency running through what would otherwise have been, on the face of it, an inconsistent pattern of decision making. In 61 per cent of its 1971–78 decisions dealing with the meaning of minor, and 68 and 61 per cent of such 1987–94 and 1995–2000 decisions, respectively, the board stated explicitly that whether or not a variance was minor depended on whether it would have an adverse impact.[128] A review of the remaining decisions suggests that impact was often a significant, if implicit, consideration in them also. Moreover, the application of this test lay behind the board's often expressed view that it was not to interpret *minor* in a mathematical sense; that is, that a variation of 10 per cent from a by-law standard was minor, but one of 11 per cent was not. It stated in *Grant*, for example, that '[w]hile it is true that minor variances must not be construed as a mathematical consideration, the board must determine any adverse effects which might flow from the granting of the application,'[129] and in *McLean* that '[t]he question of whether it is minor is something that the courts have said cannot be calculated mathematically. What is minor in one instance is not minor in another.'[130] The board took a similar position in many of the other decisions, which lead to a series of results having strong policy but little mathematical consistency. It refused to approve variances from by-law standards ranging from 7 per cent to over 100 per cent of a standard where, in the circumstances, it concluded that such variances would have an adverse impact on adjacent properties. It approved variances ranging from 16 per cent of a standard to the total elimination of a by-law requirement where it concluded that the impacts arising from such variances would not be adverse.

One difference of emphasis more than of substance between the earlier and the two later review periods was the more explicit articulation of policy often found in the 1987 and subsequent decisions. The board stated in *Glinert* that 'this board and committees of adjustment have, for the past 25 years or more, been essentially using the criteria of impact on surrounding land users as the measure of whether or not a proposed variance is minor.'[131] It was unusual for the board to be so explicit about its policy-making role.

The cumulative impact test is a variant of this test, which reflects the importance of overall impact rather than the magnitude of any individual variance requested. Applications were frequently made for multiple variances to enable a development project to proceed, and the board held on a number of occasions that, while any one variance might not cause a problem, 'the cumulative effect of this series of variances must be considered when assessing impact.'[132]

Despite its consistent focus on balancing the private interests of applicants and neighbours in minor variance applications, the OMB has occasionally given consideration to a broader aspect of interest evaluation, its perception of a public interest in the integrity of the planning process. It has occasionally concluded that a proposed variance was not minor because it would, inter alia, impinge on the integrity of a zoning by-law. It noted in refusing to approve a minor variance that the intent and purpose of a zoning by-law 'is to preserve and protect established neighbourhoods and the rights and privileges of property owners therein, and that such purpose is frustrated by significant variances from the by-laws' provisions.'[133] The board has recently held, in the context of an application to increase the permitted size of a retail store, that a variance is not minor where the size of retail stores is the essence of the problem that the by-law seeks to address.[134] It has similarly held that a variance is not minor where it would have the effect of making an ancillary use of a property – say, video games in a billiard hall – the principle use of the property.[135] It has, without directly addressing impact, concluded that a variance to recognize the existence of a triplex within an area in which only single-family residences and duplexes were permitted was not minor because it contravened the city's policy of limiting these dwelling types to different areas.[136]

A Minor but Revealing Example of the Board's Policy Development

The Planning Act speaks only of minor variances, without providing further direction. The courts have held that the term is relative and must be flexibly applied to the circumstances of each case. The board has avoided this invitation to 'ad hocery,' and attempted to achieve a consistent approach by applying its interest evaluation policy to determine whether each variance application is minor. In the great majority of such decisions it has simply applied its adverse impact test. Where it has concluded that the impact of a proposed variance on neighbouring properties would be adverse, regardless of the percentage variance proposed from the zoning requirement, it has held the variance not to be minor. Where it has concluded that the impact would not be adverse, it has found the variance to be minor. It is of interest also that, while the board has rarely considered the cumulative impact of a series of development approvals, it has applied a cumulative impact test here. It has even on occasion recognized the public interest in the protection of zoning standards and broader planning policies. On the whole, however, it is fair to say that the board's interpretation of minor provides a specific example of how a tribunal has applied its own policy to assist in its interpretation and application of a statutory provision.

4

Policy Development in a Public Policy Vacuum

In this chapter we examine how the Ontario Municipal Board has developed and applied policies pertaining to several substantive planning matters in which it has received no policy guidance. The Planning Act does not refer to these, nor, with limited exceptions, do policy statements or other expressions of policy. Yet these are all important planning considerations and are addressed on a regular basis by politicians, planners, proponents, and others engaged in the planning process.

The matters selected for study are not the only substantive planning matters considered by the board, of course, but they represent a reasonable cross section of those which appear in its decisions. Its determination of what constitutes good planning relies heavily on its approach to interest evaluation, and reveals the tension between its public policy and private law orientations. Its policy with respect to the preservation of neighbourhood character is revealed to be a subset of its interest evaluation policy, which provides a pure example of its adoption of a private law ideology unhampered by consideration of the public interest. The board's treatment of commercial competition illustrates its development of policy with respect to a specific planning issue in which there is a clear public interest but no public policy directives. In dealing with the provision of social housing, it reveals, in a specific policy context, its subordination of a recognized public interest to the interests of property owners. It has clearly developed policies with respect to all of these matters. We examine also the board's use of the planning concept of prematurity. It has not developed a policy for determining whether or not a proposed development is premature, but it has used the concept as legitimization for decisions it wishes to make for other policy-related reasons.

104 A Law unto Itself

The Principles of Good Planning

The OMB has rightly treated good planning as an important consideration in deciding whether to approve planning applications, and it has regularly given or refused approvals on the ground, inter alia, that the proposals did or did not constitute good planning. It has so frequently used the term *good planning* without further explanation, however, that it might be seen as a mantra rather than an expression of policy. Nevertheless, the board has developed a complex policy on this matter, one reflecting a tension between its treatment of public and private interests. In its public aspect the policy has been that development which is in conformity with approved official plans is ipso facto good planning. In its private aspect the policy has been that developments which cause adverse impacts or are incompatible with their neighbours do not represent good planning, even if they are in conformity with official plan policies. Most tellingly, where these two elements have been in conflict the private aspect has prevailed.

Table 4.1 confirms that the OMB regularly addressed the matter of good planning during all review periods. It greatly underestimates the extent of the board's consideration of the matter, however, as it includes only those decisions in which the board made specific reference to the term and gave reasons for concluding that an application did or did not represent good planning. The data show consistency in some aspects over time. Good planning was discussed most frequently in the context of official plan and zoning by-law applications. The mixture of owner support and neighbour opposition in those hearings in which it was addressed remained the same throughout the review periods. Good planning was frequently addressed in decisions in which the board gave direct consideration to the evaluation of interests also. This is expected, as the board has regularly cited the public interest and good planning, or the lack thereof, in the same breath, as being reasons for approving or refusing to approve applications before it. There were also changes during the period. The pattern of municipal support was unchanged during the first two review periods, but after 1994 the patterns of municipal support and opposition were reversed. The percentage of decisions in which approval was given has reflected the Board's greatly increased overall approval rate during the 1995–2000 period.

Grappling with the Term

It goes without saying that a planning appeal tribunal should promote

TABLE 4.1
Good Planning – Decision Data

	1971–78		1987–94		1995–2000	
	No.	%	No.	%	No.	%
Total decisions	73	100	95	100	28	100
Application types						
Official plan	16	22	38	40	13	46
Zoning by-law	43	59	57	60	18	64
Severance	19	26	12	13	3	11
Minor variance	3	4	14	15	4	14
Supporters						
Province	–	–	1	1	–	–
Municipality	42	58	51	54	11	39
Owner	62	85	77	81	21	75
Neighbour	6	8	11	12	1	4
Opponents						
Province	5	7	13	14	2	7
Municipality	27	37	38	40	14	50
Owner	5	7	15	16	2	7
Neighbour	51	70	56	59	16	57
Other board policy areas						
Approval procedures	4	5	6	7	–	–
Decision making	11	15	12	13	1	4
Interference	19	26	5	6	1	4
Interest evaluation	39	53	52	55	16	57
Neighbourhood character	19	26	16	17	3	11
Prematurity	15	21	10	11	1	4
Decision						
Approve	30	41	43	45	18	64
Refuse to approve	43	59	52	55	10	36

good planning. Yet *good planning* has proved to be a notoriously slippery term to define, and its contents have not been susceptible to any widely agreed-upon definition or application. The Planning Act Review Committee applied the group public interest theory discussed in chapter 2, stating that 'Whether a municipality's planning is considered to be good or not depends very much on whose interests are being served. Where the provincial interest is being violated by a municipality's planning actions, the Province should be in a position to prevent or secure change in such actions. Beyond this, good planning is a matter of local norms and standards and should be left for the municipality and its inhabitants to settle among themselves.'[1] Jaffary and Makuch accepted that good planning had a political dimension, and they took the board to task for demonstrating what they considered to be an over-reliance on technical expertise in determining the contents of the term.[2] Our analysis shows that the board has accepted these political value judgments, as embodied in official plan policies, but only when they do not conflict with its own judgment with respect to impact.

The OMB has generally taken the need for good planning as a given, but has occasionally spoken explicitly of its importance and of its close relationship to the public interest. As it stated in *Ottawa-Carleton*, 'it is necessary to discuss and clarify the Board's interpretation of the principles of the planning process and of good planning generally that have been developed from the use of the *Planning Act* over many years and must be recognized as being in the interests of the public as a whole.'[3]

Despite the stated need to 'discuss and clarify,' it is not always clear what the board has meant by good planning, particularly with regard to the many decisions in which it has made only a bald statement, without further explanation, that applications do or do not constitute good planning. In some decisions, however, it has enlarged on the theme by citing matters that represent good planning, or whose absence or inadequacy constitutes bad planning. The list is extensive, including such disparate matters as the adequacy of open space, the availability of public transit, the adequacy of roads, water supply, and sewage disposal, the avoidance of piecemeal development, impacts on existing commercial facilities, conformity with adopted official plans, and public involvement in the planning process.[4] Because the elements selected are so dependent on the circumstances of each application, it can be difficult to trace common themes, but our analysis shows that they have generally fallen into the following categories: conformity with approved planning policies, impact and compatibility, and adequacy of process. The OMB has addressed the first two categories most frequently, and has often given consideration to the relative importance to be attached to each. In the third category, good planning is equated with the adequacy of planning studies supporting an application, and, less often, with the adequacy of the approval process itself, particularly public participation. There are also some substantive elements of good planning which, while linked to the above categories, are sufficiently distinct to be analysed as policy areas in their own right. Those we have selected for analysis are (1) the impact of development on neighbourhood character and on the planned commercial structure of a municipality, and (2) the determination of prematurity.

The board has, unsurprisingly, stated that good planning pertains to planning issues. It has refused to consider collateral issues that may arise, such as hardship, inconvenience, or the need to give relief after unauthorized development has taken place, as relevant to whether a proposal constitutes good planning.[5]

Conformity with Approved Planning Policies

The OMB has treated conformity with an official plan an important but not determinative element of good planning. In the *Ottawa-Carleton* decision it stated that it must accept that official plan policies 'reflect the objectives and purposes intended in the plan to the best of council's ability under the circumstances at the time of its decision.'[6] Yet it immediately conditioned this statement with the following caveat: '[t]his does not mean that the board need agree with any specific statements in the plan.'[7] While the board thus accepted the centrality of official plan policies in determining good planning, it did not limit itself to a mechanical application of those policies. In *Oshawa* it noted, in approving a zoning by-law, that the by-law was in conformity with the official plan, but went on to say that '[t]he findings in respect of conformity with the official plan do not mean some automatic acceptance of a zoning by-law. The board must still direct itself to whether the by-law is consistent with accepted principles of community planning.'[8] It has accepted that good planning includes matters independent of conformity with the official plan, and might well provide grounds for overruling this adopted statement of policy.

In both decisions noted above, the OMB was dealing with the approval of municipally adopted zoning by-laws. In *Metcalfe*, an appeal from a refusal of council to pass a requested amendment to a zoning by-law, it established an even stronger distinction in the tests the appellants had to meet to succeed in persuading it to reverse council's decision: '[f]irst, the development as proposed must conform with the official plan ... Secondly, the proposed use must, on the application of good planning principles, be compatible with adjacent uses permitted in the R2 zone.'[9] Despite the board's expressed reluctance to rely solely on official plan policies, however, it regularly concluded that applications did or did not represent good planning because, inter alia, they were or were not in conformity with policies in official plans. Examples of this, drawn from the entire review period, include compliance of a senior citizens' apartment building with official plan guidelines for high-density development,[10] failure of a severance to comply with official plan policies with respect to retention of good agricultural land,[11] failure of a shelter for battered women proposed for a single-family residential area to conform with official plan policies for such areas,[12] conversion of a vacant commercial building into a residential condominium implementing official plan policy to encourage housing intensification,[13] residential development implementing official plan policies to make effective use of existing infrastructure,[14] and conformity with official plan policies for the evolution of a property from a shopping centre to a mixture of commercial and residential uses.[15] Moreover, throughout the entire review period the board has consistently approved applications which it concluded were in conformity with official plans, and refused to approve applications which were not. It has held that lack of conformity with an official plan is in itself sufficient reason to reject an application,[16] even where the evidence showed that the proposed development was otherwise good planning.[17] Other policies were also addressed in these decisions, of course, so it cannot be said that conformity was the only issue, but it was clearly of significance.

The board has drawn a clear distinction between policies in approved official plans and policies under consideration for inclusion in official plans. It has stated that it can consider only the former as relevant, as emerging policies do not yet represent public policy and may never be adopted or approved.[18]

The OMB has on occasion considered the relationship between provincial policy and good planning. During the 1971–78 period it associated provincial policy with good planning, but was unclear as to the nature of the association.[19] The few 1987–94 decisions in which it addressed this matter revealed a greater awareness of government policy as an element of good planning but did nothing more than treat it as being the equivalent of official plan policies. Conformity with provincial policy was thus one matter to be considered, but, as with official plans, it was not in itself determinative of good planning. The board thus held that applications were not good planning because they were not in conformity with either government policy or official plans.[20] During the 1995–2000 period it often spoke of good planning and conformity with official plans and provincial policy statements in the same breath. As in the earlier review periods, however, it was not generally clear whether it meant that conformity with these expressions of policy was in itself good planning, or whether conformity was something in addition to good planning, with the content of the latter to be found elsewhere.[21]

The board has noted the same conflict between government policy and good planning as between official plan policies and good planning, stating that '[t]he board ... finds it a most difficult problem to resolve a confrontation between government policy [the Food Land Guidelines] and "good planning" in the opinion of qualified planning experts. It creates a "no win" situation.'[22] Despite this comment, it rarely found a conflict between the provincial policy and good planning. Its true opinion of the relationship between the two is seen in its treatment of the provincial housing policy statement, whose objective was to foster municipal planning practices responsive to housing needs. It regularly concluded that where the housing policy goals of the statement and good planning are in conflict, the latter will displace the former; that its own determination of what constitutes good planning will outrank even formally adopted provincial policy where it sees a conflict.

Impact and Compatibility

Despite the OMB's acceptance of official plan policies as representing good planning, it has to a great extent treated the term as a subset of its underlying policy for the evaluation and balancing of private interests. Its determination of what constitutes good planning has frequently been derived from the application of its adverse impact test.

The board has always been ambivalent about merely accepting conformity with an official plan as the sole determinant of good planning. It has developed its own views as to what constitutes good planning, which are independent of official plan policies and which it has applied in its evaluation of development proposals. It has regularly used the terms *impact* and *compatibility* in the majority of the decisions throughout the review periods in which it specifically addressed good planning. These terms have related, but not identical, meanings. *Impact* means operational in nature: the effect the actions of A have on B. *Compatibility* refers to a state of being. It may be defined in this context as a harmonious relationship between different uses of land, such that one use will not have adverse effects on other uses or on the ability of the occupants of other lands to use or enjoy them. An example of the differing meanings given to these terms is found in *Sarnia*, in which the board approved the use of a former convent as a group home for mentally handicapped adults. It stated with respect to impact that the building was in existence and was therefore not an invasion of a single-family area, and with respect to compatibility that evidence showed that group homes were compatible in other residential areas.[23] The board has applied the terms in various decisions in which it has explicitly addressed good planning, to encompass a range of impacts on property and persons which fall into two categories: those affecting immediate neighbours and those affecting a larger area. With respect to the former it is clear that where the board has been faced with development proposals which it believes will have unacceptable adverse impacts on adjacent properties, it has held them not to be good planning, and has either refused to approve them or has approved them with modifications to reduce these impacts to what it considers an acceptable level. These impacts have generally been of a physical nature, involving the design, bulk, or density of proposed buildings which would create shadowing or affect the privacy of adjacent properties,[24] particularly of single-family residences.[25] With respect to the latter, it often concluded that applications which would have adverse impacts on the neighbourhoods within which the proposed developments were to be located, and, less frequently, on the larger community, also failed to constitute good planning. Given the larger areas affected, however, the types of impacts differed from those affecting immediate neighbours. One important element of the test was compatibility with the surrounding area.[26] Traffic impact has often been addressed also.[27] In a broader context, the location of the proposed development in relation to other uses in the neighbourhood,[28] the availability of public transit,[29] the adequacy of existing schools, parks, and other municipal soft and hard services,[30] and the impact of the proposed development on these services,[31] have also been addressed as elements of good planning. In the majority of the decisions in which good planning has been addressed, however, the board has made reference to impacts which may adversely affect property, either in the immediate vicinity or in the larger neighbourhood.

In its application of an impact test to determine what constitutes good planning, the OMB, despite its obligation to address a wide range of policy issues, has engaged in an activity which is tantamount to the hearing of private actions in nuisance. In doing this, it has seen its role as one of protecting the interests of property owners. Its activities illustrate an increasing judicial orientation being given to the planning review process, with the consideration of private property rights given pride of place. The following statement appears to underlie its consideration of impact, even where not so explicitly stated: '[g]ood planning implies, firstly, a recognition of property rights, and secondly, fairness. There is no doubt that, in the planning field as elsewhere, justice must not only be done, it must appear to be done.'[32] The term *justice* appears to mean, in this context, the protection of private property from undue adverse impacts which may be generated by new development. Good planning is thus reduced to an adjunct of property rights protection, with the board treating consideration of the larger public policy elements that the term might be expected to encompass as being secondary to the application of its impact policy.

The Tension between Public and Private Interests

The OMB's treatment of good planning reveals the tension between its public policy and private law orientations. Our analysis shows that it has consistently identified two sometimes conflicting elements as constituting good planning. The significance it has attached to the first of these, conformity with official plans, has been in keeping with its views as to what constitutes the public interest. Its decisions reveal that it has accepted an equivalence between good planning and the public interest, with the nexus being the approval of the policies contained in an official plan adopted by an elected local council. In requiring conformity with an official plan as an element of good planning, it has been engaged, in its role as a provincial planning review tribunal, in the interpretation and application of publicly determined planning policies to the matters before it, and an approved official plan may be considered a form of localized provincial policy. Thus, as the board is required to have regard for provincial policy, it is equally required to have regard for public policy as expressed in official plans. If it had identified good planning as only conformity with official plans, the logical conclusion of this would have been its acceptance of compliance with official plan policies as determinative in any hearing, yet it has clearly not done this. It has retained the discretion to consider official plan policies, but also to address other matters it considers to be elements of good planning. More specifically, it has regularly identified the absence of adverse impacts as the second element of good planning, and, when conflict has arisen between the two elements, it has not hesitated to give priority to impact over conformity. Thus, where applications have failed the impact element of the good planning test, findings of conformity with official plans have not been sufficient to warrant their approval.

The Protection of Neighbourhood Character

The OMB's policy with respect to the preservation of neighbourhood character, a subset of its interest evaluation policy, provides an example of private interest protection largely unhampered by consideration of the public interest. It provides an example also of the board's shift of emphasis in recent years from 'consumers' of property rights to 'producers'; that is, from supporting those residing in a neighbourhood to supporting owners wishing to develop their properties. During the first two review periods it exhibited a strong bias in favour of the protection of low-density residential neighbourhoods. During the post-1994 period this policy did not appear to change, but its application certainly did, with the board showing, as it did generally, a greater propensity to approve development applications.

The Background to Neighbourhood Protection

The protection of neighbourhood character has always loomed large in land use control. The protection of residential areas, particularly prime residential areas of substantial single-family homes, from the smoke, noise, and general incompatibility of industrial, commercial, and higher-density residential uses was a major reason for the creation of zoning and other development control tools. In Ontario, the authority to pass zoning by-laws was given to local municipalities in 1921. The Ontario Railway and Municipal Board was given a controlling role at that time, as such by-laws were not to come into force without its approval. The nature and purpose of zoning by-laws was made clear in the legislation: 'For prohibiting the use of land or the erection or use of buildings within any defined area or areas or abutting on any defined highway or part of a highway for any other purpose than that of a detached private residence.'[33] Since then, the scope of zoning control has been widened to include all land uses, but the protection of residential areas, particularly single-family and other low-density residential areas, has remained an important component of planning, and of the board's review of local planning decisions.

The OMB engaged during the 1960s in an important debate, revelatory of its policy development activities, regarding how to deal with

Policy Development in a Public Policy Vacuum 113

more contemporary intruders into prime residential neighbourhoods than smoky or smelly factories. During this period there was substantial pressure in larger urban centres for approval of site-specific rezonings to permit high-rise apartment buildings in single-family residential areas. This became a matter of major concern for the board, a concern reflected in both its decisions and its private deliberations. While this period predates our review period, it is useful to note the board's deliberations on the matter, both as an indicator of its thinking with respect to this aspect of neighbourhood protection and as background to the analysis of its later decisions. It was attempting even at this time to develop a consistent policy of neighbourhood protection. Thus, in 1962:

> The consensus of [Board members'] opinion appeared to be that it is sufficient to prevent the construction of higher density residential buildings if it appears that the amenities of the neighbourhood will be affected injuriously and that the character of the street will be changed. Of course a far greater danger exists always in cases where the by-law or proposal, as the case may be, would result in spot zoning for higher density use in a lower density area and especially in a single family area.[34]

Note how the importance of providing protection increased as residential density decreased. The discussion continued, and, in 1964:

> The chairman also reported to the Board that he had discussed with the Minister of Municipal Affairs the policy presently being followed by the board with respect to high density residential development and with respect to higher density redevelopment. He had reported to the Minister that, in the case of the first, the Board is moving gradually toward a policy that high density use will not be approved unless such a by-law is passed or sought before the low density development occurs in the immediate vicinity. This same principle would apply in the case of commercial or industrial development that might harm the amenities of residential use nearby.[35]

> Higher density and apartment development was again the subject of discussion. The chairman reported that he had suggested to the Minister that if the Board is to hold its present policy against strong pressure the Board would expect the Cabinet [on petitions to it from Board decisions] to uphold these decisions should objections be made. The Minister has indicated that he supports the policy of the Board in this regard.[36]

114 A Law unto Itself

The application of this policy was noted at the time by an active participant in the board's process:

> The Board's decisions have certainly made it clear that the Municipality must regard legitimate complaints and rights of neighbouring property owners. For instance, all of you know that if the facts and circumstances in a particular area have not changed from the time a subdivision is developed in a single family area, that you have practically no chance at all of getting an apartment zone in the middle of it because the Municipal Board will not approve it.[37]

The accuracy of this observation, and of the existence of a clear board policy, was reinforced in a 1973 decision:

> It is merely following policy laid down in a long list of decisions of this board to say that the intrusion of this 23-storey building in such close proximity to these residences will change the character of the area to a degree that the owners and other residents in the area should not be obliged to accept.[38]

The only drawback with these statements is that they did not go far enough. The OMB's policy has been one of protecting low-density neighbourhoods from development far less intrusive than twenty-three-storey apartment buildings.

Decision Data

Table 4.2 illustrates the patterns during the three review periods of the decisions in which the OMB addressed neighbourhood character. This table plus other data reveal little change in some respects among the periods. Neighbourhood character was regularly addressed, being considered in 22 per cent of the 1971–78 decisions, 16 per cent of the 1987–94 decisions, and 19 per cent of the 1995–2000 decisions. The applications considered were predominantly for residential development, 84, 85, and 77 per cent for the three periods, respectively. As befits the fact that it was primarily private interests that were at stake in these hearings, most of them involved residential owners seeking approvals to build and their neighbours opposing them. The data are indicative also of the province's largely hands-off role with respect to substantive planning issues, as it did not appear as a party in any of the

TABLE 4.2
Neighbourhood Character – Decision Data

	1971–78		1987–94		1995–2000	
	No.	%	No.	%	No.	%
Total Decisions	75	100	52	100	39	100
Application types						
Official plan	5	7	9	17	9	23
Zoning by-law	41	55	22	42	14	36
Severance	19	25	9	17	10	26
Minor variance	16	21	26	50	19	49
Supporters						
Province	–	–	–	–	–	–
Municipality	35	47	10	19	7	18
Owner	65	87	49	94	36	92
Neighbour	5	7	5	10	–	–
Opponents						
Province	–	–	–	–	–	–
Municipality	25	33	29	56	16	41
Owner	4	5	3	6	2	5
Neighbour	65	87	42	81	28	72
Other board policy areas						
Interest evaluation	41	55	26	50	16	41
Good planning	19	25	16	31	3	8
Minor	6	8	11	21	3	8
Decision						
Approve	32	43	20	38	24	62
Refuse to approve	43	57	32	62	15	38

decisions in which neighbourhood character was an issue in any of the review periods.

The data do, however, reveal changes over time with respect to decisions in which neighbourhood character was addressed. Decisions involving official plan and/or zoning applications declined from 59 per cent of the total in 1971–78 to 42 per cent in 1987–94 and 44 per cent in 1995–2000. The difference was more than made up by the increasing frequency, from 21 per cent in 1971–78 to 50 per cent in 1987–94 and

49 per cent in 1995–2000, with which the OMB considered minor variance applications, the most 'local' type of application. This suggests an increasing importance of minor matters in the determination of neighbourhood character. One distinct subset of decisions dealt with severances, and, in almost every instance, the issue was the appropriateness of the proposed lot size within the neighbourhood. The pattern of municipal involvement changed also. Municipal support of applications in which neighbourhood character was an issue declined from 47 per cent during the 1971–78 period to 19 and 18 per cent during the later periods. Municipal opposition was more variable, increasing from 33 to 56 per cent during the first two periods, then declining to 41 per cent during the most recent period. These changes suggest a heightening of municipal awareness of neighbourhood character concerns and a greater willingness to act to protect such character.

By far the most important change occurred in the board's approval rates for decisions in which neighbourhood character was addressed. The approval rates for the first two periods were 43 and 38 per cent. The rate for the post-1994 period increased to 63 per cent, a figure reflecting the board's overall approval rate of 59 per cent for this period. Its approval rates in hearings involving low-density residential neighbourhoods also reflected this change. During the two earlier periods the board exhibited a protective attitude towards the interests of opposing neighbourhood residents in these hearings. There were 55, 35, and 24 such hearings during the three review periods. The approval rates for these applications during the two earlier periods, 29 and 31 per cent, were below the respective approval rates for all neighbourhood character-related decisions of 43 and 38 per cent, and were well below the respective overall approval rates of 44 per cent and 47 per cent. During the 1995–2000 period the board gave its approval in 63 per cent of the low-density-related decisions, a figure which was very close to its 62 per cent rate for neighbourhood character-related decisions and its overall approval rate of 59 per cent for the same period.

This change is shown also by the manner in which the board has treated municipal opposition to development applications in neighbourhood character-related decisions. During the first two review periods it approved only 24 and 21 per cent, respectively, of those applications to which municipalities were opposed. Municipal opposition was much less significant during the 1995–2000 period, as the board gave its approval in 63 per cent of these decisions.

Neighbourhood Character: Physical Elements and Planning Standards

One might imagine that the prime determinants of neighbourhood character would be physical, relating to its appearance and amenities. The OMB has certainly treated these as important, but the heart of its policy of neighbourhood protection, at least until more recent years, involved responding to adverse impacts on the more abstract concerns of property owners. It positively addressed the desire of owners, particularly of single-family homes, that neighbourhood stability be maintained and that the type of development now being permitted, and by extension the socio-economic standing of the residents the development would accommodate, be as close as possible to that currently existing within the neighbourhood. Moreover, its espousal of this position was so strong that it overrode development rights enshrined in zoning by-laws in order to ensure that development considered inappropriate by current owners did not occur.

While the board has often referred to the character of neighbourhoods, the components of this character have been difficult to pin down. In the 1971–78 period, character, at least that of a single-family or otherwise low-density neighbourhood, appeared to be anchored in the amenities experienced by its residents. The board stated, in refusing to extend commercial parking into a single-family residential area, that it 'must attempt to decide whether or not the residential amenities of the single-family user will be adversely affected by what is proposed.'[39] Similarly, in approving higher density development close to a low-density residential area, it stated that '[i]n such cases this board has, in the past, made it quite clear that such intrusion is not in keeping with a proper planning concept, particularly where the residential amenities of the abutting neighbours are going to be seriously interfered with.'[40] These amenities were, at one level, the lack of adverse impact addressed in the context of the Board's interest evaluation activities. These included such tangible matters as traffic, noise, and overshadowing by larger buildings. During the 1987–94 period the board described more specific indications of character, again primarily physical and design-oriented in nature. It often refused to approve smaller lot sizes and frontages than were customary in an area.[41] It addressed the general size and appearance of houses, particularly where 'monster homes' were proposed in areas of much smaller houses.[42] Despite its earlier concern with high-rise residential development, it dealt most frequently and often refused approval to moderately higher-density residential structures, such as semi-detached or row houses.[43] During the 1995–2000 period the board continued to refer to physical characteristics as central to neighbourhood character. It noted, in considering appropriate frontages for severed lots in an established residential neighbourhood, that such factors as lot sizes, built form, and streetscape should be given weight.[44] It considered whether proposed lot sizes or building dimensions would be in keeping with the established character of neighbourhoods.[45] The difference during this period was that the board was more likely than previously to find that proposed developments were in keeping with the character of neighbourhoods.

The OMB has dealt with applications to permit reduced area, frontage, and setback requirements through the application of what might be referred to as the 'preponderant character' test.[46] This test is a specific example of the board's application of its adverse impact test, as it provides a rationale for its frequent conclusion that reduced lot sizes or frontages should be approved only if they are generally in keeping with existing standards within a neighbourhood. Conversely, the board has generally refused to approve reduced lot dimensions which were below the existing standards in the neighbourhood. Its statement in *Richmond Hill*, that 'what is proposed in the creation of two smaller lots would not be in conformity with the lots in the subdivision as a whole, and would thus adversely affect the character of the neighbourhood,'[47] clearly shows how its adverse impact test has been applied to what is primarily a matter of perception, a smaller lot located within an area of larger lots, rather than a physically measurable impact. Allied with this has been the view that a house built on a smaller lot could not be in keeping with existing houses on larger lots.[48] This view was implicit in another decision in which it held that the proposed 'long narrow lots' in an area of much larger lots containing 'good quality residential houses' would, because of their size and configuration, not allow for the construction on them of houses in keeping with the character of existing dwellings.[49] The board has applied this test to refuse approval of reduced lot requirements even where the resultant lots would meet or exceed the minimum by-law requirements. It has thus refused to approve the creation of a lot in an area of 'fine old homes' in which the setbacks would be well in excess of the by-law requirements, on the ground that a building located on it could not provide sufficient setbacks to fit into the character of the area.[50] It held recently that such factors as lot size, built form, and streetscape should be given greater weight than 'mere compliance with minimum zoning standards.'[51] The board did not adopt this position consistently, as illustrated by *Hamilton-Wentworth*, where it approved development on lots exceeding minimum by-law requirements but that were smaller than those in the neighbourhood, on the ground that 'it would be unreasonable to impose a zoning category on the subdivision lands having greater lot size restrictions than the existing zoning standards on the neighbouring lands.'[52] Nevertheless, its approach throughout the entire review period has been generally that size, frontage, and other standards prevailing in a single-family area should take precedence over lesser requirements in zoning by-laws where adherence to the latter would, in its opinion, have an adverse impact on the character of the neighbourhood.

The Rise and Decline of the Expectations Rationale for Neighbourhood Protection

During the pre-1995 review periods it was the OMB's response to the perceptual and psychological concerns of residents that underlay its consideration of the physical and land use attributes of neighbourhood character. The residents of low-density neighbourhoods, primarily owners, were seen as having expectations that the physical environment they had bought into and become accustomed to would be preserved.[53] While the board was never explicit in this regard, there was an underlying socio-economic dimension to its determination of neighbourhood character, a dimension inherent in zoning from its inception. Single-family properties and their owners were often afforded protection, not just from small-scale and unobtrusive commercial uses,[54] but from other types of residential use considered less desirable, such as high-rise apartments, townhouses, and mobile homes, or from the imposition of smaller lot sizes than were customary in the area. The board thus refused to approve some uses which were of a residential nature or least closely associated with residential use, such as a nursing home, daycare centre, and shelter for battered women.[55] It spoke generally of the incompatibility of these uses, or of the loss of amenities they would impose on their low-density neighbours.

The OMB's adoption of an expectations rationale for the preservation of the character of low-density residential neighbourhoods led, as a further development of its private rights-driven ideology, to the creation of a 'property owners' right' to the preservation of the character of their neighbourhoods. The emergence of such a right represented a move beyond the protections embodied in the law of nuisance. More tellingly, for a tribunal deriving its jurisdiction from legislation, it represented the development of protection for property owners beyond that mandated by the Planning Act. A major function of the latter is to provide a process for the mediation of land use changes. The board has, as a matter of policy, adopted an approach to the protection of neighbourhood character, which, allowed to follow its logical progression, would have militated against any but the most inconsequential land use changes. The board has variously characterized this 'right' as a public interest, and, more frequently, as a form of property interest which adheres to the ownership of a single-family dwelling. This rationale was expressed briefly in 1977 and 1978 as a matter of the public interest: 'the public interest is to develop residential neighbourhoods as pleasant places for the inhabitants to reside in,'[56] and there is a public interest in the 'openness and space, pleasant surrounding, lack of fences, well manicured lawns [which] were the order of the day in this neighbourhood.'[57] This interest was linked also to the public interest inherent in enacting zoning by-laws 'to preserve and protect established neighbourhoods and the rights and privileges of property owners therein,'[58] a statement indicating the board's continuing adherence to the original rationale for zoning controls.

Nevertheless, the more significant line of decisions which appeared during the two earlier review periods applied the expectations rationale directly. This is of interest for two reasons. Firstly, it illustrated the board's solicitude towards low-density residential property, as it was cited in every instance in connection with the protection of such property from the adverse impact of 'out-of-character' development. Secondly, it illustrated in specific circumstances the amorphous nature of the board's distinction between public and private interests, as addressed in chapter 2. The rationale was, early in the review period, based on the right of property owners to expect the continuation of the zoning protection which was in place when they purchased their properties.[59] The public interest lay in the protection of the integrity of the zoning by-laws, while the private interest lay in the protection the by-laws provided to owners in low-density areas against unexpected and potentially adverse development. This later developed into a more general rationale based on the expectations of low-density buyers at the time of their purchases, and was clearly expressed in *Martin*: 'It is clear to the board that when a person moves to a rural area to live in a relatively large single-family residence, he expects some "quiet life."'[60] Similarly, the board refused to approve the severance into four lots of a five-acre parcel on the ground that the severance 'would seem unfair to the owners of all the other lots on the plan, who presumably purchased their property knowing that the minimum area at the time of purchase would be about five acres.'[61]

A different emphasis appeared in the board's decisions during the 1995–2000 period. Consideration of the impacts on neighbouring properties was still important, but the board showed a greater willingness to accept change within even low-density residential areas and to shift the emphasis from the protection of owners' expectations. In *Keewatin*, in approving townhouses within a single-family neighbourhood, it held that the regulations and standards contained in zoning by-laws must be reassessed over time in light of new circumstances, and that the test to be applied in assessing these changes is the intent of the by-law, not the preservation of existing quantitative standards.[62] The board held similarly in *Brookvalley* that a village had lost its small-scale, low-density 'innocence' when its regional government allocated a share of the overall regional population growth to it and approved policies for the appropriate servicing of that growth.[63] These and similar decisions did not represent a wholesale move away from the protection of neighbourhood expectations, but they made clear that these expectations could and would be overridden where warranted by changing circumstances. There have been too few recent decisions, however, to enable us to determine if this represents a lasting policy shift.

The Board's Treatment of Mixed Use and Marginal Neighbourhoods

The contrast between the OMB's approach to preserving the character of low-density residential neighbourhoods and that of other types of neighbourhoods is striking. In the former situation, its focus has been on the protection of private interests. In the latter, it has shown little solicitude towards private property interests, and, by implication at least, has placed much greater emphasis on the public interest in having land use changes occur in an orderly fashion. This policy has, moreover, remained unchanged throughout the entire review period.

Mixed use neighbourhoods are those containing a mixture of residential, often single- and multiple-family, institutional, commercial, and possibly other uses. They are generally older areas and are often close to city or town centres. The term *marginal area*, rarely used by the board, applies to neighbourhoods in which a significant portion of the building stock is poorly maintained, if not vacant, little or no redevelopment or renovation is occurring; and, frequently, the types of uses are changing. The two terms do not necessarily overlap, as mixed-use areas are often stable areas with well-maintained buildings.

The board's treatment of mixed-use neighbourhoods has been the obverse of its treatment of low-density residential neighbourhoods, and serves to heighten its policy of protecting the latter. Its position was clearly stated at the beginning of the review period and remained unchanged throughout. In *Oakville* it permitted the establishment of a home for mentally handicapped adults and day nursery facilities in a mixed-use area. The board showed its differing approaches to the protection of low-density and other neighbourhoods in stating that 'If this were an application to inject a use into a neighbourhood where its compatibility with existing homes was in some doubt, I would have no hesitation in approving only part of the application ... I am satisfied that in this particular area with its mixture of residential, commercial and institutional uses, albeit some of them non-conforming, the use proposed does not represent a depreciation in the existing amenities of the ratepayers living in the area.'[64] Similarly, in *St Catharines*, it approved a detoxification centre on lands adjacent to a hospital and a residential area, stating that the use would not alter the established character of the neighbourhood because much of it was 'not used for detached dwellings but for other purposes, namely, multiple dwellings, institutional and commercial.'[65] In these decisions, which involved the insertion of uses previously not in the area, the board's concern for compatibility and the avoidance of adverse impact – which lay at the heart of its treatment of low-density residential neighbourhoods – was addressed, but was more loosely applied than in its dealings with the latter. One variant of this position was that, as the areas already contained uses that would be incompatible in a purely residential area, none of the uses, including any single-family dwellings, were entitled to protection from new uses. It held similarly, in considering semi-detached and apartment applications in areas already containing those uses, that the neighbourhoods affected were already of a mixed residential character and the proposed developments would for that reason be compatible.[66] Another variant was that, where neighbourhoods were already undergoing change, development proposals that would maintain the general character and stability of such neighbourhoods should be approved.[67]

The obverse of the OMB's treatment of low-density residential neighbourhoods is seen also in its views with respect to protecting the character of marginal neighbourhoods. There are no decisions dealing directly with neighbourhoods so identified, but there are decisions giving indications of its approach to dealing with them. In *Ashland* the board refused to approve a rezoning to legitimize an existing asphalt plant located in an industrial zone near a residential area, stating that '[t]he board does not find that this residential area [where objectors lived] is marginal. The houses, while not luxurious, appear from photographs to be well-maintained in a well-treed area.'[68] The implication here seems to be that, if the board had found the residential area to be marginal, it might not have considered the noise, dust, odour, and traffic impacts emanating from the asphalt plant to be sufficiently adverse to warrant refusing the application. In *Darte* it refused to approve a funeral home in a largely single-family neighbourhood, but this refusal was conditional on that single-family character being maintained.[69] The Board's reasoning suggests that its policy of protecting the amenities of single-family and other low-density residential development was meant to apply only to relatively 'pure' versions of such development, and that it believed there to be a tipping point in neighbourhood change beyond which the remaining single-family and other low-density residences would no longer be entitled to such protection.

Summary

Our analysis of the OMB's policy with respect to the protection of neighbourhood character reveals how far a tribunal, while not receiving specific public direction, has been attuned to and followed the policy underlying statutory provision. A major reason for establishing planning controls, particularly direct land use control mechanisms such as zoning, has been to protect good residential areas from the unwanted impacts of other types of development, ranging from multi-family residences to heavy industry. The board has long taken this to heart. As Palmer and Erkkila noted in 1972, 'it seems that the OMB concerns itself primarily with the protection of property owners in low-density residential areas.'[70] The board's development and application of the expectations principle shows how a tribunal can advance beyond the protections provided by the courts into new and legally uncharted areas. Its decisions, at least until recent years, have shown no significant evidence of changes in its approach to this matter.

There is insufficient evidence for saying that the board's policy in this regard has changed in recent years, but there has been a shift of evidence from the rights of those owners who oppose change to the rights of those owners who wish to develop their property in various ways. This is, however, a shift that has occurred within the unchanging context of the board's impact policy. Although the board has proved more open to accepting change in recent years, and has made little reference to the expectations of neighbouring property owners, it continues to base its decisions on its evaluation of the impact of the proposed changes on those neighbouring owners.

Commercial Competition

The OMB's treatment of commercial competition provides a clear example of the evolution of policy in a specific area of planning, a policy clearly articulated by a tribunal in the absence of any guidance by way of statutory provisions or government directives. It reflects also the tension between the board's espousal of a strong private law ideology and its need to give credence to public policy considerations.

Commercial competition was not an issue in the majority of commercial land use applications heard by the board. These generally involved the impact of small-scale commercial facilities such as service stations, convenience stores, and neighbourhood shopping malls on their immediate neighbours, and it applied its adverse impact test here as it did to applications involving other land uses. Competition was specifically addressed in less than one-third of the commercial land use applications reviewed for each review period, but it became a central issue in a number of large-scale shopping centre development or expansion proposals. These proposals had the potential to greatly affect commercial functions and associated land uses in the municipality as a whole, and the board was required to consider how they might affect either existing commercial uses or official plan policies with respect to the municipality's commercial structure. The specific issue it has had to address in these decisions has been the nature of commercial competition that should be allowed, and it has dealt with this by developing and applying a policy regarding competition which has undoubtedly had some bearing on urban form and functions within the province.

The OMB has addressed the issue of commercial competition throughout the three review periods, in 19, 20, and 14 decisions, respectively. Most of the applications were for substantial commercial facilities, and thus required both official plan and zoning by-law amendments. Table 4–3 shows a pattern of party involvement considerably different from that observed overall. The protagonists were almost exclusively municipalities and property owners. One unusual feature, which indi-

TABLE 4.3
Commercial Competition – Decision Data

	1971–78		1987–94		1995–2000	
	No.	%	No.	%	No.	%
Total decisions	19	100	20	100	14	100
Application types						
Official plan	11	58	17	85	10	71
Zoning by-law	15	79	17	85	13	93
Supporters						
Province	–	–	–	–	–	–
Municipality	16	84	13	65	11	79
Owner	7	89	17	85	14	100
Neighbour	1	5	2	10	–	–
Opponents						
Province	2	10	–	–	–	–
Municipality	7	37	11	55	2	14
Owner	2	10	5	25	–	–
Commercial neighbour	15	79	15	75	11	79
Residential neighbour	1	5	2	10	1	7
Other board policy areas						
Approval procedures	–	–	2	10	–	–
Adequacy of decision making	1	5	2	10	–	–
Interference	5	26	2	10	–	–
Prematurity	5	26	–	–	–	–
Interest evaluation	5	26	6	30	6	43
Good planning	5	26	8	40	3	21
Decision						
Approve	11[1]	65[2]	15	75	11	79
Refuse to approve	6	35	5	25	3	21

1 Excluding two decisions which involved approval of one application and refusal of another.
2 Based on 17 decisions equalling 100%.

cates the importance of the commercial interests in dispute in these hearings, is that municipalities were frequently on both sides of the disputes, in five of the 1971–78 hearings and in six of those in 1987–94. This rarely occurred in other types of hearings, and it reflects two things: the fact that large- or even medium-scale commercial development proposals can have impacts on the viability of commercial facilities in neighbouring municipalities, and that policy differences between upper- and lower-tier municipalities are expressed in their respective official plans. Property owners, when in opposition, were generally the owners of other commercial properties who were opposed to development proposals primarily on economic grounds, the adverse impact they feared on their own or their tenants' sales. The province, as usual, took no direct role in any of these hearings, although the Ministry of Municipal Affairs would have submitted comments to the board on proposed official plan amendments.

Municipalities have generally been supportive of commercial development proposals throughout the entire review period, as they have seen such projects as valuable additions to their assessment rolls. They have also, however, opposed such development when they feared the impact of such development on the continuing viability of their central business districts. The question of commercial competition has arisen most frequently with respect to proposals in towns and small to medium-sized cities, not major metropolitan centres. This most likely reflects the fact that smaller municipalities have smaller and less complex commercial structures than larger centres, and that the impact of a single commercial proposal is likely to be greater on their current or planned commercial structures.

The board was generally supportive of applications in which commercial competition has been addressed, as it approved 65, 75, and 79 per cent during the three periods, respectively. Moreover, commercial competition was an important consideration where it arose. It was the only one of the board policies under review here which was addressed in 47, 40, and 55 per cent, respectively, of these decisions during the review periods. The importance of public interest evaluation increased over time, being a matter addressed by the board in 26, 30, and 43 per cent of these decisions during the same periods.

General Elements of the Board's Commercial Competition Policy

There is an important distinction between these commercial competition-related decisions and others. In the latter, parties usually opposed development proposals because they considered them not to be good planning, or were concerned about the direct impact of the proposals on their properties. In these decisions the opposition has been based primarily on economic grounds. Other commercial property owners or merchants have been concerned about the impact of the proposed projects on their sales. Municipal councils have been concerned about their impact on the economic health of existing or currently planned commercial development within their boundaries.

The policy with respect to commercial competition developed by the OMB has consisted of two elements, one specific to commercial development applications and the other representing a sophisticated, public interest-related variant of its adverse impact test. Both of these elements appear to have been well established prior to 1971, as they were regularly addressed during the 1971–78 review period, but the latter showed evidence of evolution between then and the post-1987 period. The first element has been that the board does not have the duty or the function to regulate or control commercial competition per se.[71] Its consistently stated policy, based on its perception of its role in the land use planning process, is that it must decide on planning rather than on economic grounds. As it has pungently stated, 'The role of the board is restricted to planning matters and not to the competitive factors in the marketplace ... It is not the board's function to participate in the predatory market policies of the food store industry.'[72] The impact-related elements of the board's policy have been rather more complex. It has recognized that commercial development will have an impact on existing commercial operations, but that such an impact must be accepted because it is economic rather than physical, and is inherent in the operation of the free market system.[73]

1971–78: A Focus on Economic Impact

The OMB's policy during the 1971–78 review period revealed a partial abdication of its planning role when considering substantial commercial development proposals. Broader aspects of planning policy were reduced to a consideration of the economic impact of these proposals on existing commercial operators and property owners. It was only with the emerging focus on impacts on central business districts (CBDs) that these wider policy implications of approving shopping centres began to emerge in its decisions. During this period, the Board's approach was one of technical orientation to commercial competition based on market studies. These studies were objective in that they made use of data pertaining to such matters as the demand for different categories of retail products, sales per square metre for different types of stores, and population growth projections within defined catchment areas to determine whether a commercial proposal, generally a shopping centre, could in theory be supported within a given market area. 'Support' in these studies meant that there would, again in theory, be enough retail business potential within the market area to support both existing and proposed commercial centres. The studies were aspatial in that they looked at market areas as a whole and did not consider where within them the proposed commercial facilities might best be located.

Despite this apparent objectivity the data relied upon were generally the competing assumptions of expert witnesses for the parties, not truly objective, agreed-upon information. The board determined whether there would be a sufficient demand within a market area to support a proposed development, and gave approval if satisfied that there was.[74] Later during this period it began to adopt a more spatially focused approach by addressing the impact of proposed commercial development, as revealed by market studies, on the CBDs of affected municipalities rather than on market demand generally within them. In doing this it was reflecting an increasing concern at this time that substantial commercial development on suburban and rural sites was undermining the function and viability, and leading to the deterioration, of the traditional CBD in many cities and towns. As a result, the board approved shopping centres in each instance where it had concluded that their impact on the CBD, as determined by market studies, would be limited,[75] and refused approval in each instance where it concluded that the impact would be adverse.[76]

1987 and Following: A Focus on Planned Commercial Structure

By 1987 the OMB had abandoned its reliance on market studies and had focused on the impact of proposed commercial developments on the planned commercial structure of municipalities. There appear to have been two reasons for this: a disillusionment with market studies, and an increasing awareness that the nature and location of commercial land uses should be treated as an important aspect of public policy rather than primarily a marketing exercise.

By this date the board was showing evidence of disillusionment with the market studies it had earlier relied on so heavily. It concluded that such studies, which were developed as a tool by retailers to assist them in locating and expanding their operations, were too narrowly focused to be treated as the prime determinant of what should be a public policy decision, taking a much wider range of matters into account. These

Policy Development in a Public Policy Vacuum 129

studies were to continue to play a role, but a subordinate one. As the board stated in one decision, 'the only role of market evidence is to assist in reaching a sound planning decision to guide orderly development in the best interests of the community, consistent with the broad policies of the official plan.'[77] The planning-oriented policy which the board had developed by this time was clearly articulated in several decisions. In refusing to approve a major retail and wholesale food distribution centre on the ground, inter alia, that it would be too disruptive to the existing fabric of commercial development, it stated that 'the board will use the market evidence before it not for the purpose of regulating competition but for the purpose of assessing whether the impact of the new store will have the effect of destroying or undermining the *planned function* of existing land uses.'[78] In another decision approving a commercial mall in a central area, it stated that '[t]he central issue in all these cases [involving commercial developments] is, will the proposed development undermine the planning function of the existing centres.'[79] It further articulated the manner in which it was prepared to apply its general 'adverse impact' test to the impact, not on particular properties, but on a municipal policy as expressed in an official plan: 'The board intervenes only when the impact is "deleterious or harmful" to existing facilities to the extent that the development would "jeopardize" or, as this board has said elsewhere, "undermine or destroy" the proper planned function of existing land uses and the planned commercial structure of the community.'[80]

These decisions illustrate the board's development of a more sophisticated version of its impact test, which can be paraphrased as follows: 'A municipality, through its official plan, codifies the commercial land use policies it wishes to pursue. This involves the assignment of different functions in the commercial hierarchy to different areas within the municipality. Implicit in these policies is the understanding that they will be implemented only if the development they envisage is commercially viable. Any development that threatens this viability, and, with it, the functions planned for a given commercial area in an official plan, will threaten these elements of the official plan and should not be approved.' In following this policy, it has placed emphasis, not on the economic impact on competing commercial property owners and store operators, but on the public interest inherent in ensuring that official plan policies can be successfully implemented without being put at risk by subsequent approvals. This concern is applicable to other types of land use also, but the board has concluded that the nature of commercial land uses and of the retail hierarchy within a municipality makes such uses particularly susceptible to harm. It has not attempted to roll back the tides of change that have overtaken retailing, the shifts from store-lined streets to shopping centres, and, more recently, the emergence of large retail warehouse outlets known as 'big boxes.' It has followed this policy, variously expressed, with the decision to approve or refuse a proposed commercial development turning to a great degree in each case on its application of this variant of its impact policy.[81]

The board has generally followed this policy during the 1995–2000 period, but with variations. On the one hand, it has accorded greater importance to market studies, and explicitly based its decisions on its assessment of market impact as derived from those studies.[82] It has refined its assessment of impact, noting that adverse impact refers in this context to the social impact of harming the functioning of the commercial structure, not the impact on individual store owners or operators.[83] Yet it has also placed considerable emphasis on the threat that commercial development can cause to the public interest in the preservation of strong CBDs.[84]

A Clear Example of Policy Evolution

During the 1971–78 period the OMB functioned as a mediator of retail interests with respect to commercial applications and their opponents. Its decisions were based primarily on its acceptance of the market study tools used by the retail industry to assist in making locational decisions, and consideration of other planning matters was infrequent. By the 1987–94 period its competition policy exhibited a strong public policy orientation through its focus on commercial functions as provided for in official plans. Nevertheless, the board was prepared to and often did override the planned commercial functions in official plans by approving new or additional commercial development. In so doing it was engaging in its 'traditional' activity of allowing property owners to develop their land as they saw fit, subject to refusal only where the impact on other owners and business operators – that is, those in existing and planned commercially designated areas – was considered to be adverse.

Why did the board develop this policy? Firstly, it understood its jurisdiction under the Planning Act as one requiring it to apply land use planning criteria and standards to development proposals, but not to consider their economic viability. Secondly, the policy provided it

Policy Development in a Public Policy Vacuum 131

with the ability to both transcend the issue of competition and take a consistent approach to dealing with these applications. Moreover, its approach has been consistent with its underlying policy of evaluating the interests of the parties before it, and of the public, in accordance with the degree of impact imposed upon them by development proposals. This policy evolved from the relatively simplistic approach seen during the 1971–78 review period, which was really only one step removed from deciding on the basis of private economic impact, to one focused on the public policy aspect of commercial development.

An analysis of the effect of this policy on the pattern of commercial land use development in the province is beyond the scope of this book, but its application has likely had some bearing on the commercial structure of municipalities by providing a steadying influence on this volatile area of planning. Commercial development is favoured by municipalities because of the economic and assessment benefits it brings, often with little countervailing public expense, and the temptation is therefore strong to approve such proposals. It is true that, throughout the review period, the board gave approvals in the majority of the applications in which it addressed commercial competition. Nevertheless, by imposing its impact test, particularly in the form to which it had evolved by 1987, it has required municipalities, proponents, and opponents to address the public policy implications of such proposals.

The Provision of Social Housing

The OMB's treatment of social housing illustrates how a tribunal has subordinated a recognized public interest to its regular planning evaluation. The provision of various categories of social housing has, during the entire review period, been recognized by the board as being in the public interest. For the more recent periods, the provision of affordable housing has been a matter of formally stated government policy also. One might therefore have expected it, as a tribunal responsible for the furtherance of the public interest generally and provincial policy specifically, to have made this a fundamental element of its decision making, but its decisions dealing with this matter show that it has not done this.

The term *social housing* encompasses a wide range of facilities: group homes, seniors' residences, shelters for specified classes of persons such as troubled youth, ex-mental patients, or battered women, and housing to be made available at lower than market rents, variously referred to as assisted, low-cost, or non-profit housing. During the 1971–78 review period the board, in its few decisions dealing with social housing proposals, treated them no differently than it did other types of housing. During the 1987–2000 period it exhibited a mixed response to such proposals. It recognized the public interest in providing social housing, but continued to base its decisions on the application of its adverse impact test. Yet at the same time it gave procedural recognition to the provincial interest in the provision of affordable housing, as set out in the province's policy statement, by working with the Ministry of Municipal Affairs and Housing to 'fast-track' applications involving such housing.

Table 4.4 summarizes the data with respect to those decisions in which the OMB considered the provision of social housing. There was very little activity during the 1971–78 review period, and the few decisions there were fell into a pattern of zoning amendment applications which were supported by the property owners, opposed by neighbouring residents, and frequently supported by municipalities. While the board appeared to be supportive of such applications, the number of decisions involved is too small to be determinative. The more frequent consideration of social housing during the 1987–94 review period fell largely into two categories: zoning amendments, some of which were for substantial developments, and minor variances to permit the provision of social housing on individual properties. Municipal involvement became less frequent, as municipalities were rarely parties to minor variance appeals. The comparable patterns for 1995–2000 showed little change. Once again the province took no active role, with one exception, in supporting applications involving social housing, even during the post-1987 period when its housing policy statement encouraging the provision of affordable housing was in effect.

During the 1971–78 review period the OMB received little policy direction with respect to social housing, and was, in any event, rarely called upon to consider the matter. Various government housing funding programs were in operation, which were themselves an expression of provincial policy, but the province did not address housing in a planning policy context. The board did, however, show some recognition of the public policy aspect of providing social housing. It noted, in approving a non-profit town house project over strong local opposition, that there was a public interest in increasing the stock of low-cost housing.[85] It overrode objections to senior citizens' housing based on excessive density on the ground that the proposal was for non-profit housing.[86] It noted that there was evidence of need for group housing for mentally handicapped adults,[87] and for low-rent housing.[88] For the most part, however, there

TABLE 4.4
Social Housing – Decision Data

	1971–78		1987–94		1995–2000	
	No.	%	No.	%	No.	%
Total decisions	8	100	31	100	14	100
Application types						
Official plan	1	13	5[1]	16	2	14
Zoning by-law	7	87	15	48	8	57
Minor variance	–	–	13	42	4	29
Supporters						
Province	–	–	1	3	–	–
Municipality	5	63	11	35	2	14
Owner	8	100	26	84	12	86
Neighbour	1	13	5	16	–	–
Opponents						
Province	–	–	–	–	–	–
Municipality	3	38	10	32	10	71
Owner	–	–	2	6	–	–
Neighbour	8	100	21	68	7	50
Other board policy areas						
Approval procedures	–	–	4	13	–	–
Adeqacy of decision making	2	25	4	13	–	–
Interference	2	25	1	3	1	7
Interest evaluation	5	63	18	58	10	71
Good planning	5	63	15	48	3	21
Neighbourhood character	3	38	7	23	3	21
Decision						
Approve	7	87	20	65	10	71
Refuse to approve	1	13	11	35	4	29

1 Includes one comprehensive official plan.

was little to distinguish its treatment of social housing during this period from its treatment of development applications generally. While the fact of a development proposal being for social housing was clearly addressed, its decisions were based on the matters it considered in all applications: the lack of adverse impact and its satisfaction that the proposals were in accordance with the principles of good planning.

In contrast to the earlier period, social housing programs were a feature of government housing and planning policy throughout the 1987–94 review period, and the OMB responded to this changed policy environment. The most significant new element was the provincial government's approval in 1989, under section 3 of the Planning Act, 1983, of the housing policy statement Land Use Planning for Housing. As the following chapter shows, the board dealt with this policy statement largely by subordinating it to the application of its adverse impact test. It continued to deal at the same time with applications for other forms of social housing, and, in addition, with affordable housing applications in which the policy statement was not addressed. It is these decisions which are primarily addressed here.

During the 1987–94 review period the board continued to subordinate the provision of social housing to its primary concern of ensuring that proposed developments did not have an adverse impact on their neighbours. In many of these decisions the social housing proposal, be it for a group home, a low-rental apartment building, or the conversion of an existing residence to provide additional affordable units, was subject to the same criteria as were other residential applications. This is not to say that the board did not address the matter of social housing at all. It recognized that there was a public interest in the provision of various forms of such housing, and, subject to the application of its overriding impact policy, it sought to further this interest. The fact that it approved 65 per cent of the applications involving social housing during this period, as contrasted with its overall approval rate of 47 per cent during the same period, is indicative of this. It referred in many of its decisions to the need for the type of social housing for which approval was being sought, thus recognizing that even if there was no formal policy statement in place, there was a general public interest in the provision of such housing.[89] It noted that applications were in conformity with official plan policies pertaining to social housing,[90] or were supportive of more general municipal social housing policies.[91] It noted the need for additional density in order to make social housing projects economically viable, a statement in contrast to its usual refusal to address the economic viability of other types of development.[92] It responded to the element of opposition, particularly common in opposition to group homes, based on fear of the occupants of these facilities rather than on the impact of the proposed structures themselves, by noting their concerns but applying its policy of deciding on the basis of impact and good planning.[93]

In a number of decisions dealing with affordable housing applications, the OMB addressed also the balance between the public interest in providing such housing and the need to ensure that these proposals did not cause adverse impact or that they represented 'good planning.' It did so independently of its consideration of provincial policy: in only one of the eight 1987–94 decisions in which it considered affordable housing proposals did it make even a passing reference to the housing policy statement.[94] While most applications involved the provision of new social housing, the board showed concern with preserving existing affordable housing also. It thus refused to approve the replacement of a small bungalow with a monster home, citing the need to retain affordable housing.[95] It furthered the provision of social housing where possible, but did not allow this to override the application of its own policy.

There was another indication of support for the province's housing policy statement which is not evident in the decisions themselves. In the early 1990s the board, working in conjunction with the Ministry of Municipal Affairs and Housing, adopted 'fast-track' procedures to further the achievement of the goals of the housing policy statement. Applications involving the provision of at least some affordable housing were brought forward for hearing more quickly than were other applications, including other residential applications. This was a significant innovation which the board had not previously adopted for other categories of application. It is indicative of the ongoing relationship between it and the province in operational matters – a relationship which has certainly not prevented it from giving priority to its own policies.

The OMB's treatment of social housing changed little during the 1995–2000 period. It continued to consider applications for group homes, seniors' buildings, and development involving affordable housing. Again, its decisions were based on its assessment of impact and of conformity with official plans. It continued to make reference to the public interest in the provision of affordable housing, but did not allow this to override its focus on the traditional planning issues.

The provision of various categories of social housing has, throughout the entire review period, been clearly recognized by the OMB as being in the public interest. The provision of affordable housing has been a matter of formally stated government policy since 1989. One might therefore have expected it, as a tribunal responsible for the furtherance of the public interest generally and provincial policy specifically, to have made this a fundamental element of its decision making. The board has not done this. It has in recent years shown its recognition of the need for affordable housing by fast-tracking applications involving such housing. Once these and applications involving other types of social housing were before it, however, it recognized this public interest but at the same time followed its customary policy. Moreover, the board has rarely even referred to the provincial housing policy statement. It subordinated the provision of social housing to the interests of adjacent property owners by refusing to approve applications which would have adverse impacts on those owners.

Prematurity

The OMB had by 1971 adopted a policy of using prematurity as a legitimation for decisions it wished to make for a range of other policy-related reasons. Our analysis shows that it has treated prematurity as a reason for refusing approval even in those situations where there was no statutory requirement that it do so. The board has frequently been called upon to decide whether an application was premature, or, as it often stated, was premature and not in the public interest. A review of the decisions shows that it has used prematurity in different ways: as a ground for refusal of planning applications in its own right, and as a portmanteau word encompassing, if not always specifically referring to, its own procedural or substantive planning policies.

The board's consideration of prematurity differs from the other matters analysed here in two ways. Firstly, prematurity has been used to determine, not whether an application should be approved at all, but whether it should be approved *now*. Implicit in this decision is that, if the matters causing an application to be found premature are resolved, it could then be reconsidered. Secondly, prematurity is a hybrid matter. The areas of policy development we have reviewed pertain to either procedural or substantive elements of planning. The board's treatment of prematurity has encompassed both elements, although primarily the procedural. Acting with limited statutory guidance and no policy direction, it has found planning applications to be premature in certain well-defined circumstances.

The board has received some statutory and judicial direction with respect to prematurity, and has throughout the review period had an obligation to consider prematurity when dealing with certain types of applications. The Planning Act requires the approval authority for a plan of subdivision, which includes the board on an appeal of a plan or of conditions of approval, to have regard to 'whether the proposed subdivision is premature or in the public interest' (clause 51(24)(b)). Similarly, in deciding whether to approve a consent to sever, it must have regard to the matters set out in subsection 51(24) (subsection 53(12)). It must, however, exercise its discretion judicially when deciding whether a proposed subdivision is premature or whether the other conditions in subsection 51(24) have been met. The Court of Appeal held in *Highbury* that the board had erred in deciding that the provision of adequate school facilities was a matter to be addressed in determining whether a plan of subdivision was premature. It stated:

> 'it is clear ... that "premature" as used in cl. (b) [now clause 51(24)(b)] means that a proposed subdivision may be premature in the sense that it is presented too soon for any real need or demand for housing of the type contemplated or is perhaps being put forward before finalization of a pending official plan as defined in the act or before final determination of zoning provision under current consideration in a municipality.'[96]

The board has subsequently applied these considerations in deciding whether an application is premature, but it has also taken full advantage of the caveat to bring other considerations to bear also. It stated in *Clutterbuck* that the minister's (and, on appeal, the board's) decision with respect to prematurity was a matter of judgment,

> 'having regard to possible financial difficulties to which the development might commit the township, the undesirability of permitting new developments where they cannot be serviced economically and the requirement of the local Council and Ministry of Housing to endorse the most suitable development of the locality in the public interest.'[97]

As table 4.5 illustrates, the board addressed the question of prematurity during the review period, but with decreasing frequency. It addressed the matter in 18 per cent of its 1971–78 decisions, but only 9 per cent of its 1987–94, and 5 per cent of its 1995–2000 decisions. It had a statutory obligation to address prematurity only when hearing appeals of plans of subdivision and severances, but these represented only 43, 48, and 36 per cent of the decisions in the three review periods, respectively, in which it did so. Most of the remaining decisions were with respect to official plan and zoning amendments. The board had no obligation to consider prematurity in dealing with these

TABLE 4.5
Prematurity – Decision Data

	1971–78		1987–94		1995–2000	
	No.	%	No.	%	No.	%
Total Decisions	62	100	29	100	11	100
Application types						
Official plan[1]	14	23	5	17	3	27
Zoning by-law[2]	28	45	11	38	5	45
Plan of subdivision	4	6	3	10	2	18
Severance	23	37	11	38	2	18
Minor variance	2	3	2	7	1	9
Supporters						
Province	–	–	–	–	–	–
Municipality	31	50	10	34	3	27
Owner	56	90	24	83	10	91
Neighbour	–	–	2	7	1	9
Opponents						
Province	6	10	7	24	2	18
Municipality	37	60	12	41	6	55
Owner	–	–	5	17	1	9
Neighbour	34	55	14	48	7	64
Other board policy areas						
Approval procedures	2	3	4	14	–	–
Adequacy of decision making	17	27	5	17	–	–
Interference	9	15	1	3	–	–
Interest evaluation	18	29	14	48	3	27
Good planning	15	24	10	34	2	18
Neighbourhood character	3	5	3	10	–	–
Decision[3]						
Approve	12	19	10	34	2	18
Refuse to approve	51	82	19	66	9	82

1 Includes both comprehensive official plan and official plan amendment referrals.
2 Includes both comprehensive by-law and by-law amendment appeals.
3 One 1971–78 multiple application involved both approval and refusal.

applications, but it clearly believed that prematurity was a legitimate concern even here.[98]

The pattern of the OMB's refusal and approval of planning applications is of interest. During the 1971–78 review period 82 per cent of the decisions in which it addressed prematurity were refusals, a figure well in excess of the overall refusal rate of 56 per cent. The disparity still existed during the 1987–94 review period but was less marked, the refusal rates being 66 and 53 per cent respectively. The 1995–2000 period represented a return to the initial period, as 82 per cent of the decisions were again refusals, in strong contrast to the overall refusal rate of 41 per cent. It is difficult to determine the influence of prematurity itself on the board's decision making during the two earlier review periods, as in most instances other policy considerations were also addressed. It was clearly of great importance during the most recent period, however, as it was the only policy considered in more than half of the prematurity-related decisions. There are other data also which suggest the importance of prematurity to the board. In every decision, in all three review periods, it refused to approve an application it considered to be premature. It gave approvals, where the issue of prematurity was raised, only when it concluded on the evidence that an application was not premature. There is no doubt that it has consistently found prematurity to be a bar to approval. The circumstances under which it has found prematurity to exist are described below.

Procedural Elements of Prematurity

The OMB has most frequently considered prematurity in connection with the planning process. The areas it has addressed pertain to the status of official plans and planning policies generally, the existence of planning studies pertaining to the matters before it, and, to a lesser extent, the adequacy of certain types of applications.

The board has always considered it important that planning applications be supported by a municipality's planning policies, particularly those in its official plan. This is not notable in itself. The preparation and approval of an official plan lies at the heart of the planning process, and the board has an obligation to consider the application of official plan policies to the matters before it. The Planning Act is static, however, in that it deals with the formal status of official plans but does not address the dynamic of their application. It provides no guidance as to how the board is to deal with appeals in the absence of any local planning policy or official plan, or where policies and plans are under consideration, but have not reached the stage of approval or adoption. It is in responding to applications made when these circumstances occur that it has made creative use of what might be termed the doctrine of prematurity.

During the 1971–78 review period, when the use of official plans was not as widespread as it later became, the board occasionally held the lack of planning controls to be an indication of prematurity.[99] It held that plans of subdivision were premature because, inter alia, the municipalities lacked any planning controls,[100] or lacked a development plan upon which to base the required zoning by-law for the subdivision.[101]

The board has often, throughout the entire review period, been called upon to consider the application of planning policies which are being developed or are contained in official plans for which approval is pending. It has generally held that it would be premature to approve applications while official plan policies are still being developed.[102] This was particularly so where a proposed development, while not currently prohibited, would run counter to policies currently being considered for inclusion it in an official plan.[103] Calling an application premature was, in this context, a useful shorthand expression of its view that planning is an ongoing activity, and that the interests being expressed through the development of local planning policies should not be frustrated by the approval of applications which might prove to be incompatible with those policies.

By 1987 the board had developed a further variant of this approach in response to developments in planning tools. It was becoming common by this time for municipalities to prepare secondary plans containing detailed policies to govern the development of specified areas, although these were not necessarily to be adopted as official plans. The board's finding of prematurity in decisions where secondary plans were required by an official plan, but had not yet been prepared, appears to have turned on the nature of the applications before it. Thus, in a zoning application which it concluded would have an adverse impact, it held that approval was premature until the secondary plan had been prepared.[104] Where it was dealing with official plan amendments setting out general development policies, it held that it was not premature to approve these in the absence of the called-for secondary plans, as the latter were required later when specific development proposals were brought forward.[105] The board has, on occasion, further extended this application of prematurity by using it as a reason for refusing to approve applications which were in conformity with official plans currently in force but which might run counter to newer, emerging policies.[106]

A variant of this has been to find development proposals premature until the appropriate development controls are in place. The board has thus determined that seasonal shoreline residential development was premature until an agreement dealing with environmental concerns was in place.[107] Yet in a recent decision the board took a very different approach and made an uncharacteristic leap of faith. It approved an official plan amendment that would permit the creation of a community of 30,000 within a largely agricultural area, without knowing the particulars of when and how water, sewer, and highway requirements were to be met, on the understanding that adequate control mechanisms would be in place at the appropriate time to prevent premature development.[108]

The board has on occasion used prematurity as a policy tool. In the *Scarborough Transportation Corridor* decision, it refused to approve a strongly opposed application for funding to purchase portions of a proposed expressway corridor not yet in private ownership. The ability of Metropolitan Toronto to finance the purchase was not in issue. The construction of the expressway had not yet been approved, and the board concluded that the application was premature until the ultimate use of the lands to be acquired had been determined.[109]

The OMB has frequently, throughout the entire review period, held applications to be premature on the ground that they were not supported or justified by planning studies. Its use of prematurity in this context has served to shed light on its understanding of the planning process. Its approach has frequently been project-focused, in that it has held applications to be premature when their proponents have failed to provide evidence of planning studies justifying them and responding to objections, particularly objections based on adverse impact. The board has also taken a broader outlook focused on planning policy development, holding that applications are premature because they are unsupported by any planning policy studies.[110] In some of these decisions it held approvals to be premature until studies under way had been completed. Examples include studies to determine long-term residential use patterns,[111] to determine shoreline parks requirements,[112] to establish boundaries for the expansion of urban development,[113] to establish adult entertainment policies for inclusion into an official plan,[114] and to establish front yard parking policies.[115] It appears that, in these instances, it was unknown at the time of the hearings if these studies would support the applications. The equation applied by the board appears to have been that prematurity arises from the uncertainty regarding land use policies that will ultimately be developed and applied, and uncertainty as to whether approving an application now may create long-term land use incompatibilities and other problems.[116]

In most of the decisions in this area, however, studies were not underway, and the board went further by stating that applications were premature because studies it considered necessary had not been undertaken. This occurred frequently during the 1995–2000 period. The board has thus held that it would be premature to approve waterfront development which might interfere with land uses found desirable once planning studies had been completed,[117] to approve high-density residential development in a mixed use area until the municipality had undertaken studies to determine a reasonable land use pattern for the area,[118] to permit a new shopping centre before the council had determined the total amount of acreage to be set aside for shopping centre development,'[119] to approve rezoning of a large area for industrial development until an overall plan for the development and servicing of the lands has been undertaken,[120] or to approve development in environmentally sensitive areas until the necessary hydrogeological and other studies have been undertaken.[121] While the board treated the lack or inadequacy of planning studies as determinative of prematurity, the need for or adequacy of such studies remained a matter for it, not objectors, to determine. Thus, it refused to await completion of studies for adjoining lands before approving a high-density residential designation.[122] It approved residential development within an environmentally sensitive area where it was satisfied that environmental matters had been exhaustively reviewed and addressed.[123] It refused to hold the approval of a large-scale redevelopment scheme to be premature on the ground that only a part of the entire planning area was included.[124]

The OMB has occasionally used prematurity as a ground for refusal when it has not been satisfied that the type of application before it provides sufficient opportunity for the full consideration of planning issues. It has addressed this also as a matter of the adequacy of approval procedures as discussed in chapter 3. It has refused to approve multiple severance applications on the ground that they were tantamount to a subdivision and should be subject to the consultation with various agencies that would be required by a plan of subdivision.[125] It has found multiple severances requiring an amendment to a zoning by-law to be premature on the ground that the in-depth study required for approval

Policy Development in a Public Policy Vacuum   143

of a by-law had not yet been undertaken.[126] After 1987, by which time site planning was an established planning process,[127] it refused to approve zoning by-laws which left much of the detail with respect to design, servicing, and traffic matters to be resolved in the site plan review process.[128] In both types of decisions prematurity arose from the fact that the application type selected did not provide an adequate process for the consideration of matters that had to be addressed before approval could be given.

Substantive Elements of Prematurity

While the OMB has most frequently considered prematurity in the context of the planning process, it has also applied the term in addressing a substantive planning issue, the provision of municipal services. For the most part, its concern has been with the provision of hard services – water, sewers, and roads – so as to ensure that new developments can be serviced economically.[129] It has thus held that it was premature to approve development applications where municipal services were not available,[130] where existing services were recognized as being inadequate,[131] or where the provision of services required for the proposed developments had not yet been resolved.[132] Where, on the other hand, it has concluded that existing services were adequate, even such privately provided services as septic tanks, it has rejected claims of prematurity and given approvals.[133] More recently, taking a broader policy perspective, it has held development proposals in unorganized territory to be premature because services would have to be provided by nearby municipalities which had no responsibility for them and had not agreed to provide them.[134] The board occasionally found applications to be premature in other circumstances also, such as where applicants for farm retirement lots were not planning to retire in the foreseeable future,[135] or where there was no evidence that a rezoning transferring high-quality agricultural land from farming to commercial use was in the public interest.[136] In the great majority of these decisions, however, lack of services provided the rationale for a finding of prematurity.

Prematurity: Available When Needed

It has been difficult to find an easily discernable pattern in the OMB's use of this concept. It has held the approval of development proposals in areas lacking planning controls to be premature, yet at the same time it has given approvals in similar circumstances. It has frequently treated prematurity as an additional reason for refusal where it felt that others of its policies were being contravened. On the other hand, where planning controls existed, it has refused to approve applications which complied with older but approved official plan policies while running counter to emerging but as yet unapproved policies. Prematurity has thus provided legitimation, in these instances, for the board's decision not to apply the 'law,' that is, the approved official plan policies, but to give weight to emerging policies which lack any formal status. It has linked prematurity to its policy regarding the adequacy of decision making in holding applications lacking adequate supporting planning studies to be premature for that reason. It has also linked prematurity to its policy regarding the adequacy of planning procedures by holding applications which provide insufficient opportunity for a full consideration of planning issues to be premature for that reason. Moreover, it has not limited prematurity to consideration of the adequacy of or compliance with statutory procedures, but has extended the term to encompass certain of the elements within the planning system from which applications derive their justification. These elements provide a threshold that applications must achieve if they are to be considered for approval, and, by extension, a window into the Board's thinking as to what the planning process requires. By calling applications premature because certain elements of the process have not been undertaken, are not yet completed, or are inadequate, it has been saying that, as a matter of policy, it requires planning applications to meet certain minimum process requirements.

5

The Treatment of Provincial Policy

This chapter examines the manner in which a tribunal interprets and applies the policies of its senior level of government. It shows how the Ontario Municipal Board has addressed the provincial policies which have been in effect from time to time, and, of equal importance, how it has subordinated these policies to policies of its own.

A central feature in the examination of the relationship between a tribunal and its senior government is the manner in which the former responds to the latter's policy pronouncements. The results of such an examination tell us much about both the nature and the degree of independence exercised by the tribunal. To put the matter in the language of regulatory theory: Does the tribunal act primarily as an agent of the government, making decisions the government wants but does not wish to make itself? Does it interpret the interests of the government, as expressed through its pronouncements, as the public interest? The more specific question being asked in the context of this study is: Can the manner in which the OMB interprets and applies provincial policy itself be characterized as policy?

It would appear natural that a tribunal created by a provincial legislature would seek to implement the policies of successive governments that fall within its area of jurisdiction. The Macbeth Committee stated in 1972 that it 'is satisfied that the OMB tries to follow government policy in making its decisions.'[1] The OMB itself has regularly taken the position that it must 'have regard to' provincial policy, even before the enactment of section 3 of the Planning Act, 1983, made this a requirement with respect to formally adopted statements of provincial policy. In its *71st Annual Report*, issued in 1976, it stated that '[t]he decisions of the board are independent and are governed by the statutes and when not in statutory conflict have regard to government policy.'[2] Yet these are misleading statements, as they suggest that the board has, as a matter of policy, given greater weight to provincial policy than this chapter will show to have been the case.

The terms *provincial policy* and *government policy*, both frequently used, are to some extent interchangeable, but the former has a broader meaning. It encompasses both government policy, which technically means policy which has received cabinet approval, and ministry policy, those internal and often unpublished guidelines and standards developed by individual ministries and applied by them when, inter alia, reviewing planning applications. The distinction between these two terms cannot always be clearly drawn, but the term provincial policy will generally be used here.

One must keep in mind the limited extent of provincial policy related to land use when analysing the OMB's treatment of it. The Planning Act has never given much policy guidance. Governments have expressed policies dealing with some specific aspects of planning, but they have said little with respect to many procedural and substantive planning matters. The board has developed and applied its own policies in these areas; it has also had to respond to provincial policies where they do apply. This chapter illustrates the manner in which it has treated these policies where they do exist.

Sources of Provincial Policy

The sources of provincial policy are many and varied. Government is not a monolith. While the cabinet, acting formally as the Lieutenant Governor in Council, clearly speaks for the government, its statements pertaining to land use and development issues are, of necessity, very general in nature. Its only opportunity to make decisions on specific planning applications was removed in 1983 when the right to petition the Lieutenant Governor in Council from a board decision under the Planning Act was abolished. The day-to-day activities of government which impinge most directly and frequently on planning matters are those of individual ministries, each of which has its own mandate and agenda. Within each ministry, policy pronouncements can include statements issued by the minister pertaining to either general policy or specific matters, and policy guidelines formally issued by the ministry. These are published documents and are thus available to the general public. In addition, ministry staff frequently develop internal guidelines and standards to assist them in evaluating individual development applications. These are generally unpublished, are likely to be known only by persons actively involved in development, and are subject to change at any time. The ministries which have been most directly involved with the planning and development matters coming before the OMB have changed over time with government restructuring, but are currently the Ministry of Municipal Affairs and Housing, the Ministry of Energy and the Environment, the Ministry of Natural Resources, the Ministry of Agriculture, Food, and Rural Affairs, and the Ministry of Transportation.[3]

The province has been involved in the development of planning policies applicable to major growth areas, and to the province as a whole, but its interest in such activity has varied greatly over the study period. In the late 1960s and early 1970s it engaged in a large-scale regional planning exercise to establish broad, long-term development patterns within the Toronto-Centred Region (TCR). This was undertaken without a specific statutory basis, but was intended to provide the framework for local planning activities undertaken under the ambit of the Planning Act. This exercise in regional planning had little impact on subsequent development in the TCR,[4] but there remained support for the belief that there was a provincial interest in planning and development activities that transcended local interests, and that this interest should be given voice in more than ministry reviews of individual applications. During the 1970s the government gave consideration to limiting indiscriminate urban growth in rural areas and to protecting good agricultural land, which led to the adoption of policies embodied in Urban Development in Rural Areas (UDIRA) and the Food Land Guidelines (FLG), respectively. This support for a provincial role in determining the general parameters of growth was expressed also in an extensive review of the planning process during the 1970s and early 1980s, which proceeded through various studies and government position papers. The last of these, the White Paper on the Planning Act, concluded that a general statement of broad provincial interests should be incorporated into the act and that '[t]o elaborate on defined provincial interests, the act will authorize the minister, either independently or jointly with other ministries, to publish policy circulars. In addition, the legislation will be supported by regulations and planning guidelines.'[5] The culmination of this process was the enactment of the Planning Act, 1983. While the major purpose of the act was to enhance local responsibility for planning, it also defined a provincial role. Section 2 required that the Minister of Municipal Affairs have regard to substantive matters of provincial interest, examples of which were set out in the section. Section 3 provided for the adoption by the Lieutenant Governor in Council of policy statements on municipal planning matters considered by the Minister of Municipal Affairs to be of provincial interest, and, once these were adopted, municipalities and the board were required to have regard to them. Such policy statements, it should be noted, were not limited to the matters of provincial interest listed in section 2 of the Planning Act.

Four policy statements, dealing with the protection of aggregate resources, flood plains, and wetlands, and the provision of housing, were adopted by the Lieutenant Governor in Council between 1986 and 1992. These statements, plus the Food Land Guidelines, which were treated as a policy statement but never adopted as such, were modified and combined by the New Democratic Party government of the day and adopted as the Comprehensive Set of Policy Statements. This document came into effect early in 1995, but was replaced with a new and very different document, the Provincial Policy Statement (PPS), little more than a year later by the newly elected Progressive Conservative government. The nature of these various policy statements, and the board's treatment of them, is addressed below.

Early in the 1990s the provincial cabinet endorsed the guidelines as part of a provincial strategy to speed up the making of environmentally sound land use decisions, and, more particularly, to guide development on the Oak Ridges Moraine north of Toronto. By endorsing these guidelines the government was stating that they were matters of provincial interest under section 2 of the Planning Act. It did not, however, adopt them as formal statements of government policy under section (3) of the act.

There were other provincial decisions which reflected the differing mandates and policies of specific ministries, and which had a significant impact on development patterns in Ontario. The Ministry of Transportation has been responsible for the locating and construction of new highways, and its decisions, particularly with respect to the expressway system, have done much to determine where major urban development will occur. The Ministry of the Environment, through its approval and construction of trunk water and sewer systems, particularly the South Peel Servicing Scheme in the 1960s and York-Durham Scheme in the 1970s, has given a tremendous impetus to growth in the areas served by those schemes. The Ministry of Housing's Ontario Housing Action Program of 1973–78 was designed to accelerate residential development in areas west, north, and east of Metropolitan Toronto. These ministry activities, probably more so than formal land use planning policies, have established the context within which the OMB has exercised its responsibilities. As Frankena and Scheffman noted in describing the clash between the province's regional land use policies and its servicing and residential development programs, '[i]t is evident, however, that the province pursued its housing obligations west of Toronto in Peel without being constrained by the TCR plan.'[6]

In addition to developing general planning policies, and making investment decisions affecting general patterns of urban growth, the Ministries of Municipal Affairs, the Environment, Natural Resources, and others have been actively engaged in developing and applying ministry policy, internal guidelines, and standards to assist them in carrying out their mandates pertaining to land development.[7] They have regularly reviewed proposed official plans and amendments, and have often required them to be modified to meet ministry 'concerns,' a code word for the guidelines, internal policies, and standards applied by their officials. Ministries have been required also to comment on zoning by-laws under appeal to the board, which has often placed heavy reliance on these comments in arriving at its decisions.

Approved official plans may also be considered as indirect expressions of provincial policy. They have from their inception required the approval of the Minister of Municipal Affairs, which is not given unless formal statements of government policy are complied with and ministry guidelines and standards are taken into consideration in official plan policies. In recent years the link between provincial policy and official plans has been made more tenuous through the transfer of official plan approval authority to upper-tier regional and district municipalities, but even these give their approvals within the larger context of provincial policy where such policy is applicable.

The primary focus in addressing the relationship between the province and the OMB, as expressed through the latter's treatment of provincial policy, is on how it has dealt with such formal expressions of policy as provincial policy statements and ministry guidelines. It is important to note also the significance the board has attached to ministry evaluations of individual development proposals. These are indicators of an ongoing, everyday relationship between it and the agencies of government most directly concerned with the subject matter of its hearings. Also, it regularly considers the conformity of development applications with official plans, and we must acknowledge as well the importance of the province's indirect influence through its approval of official plans. Our purpose here, however, is to examine the board's treatment of provincial policy per se. Policy as expressed in approved official plans, while it may be considered an indirect form of provincial policy, is essentially local planning policy which has been accepted as fitting into the provincial policy framework.

The Pattern of OMB Involvement

Our analysis includes all instances in which published decisions of the OMB made reference to any provincial policy pertaining directly to land use planning. The results are summarized in table 5.1, which shows that the policy mix changed considerably as time passed. The regional planning policies of the 1970s were replaced after 1983 with policy statements adopted by the Lieutenant Governor in Council under section 3 of the Planning Act. The four initial policy statements were replaced in 1995 with the Comprehensive Set of Policy Statements, and this document was replaced in 1996 with the Provincial Policy Statement. As only two decisions involving the former were reported, they are included in the PPS data in table 5.1. The provincial guidelines dealing with growth and with the Oak Ridges Moraine were adopted during the 1987–94 period, and were considered by the board during the later years of that period and the early years of the 1995–2000 period. The UDIRA policy of the 1971–78 period had been replaced by 1987 with the FLG, which played a central role in the protection of high-quality agricultural lands during the 1987–94 period. The FLG was superceded in 1996 by the agricultural land protection policies in the PPS, and the decisions in which they were addressed occurred early in the 1995–2000 period. The Agricultural Code of Practice, placing minimum distance limits between agricultural and non-agricultural land uses, was addressed regularly but infrequently throughout the entire review period. Environmental protection policies were addressed during both review periods, although their content changed over time. A miscellany of other policies were also referred to, sometimes only in passing and without any elaboration, but they were too variegated to be susceptible to detailed analysis. This selection does, however, underrate the importance of provincial involvement, as it excludes reference to the ministry comments and guidelines which are considered by the OMB but are rarely referred to in its decisions.

TABLE 5.1
Provincial Policies – Frequency of Consideration

	1971–78		1987–94		1995–2000	
	No.	%	No.	%	No.	%
Provincial policy	64	100	103	100	70	100
Regional planning	12	19	n.a.		n.a.	
Design for development	1	2				
TCR Plan	3	5				
COLUC	8	13				
Policy statement	n.a.		37	36	36	51
Aggregates			3	3	3	4
Flood plains			2	3	–	
Housing			23	22	4	6
Wetlands			9	9	4	6
Provincial policy statement			n.a.		25	36
Provincial guidelines	n.a.		7	7	6	9
Declaration of provincial interest	n.a.		2	2	1	1
Agricultural land protection	24	38	47	46	16	23
UDIRA	11	17	n.a.		n.a.	
FLG	8[1]	13	43	42	11	16
Code of Practice	5	9	4	4	5	7
Environmental protection	10	16	19	18	11	16
Niagara Escarpment	5	9	3	3	3	4
Ministry of Environment guidelines	2	4	7	7	4	6
Environmental protection	3	5	9	9	4	6
Other	28	44	3	3	9	13

1 Including Ministry of Agriculture Strategy and Government Green Paper.

The OMB has responded with increasing frequency over time to provincial policies. It addressed such policies in 18, 32, and 35 per cent, respectively, of the reviewed decisions during the three review periods. Yet these numbers represent only a small minority of the hearings in which the board dealt with land use planning matters. There were 953 reported decisions for the 1972–78 review period in which the board dealt with such matters.[8] Of these, only 63 (one of the 64 1971–78 decisions included in the table was a 1971 decision), or 7 per cent, made reference to provincial policies. There were 645 reported decisions for the 1987–94 review period, of which only 103, or 16 per cent, referred to such policies. There were 396 reported decisions for the 1995–2000 period, of which only 70, or 18 per cent, referred to such policies. These figures reflect the limited scope of provincial planning policy and help us understand why the board found itself engaging in policy development when it so frequently lacked any provincial guidance. It did address provincial policy more frequently during the two later periods. This was indicative of the increasing importance of government policy in the planning system, arising from the introduction into the system, prior to 1987, of matters of provincial interest and provincial policy statements, and from the increasing importance of agricultural land protection and environmental protection policies.

Table 5.2 shows the infrequency with which the province has chosen to intervene directly as a party, even when its own policies have been at issue. Its overall intervention rate was low during the earliest period, increased considerably during the second, then fell off during the most recent. It appeared that during the 1987–94 period the province was prepared to be considerably more interventionist. This was largely a matter of intervention where the application of provincial policy was being addressed, as the province's rate of involvement was negligible whenever provincial policy was not being addressed. The primary reason for provincial intervention has been to oppose development which a ministry, generally the Ministry of Municipal Affairs, has concluded was in contravention of a stated provincial policy. The increase of provincial involvement between the 1971– 78 and 1987–94 periods suggests that during this time provincial ministries were according increasing importance to policies under their jurisdiction, and to the need to ensure that they were followed. The reduction in direct provincial involvement in hearings during the most recent period suggests two possibilities: either the province is satisfied that development proposals are more frequently in compliance with its policies, or it has become a matter of government or ministry policy to be less interventionist in board hearings.

The province was active in supporting some of its policies, but not others. It did not appear as a party in any of the twelve 1971–78 hearings involving its regional planning policies. It appeared in only 16 per cent of the 1987–94 and 14 per cent of the 1995–2000 hearings involving

TABLE 5.2
Direct Provincial Participation. A = all decisions during period; B = decisions in which provincial policy considered; C = decisions in which provincial policy not considered

	1971–78					
	A		B		C	
	No.	%	No.	%	No.	%
Total Decisions	348	100	65	100	283	100
Province						
Support	1	*	–	–	1	*
Oppose	16	5	11	17	5	2
	1987–94					
Total Decisions	321	100	103	100	218	100
Province						
Support	6	2	4	4	2	1
Oppose	43	13	38	37	5	2
	1995–2000					
Total Decisions	201	100	70	100	131	100
Province						
Support	2	1	2	3	–	–
Oppose	17	8	16	23	1	*

*Less than 1%.

statements of provincial policy. The province played a far more proactive role when its agricultural land and environmental protection policies were being addressed. It was a party to only 21 per cent of the 1971–78 hearings in which its agricultural policies were addressed, but in 53 per cent of such hearings in each of the later review periods. The comparable figures for its appearance as a party during the three periods when environmental protection policies were being addressed were 40, 53, and 45 per cent, respectively. The data suggest a two-fold approach. The province has been willing to support the application of its more specific policies pertaining to agricultural land and environmental protection by arguing for its own interpretation of these policies at board

TABLE 5.3
Approvals and Refusals

	1971–78		1987–94		1995–2000	
	No.	%	No.	%	No.	%
A. Total Decisions[1]	344	100	320	100	201	100
Approval	151	44	151	47	119	59
Refusal	193	56	169	53	82	41
B. Decisions in which provincial policy addressed	64	100	103	100	70	100
Approval	32	50	43	52	38	54
Refusal	32	50	60	58	32	46
C. Decisions, in (B), in which ministry in opposition	11	100	38	100	16	100
Approval	4	36	11	29	9	56
Refusal	7	64	27	71	7	44

1 Total decision data based on analysis of 344 of the 1971–78 decisions and 320 of the 1987–94 decisions. The remainder were excluded because they either involved multiple applications and included both approvals and refusals, or they involved a motion, with neither the approval nor refusal of the application itself.

hearings. It has been distinctly less willing to argue for its interpretation of the more generalized policies found in its Section 3 policy statements.

The data pertaining to provincial involvement suggest that, while the introduction of provincial policy as a matter to be considered influences the OMB's decision, it is not determinative of that decision. Table 5.3 illustrates that the board has, overall and in all review periods, shown a generally similar pattern of approvals and refusals, and that the approval rates when the application of provincial policy was being addressed differed little from the overall approval rates. What is most noteworthy is the apparent recent loss of provincial influence in these circumstances. During the first two review periods the board's approval rate was significantly lower where the province appeared as a party in opposition to development proposals. During the post-1994 period, however, the approval rate in this circumstance has differed little from the overall approval rate.

The data do not reflect the true degree of provincial involvement in OMB hearings. This often included having provincial staff appear as subpoenaed witnesses, and the submission of ministry comments to the board, particularly with respect to applications involving official plans and amendments. The data do, however, accurately reflect the province's formal, high-profile involvement as a party, an involvement resulting in each instance from a ministry decision that the matter before the board so closely involved its policies that it should play a direct role rather than rely on other parties defending them.

The OMB's General Approach

The OMB has sought throughout the entire review period to achieve a balance between the application of provincial policy and its own independent judgment with respect to the wide range of matters before it. It has frequently engaged in internal discussions of various government and ministry policy initiatives, corresponding with provincial ministries with respect to these matters, and meeting with government officials to discuss them. The available evidence is often more tantalizing than informative, suggesting the existence of a relationship between the board and the province, and of the former's recognition of the need to give consideration to provincial policy but giving little indication of content. There are some more specific references, however. Early in 1979, following the government's approval of the Food Land Guidelines as government policy, the members considered its application during an internal meeting; '[X] referred to the 'Provincial Government Food Land Guidelines' publication, which the Members should be familiar with as government policy. [Y] was appointed to review and report at the next meeting on the points in such policy that the Members should follow.'[9] The members more recently considered the application of the Growth and Settlement Policy Guidelines, and noted in the minutes of their meeting that

> Growth and Settlement Guidelines form the framework within which decisions are being made. They have been discussed by Ministers, approved by Cabinet and represent government policy ... These are not policy statements under section 3 of the act, and as a result, these guidelines do not have the same authority as a section 3 policy statement ... In the hierarchy of policy tools, guidelines such as these would rank just below section 3 policy statements. They will provide essential policy direction.[10]

The OMB's general position was expressed in a letter from it to a senior official in the Ministry of Natural Resources:

156   A Law unto Itself

> The declaration of provincial interest is a very strong tool to which the Board is obliged to give considerable weight during a hearing. However, as I emphasized at our meeting, it is not an end in itself. Unless the evidence is supportive of the provincial statement and its application in a particular hearing is clear for all to see, the matter could well fail ... As an administrative tribunal, the Board conducts hearings in an adversarial environment and the evidence we hear is always the final determinant of the adjudication.[11]

This summarizes as well as any decision the board's view that provincial policy constitutes evidence that it will consider and weigh along with other evidence, but it does less than justice to the importance it has attached to policy expressions, regardless of whether it has been required to have regard to that policy.

Evidence of the OMB's internal discussions of provincial policy is indicative of a close working relationship between it and the province, but its decisions best illustrate its view of the formal relationship between the two. The *Caledon* decision was significant with respect to the interpretation and application of provincial policy in the pre-Planning Act, 1983 period.[12] The board was asked to order the review of a proposed official plan on the ground that it contravened the TCR Plan by providing for more estate residential growth in the municipality than was contemplated by the latter. It ordered the review, and concluded that there was such a contravention. It indicated the range of sources of provincial policy:

> in the statutes, in Government regulations which have statutory force, in decisions of the executive council (the Cabinet) on appeals from the Board, and in official pronouncements by the Prime Minister or other Minister responsible in respect of the particular subject-matter.[13]

It then set out the manner, subsequently followed and variously applied by other panels throughout the entire review period, in which it was to interpret and apply provincial policy:

> This Board applies such a policy by considering and interpreting the statement of policy with the assistance of counsel after making findings of fact on the evidence before it in much the same way as the Courts apply the law by considering and interpreting the pertinent law after making findings of fact on the evidence before them. The Government states its policy as of

general application and this Board interprets and decides how that policy applies to the facts in the particular case without assistance from the Government or any member and applies that policy for reasons which are given in writing and which are subject to the Courts on questions of law and to the executive council (the Cabinet) on any question.[14]

There are two matters of interest arising from this statement. Firstly, it is very revealing as to how the board sought to establish its freedom from subordination to provincial policy. It relied heavily on a judicial model of its functions by equating statements of policy with legislation which it must, as do the courts, interpret and apply to the facts. This interpretation was strengthened by its statement that it interpreted policy 'with the assistance of counsel.' While lawyers were accepted as experts in statutory interpretation, it did not follow that they were more versed in interpreting statements of public policy than were the politicians and public officials who were directly responsible for their preparation, adoption, and administration. Yet it stated that it was to perform this function 'without assistance from the Government or any member.' Secondly, while this statement indicated the process the board was to follow in dealing with provincial policy, it did not indicate the substance of this activity. What criteria and standards was it to apply in 'interpreting and deciding'? How was it to determine the weight to give to such policy, particularly in the face of other interests and planning issues? The policy statements themselves gave no guidance regarding these questions, and the statutory requirement to have regard to them did not come into effect until the enactment of the Planning Act, 1983. To answer them, we must look to the manner in which the board responded to these policies, and, of equal importance, to the manner in which it applied its own policies.

The OMB further developed this theme in the *Grimsby* decision, in which it considered how it would deal with conflict between provincial and local policies. The issue here was the status to be granted to statements or opinions emanating from a ministry objecting to a municipality's official plan provisions and zoning by-laws. Its discussion of the relationship between local and provincial interests is indicative of its own policy of balancing interests:

It is not too difficult to imagine situations where the provincial view might differ from that of the municipal representatives, and where it is of such overriding concern that the provincial broader view should probably prevail. Sometimes a more flexible view may be required so as to not discourage a municipality adopting progressive planning legislation. Accordingly, the Board cannot lightly disregard the expressed desire made on behalf of the municipality in what it wishes to have approved.[15]

This is a clear expression of the board's need to place even provincial policy in a larger context in which both provincial and local interests would be addressed. This statement will be seen to be an accurate, although partial, expression of its 'policy' for interpreting and applying expressions of provincial policy.

The OMB's position in receiving and responding to expressions of provincial policy was addressed in lengthy and confusing fashion in a series of cases arising out of its interim order and final decision in the City of Barrie's annexation application.[16] It had held that it was bound by provincial policy as expressed in a minister's letter stating that the government had allocated a population to Barrie of 125,000, and it had refused to allow cross-examination on the letter. The cases culminating in the Supreme Court of Canada decision focused primarily on the issue of cross-examination. The court did, however, significantly limit the authority that expressions of provincial policy were to exercise over the board's decision-making discretion, stating:

> The effect of all these provisions is to leave the Board with the duty to dispose of the annexation issue 'upon such terms as it may consider expedient' without any directives, statutory standards or guidelines, and without any right in the executive branch of government to limit the Board by order in council, regulation or otherwise,'[17]

and that its receipt of such policy expressions did not affect the rights of other parties, including the right to cross-examine. The court therefore appeared to have taken the position that provincial policy should be accorded no higher status than other evidence. This position was changed, however, by the enactment of the Planning Act, 1983. The board, along with ministries, other agencies, and municipalities, was required to have regard to policy statements issued under section 3 of the act, and, when acting in place of the minister in approving official plans, was required to have regard to the matters of provincial interest set out in section 2. The potential for granting more authority to the statements of provincial policy had therefore been created, but, as noted below, its approach showed little change.

The board's position with respect to having regard to provincial policy was clearly enunciated in the *Ottawa-Carleton* decision:

> The board is directed by the legislation and the judicial authorities to give a fair hearing to all interested persons with relevant views to impart, to use its *independent* judgement on the merits of the proposal, and to see that planning decisions are made with regard to proper planning principles, while always bearing in mind and having regard to provincial policy and the fact that, as one of several factors, the board is dealing with decisions of a duly elected body exercising legitimate legislative authority.[18]

The board continued to be aware of an uneasy balance between considering provincial policy and applying its independent judgment. Despite the rationale for exercising a degree of independence expressed in both review periods in the *Caledon* and *Ottawa-Carleton* decisions, it has spoken of the subordination of its role to that of the province. In *IPCF Properties* it considered a motion that it adjourn two retail warehouse outlet hearings pending its decision in an ongoing hearing on this topic in another municipality. The rationale was that the ongoing hearing would establish general principles pertaining to this new form of retailing which could then be applied to the adjourned hearings. The board refused the adjournment on the ground that to grant it would be analogous to treating the pending decision as provincial policy, thereby usurping the role of government.[19]

IPCF illustrated two elements of the board's position. It recognized that it lacked the jurisdiction to create formal policy where that jurisdiction has been specifically granted to the province, as under section 3, and it was consistent with its oft-expressed claim that it decides matters on the basis of the evidence before it, not on predetermined policy. Yet, as evidence of its own decision-making activities indicate, both of the above must be heavily qualified. It has not made provincial policy, but, in the absence of any more specific directive than to have regard to, it has interpreted such policy as it sees fit. Where provincial policy has been silent, it has developed a consistency of jurisprudence in certain areas which could be considered, in effect, as a form of policy created by a provincial agency, even if not formally endorsed by the government.

As observers have noted, the board has created substitutes for provincial policy in many areas where the latter is lacking. Frankena and Scheffman stated that 'One of the most notable characteristics of provincial intervention in land markets is the extent to which the province has failed to provide clear statements of its policies. The lack of clear statements has resulted in considerable uncertainty among developers, municipal planners, and even provincial representatives concerning what provincial policy is, and it has given the OMB an inordinate amount of power to determine land use policy by default.'[20] The authors then recommended that 'the province provide clear policy statements for use by the OMB as well as municipal governments and landowners.' While the province eventually did this to a limited extent, the board has applied its own gloss in interpreting these as well as other expressions of provincial policy. Its 'policy' has been to establish a balance between the latter and other matters it considers important, and, as shown below, that balance is not automatically in favour of provincial policy. The following sections illustrate how the board has applied that approach in dealing with selected key expressions of provincial policy.

Regional Planning Policy

The OMB's treatment of the province's regional planning policies during the 1970s show that provincial policy played a marginal role in its deliberations and that it was already, as a matter of its own policy, treating provincial policy as evidence to be accorded little if any greater intrinsic weight than other evidence placed before it.

In the 1960s and 1970s the provincial government engaged in an ambitious program of direct involvement in comprehensive regional land use planning. This became a matter of policy, in very general terms, with the release in 1966 of the White Paper, *Design for Development*, a document asserting the province's responsibility for regional planning. This program was not intended to replace the traditional, locally oriented land use planning process in which municipalities engaged under the Planning Act, but rather to complement it by providing a general regional land use, transportation, and servicing context within which local planning would take place. These two planning functions remained separate at the provincial level. The Regional Planning Branch of the Ministry of Treasury and Intergovernmental Affairs was responsible for regional planning, while the administration of local planning remained the responsibility of the Ministry of Municipal Affairs. The province was divided by the former into regions, for each of which a general development plan was to be prepared. The first and only such plan to come into being was the Toronto-Centred Region Plan, a regional land use plan for an area of 8,600 square miles centred on Toronto, extending to Georgian Bay on the north, beyond Peterborough and Cobourg in the east, and to Hamilton and Kitchener-Waterloo in the west. The plan defined three zones: a heavily urbanized band along Lake Ontario, a commutershed to the north of this, and a peripheral area beyond that. It designated growth centres within each zone, and stated land use objectives relating to the size and spatial distribution of urban centres and to the preservation of land for agriculture and open space. The TCR Plan was unveiled as government policy in May 1970. It was followed by further measures intended to translate its general concepts into more detailed plans, and, particularly, to provide specific population allocations within the various sub-regions and growth centres. Reports in 1971 and 1972 recommended detailed population allocations, which were largely incorporated into the Central Ontario Lakeshore Urban Complex (COLUC) Task Force report of 1974. None of these specific recommendations were, however, adopted as government policy.

In the Conan Doyle story 'Silver Blaze', what Sherlock Holmes considered significant was that the dog did not bark in circumstances where barking would have been expected. Similarly, what is noteworthy here was not that the OMB considered provincial policy, which one would have expected such a tribunal to do, but the infrequency with which it was called upon to consider a significant government regional planning policy during the 1971–78 review period. The board addressed the major expressions of the policy, Design for Development, the TCR Plan, and the COLUC report, in only nine decisions, each being considered one, eight, and three times, respectively. Furthermore, these regional development policies played a limited role in its reasoning even in the few decisions where they were addressed. Design for Development was referred to only in passing. COLUC was noted in one decision, and was indicated as a reason for the decision in two others. The TCR Plan was merely noted in four of the eight decisions in which it was addressed. It appeared to provide the main reason for a decision in only the *Barrie Annexation* decision, in which the board accepted that it was bound by government policy to provide sufficient lands within the city of Barrie to accommodate the plan's target population of 125,000.[21]

Reasons for this infrequency of provincial policy consideration can be surmised. One was likely the difference in scale between the land use issues addressed in the regional planning policies and those most frequently considered by the OMB. In most applications before it, the scale of development under consideration was too small to have any effect on, or to be affected by, the general policies and land use designations in the regional policies. On occasion, however, it did consider applications involving substantial amounts of land or having substantial impact on rural areas or on the natural environment. It seems more likely that this infrequency of consideration arose from two other causes, the lack of importance accorded to the regional policies by the participants in development activities, and the essentially passive role played by the board. As a result, the parties rarely relied upon the TCR Plan or other policy statements in presenting their cases. Because of the board's understanding of its role as giving the court-like consideration of the evidence placed before it by the parties, it did not itself raise these policies, or seek to determine if they might be applicable in any given situation unless they were first brought to its attention by one or more of the parties.

The province was not a party, either in support or opposition, in any of these applications. The board did not therefore have the benefit, other than through its receipt of a minister's letter during the *Barrie Annexation* hearing, of the views of the government as to whether, or how, its regional planning policy was to be applied to the facts of a case. It was therefore left with a free hand to interpret and apply provincial policy using the approach it established in the *Caledon* decision.

The OMB was generally supportive of this policy, but normally in the context of its own policies. In *Maxine*, another decision involving the city of Barrie, it stated that the TCR Plan placed responsibility on a municipality to provide for orderly development within its boundaries, and that 'the Official Plan designations by the municipality ... are in the best public interest in view of the role that Barrie will be expected to assume under the general provisions of the Toronto-Centred Region Plan.'[22] In two decisions in the Town of Vaughan it relied to some extent on the TCR Plan. In the first, the amount of development proposed for a community within the plan's commutershed, where urban development was to be on a limited scale, was too substantial for this location, but a lesser amount of development was approved.[23] In the second, the fact that the site of a proposed theme park was within a zone in the TCR in which urbanization was to occur was a point in its favour, but what was determinative of the board's approval was its application of its own policy pertaining to the principles of good planning.[24] In *Toronto Airways* the proponent of an airport expansion argued that the COLUC studies, which provided for urbanization in the vicinity of the airport, supported its planning rationale for its expansion, but the board's deci-

The Treatment of Provincial Policy 163

sion to approve the expansion turned on the application of its own policies pertaining to the evaluation of interests and to interference with council decisions.[25] Yet it was prepared to accord substantial importance to provincial policy where its applicability to development proposals of some scale became an issue. It took an extreme position in the *Barrie Annexation* hearing. When during the course of the hearing it received a letter from the provincial treasurer, the minister responsible for the TCR Plan, stating that it was government policy that the board should order the annexation of an area that would accommodate a population of 125,000 by 2011, it stated that it was bound by the letter. The Divisional Court subsequently held that the board was right in holding that it was bound to follow the letter as government policy, and its decision subsequently reflected this.[26] In another hearing dealing with the long-term growth of a municipality within the lakeshore urbanizing zone in the TCR, the municipality took the position that it should be required to take only a limited amount of growth so as to preserve its character. The board rejected this, stating that 'because of the assigned role of Oakville by the Province in both the Toronto Centred Plan and the COLUC studies, there is an obligation on the municipality to accept its fair share of the population.'[27]

While the board addressed regional planning policy in only a few decisions, its treatment of such policy was generally consistent in treating it as evidence whose weight and applicability it was to determine in the circumstances of each case. The only exception was the *Barrie Annexation* decision, in which it treated such policy as an absolute. It took a similar approach, as we see below, in its treatment of other expressions of provincial policy.

Urban Development and the Protection of Agricultural Lands

The province has long expressed an interest in the preservation of its agricultural land base. Pressure during the 1960s for the encroachment of urban development into rural areas, particularly those having high-quality food lands, and for non-farm residential severances in such areas, led to the enunciation in 1966 of Urban Development in Rural Areas, a policy directed to discouraging scattered, minimally serviced, non-farm development in rural areas. The essence of the policy was that urban residential development should take place in municipalities that have adequate administrative organization to cope with urban problems. UDIRA was sponsored by the Ministry of Municipal Affairs, and focused on 'traditional' land use issues, the provision of proper hard services (roads, water, sewage), and soft services (schools, libraries, recreation facilities) for urban development. The Ministry of Agriculture and Food (OMAF) was also concerned with the intrusion of urban development into rural areas, but its focus was on the protection of farm land so as to maintain an economically viable agricultural industry in the province. In 1976 OMAF released A Strategy for Ontario Farmland, a statement of its reasons for protecting food lands from urban development pressures.[28] This was followed in 1977 by the government's Green Paper on Planning for Agriculture,[29] which contained draft guidelines for municipalities to use in developing official plan policies for the protection of agricultural lands. In 1978 a refinement of these, Food Land Guidelines,[30] was released as a statement of government policy. While neither the Guidelines nor its 1986 draft update, the Foodland Preservation Policy Statement, were formally adopted under section 3 of the Planning Act as a statement of provincial policy, they remained the province's policy with respect to the protection of agricultural lands until replaced in 1995 with the Comprehensive Set of Policy Statements, which was treated as tantamount to a section 3 policy statement by all parties, including the board.

Urban Development in Rural Areas

UDIRA was presented by way of speeches made by provincial cabinet ministers in 1966 and 1968.[31] The policy was therefore well in place by the commencement of the 1971–78 review period, and the chairman had stated the OMB's policy with respect to it in a memorandum to the members: 'These statements should be accepted as containing present Government policy on the subjects in question and it is suggested that they should be followed by this board as Government policy.'[32] The decisions in which the OMB considered UDIRA provide a good example of how it dealt with a stated, and fairly specific, provincial policy prior to the 1983 amendment to the Planning Act, which gave formal statutory authority to provincial policy statements. It addressed UDIRA in eleven reviewed decisions during the 1971–78 review period. The facts in these decisions were much the same, as all involved applications by owners to sever rural residential or farm retirement lots in rural areas. Opposition came almost entirely from public agencies, with the province and municipalities each opposing on four occasions. No other provincial policies were specifically addressed in these decisions. In half of the decisions, it appeared that the board was relying solely on UDIRA, while in the remainder this policy was only one consideration, with the decision being based also on its determination of interest evaluation, good planning, or prematurity. What is of note is that it refused to approve the requested severances in every appeal where UDIRA was considered.

UDIRA was not an agricultural land protection policy per se. Its focus was on the prohibition of urban development without proper services, although this could also, in practice, lead to the protection of good agricultural lands. The board's response was to treat the policy primarily as a matter of process rather than as a substantive planning tool. It articulated this position in *Rodrigues*, where, after quoting the words of the Minister of Municipal Affairs in introducing UDIRA that '[u]rban development should not, with minor exceptions, occur in rural municipalities until the municipality has proven itself capable of handling the physical, financial and social consequences of such growth,' it refused to approve a development application on the ground that the largely rural township lacked the controls to ensure orderly, integrated growth.[33] Substantive planning issues were not addressed in this decision. Rather, it was a negative element in the process, the lack of approved planning policies as required by UDIRA, which decided the matter. The board took the same position in other decisions in which UDIRA was the sole determinant.[34]

What status, then, did the OMB ascribe to UDIRA? It certainly applied the policy in each decision in which it was addressed. Because the policy dealt with the lack of approved planning controls, however, the board was not, as in the case of its dealing with other provincial policies, put in the position of having to balance provincial policy against its own policy considerations. Nor was it called upon to balance this policy against development policies spelled out in official plans. It occasionally, in a manner that might be characterized as obiter, used the existence of the policy to bolster its decision based on nonconformity with an official plan.[35] Other decisions, where it noted the existence of and relied on UDIRA, were based equally on the application of its own policies pertaining to good planning and prematurity.[36] It thus appears that the board was prepared to rely on UDIRA in the absence of other policy considerations, but was equally ready to treat it as having no greater bearing than its own policies where it considered these applicable.

Food Land Guidelines

The Food Land Guidelines emerged gradually from 1976 on, although they were a response to concerns of the Ontario Ministry of Agriculture and Food (OMAF) existing before that date. They were adopted as government policy in 1978. It is revelatory of the OMB's views with respect to the application of provincial policy that its treatment of an emerging policy in the last two years of the 1971–78 review period was no different than its treatment of a fully fledged matter of provincial interest and de facto provincial policy statement in the post-1986 period.

The board was quick to apply the province's position as set out in the OMAF Strategy and the Green Paper, even though the matters dealt with in them did not constitute government policy until 1978. During the post-1986 period, it never doubted that the FLG was government policy to which it must have regard. While the FLG was never formally adopted under section 3 of the Planning Act, the board regularly recognized the guidelines as a matter of provincial interest under section 2.[37] There was, however, an element of ambiguity in the board's treatment of the FLG, which arose from the latter's nature as a policy instrument. It contained policies which only municipalities were required to follow. The province was not required to follow the guidelines, although ministries reviewing official plans had to consider whether the agricultural land protection policies in those plans met the FLG requirements. Its introduction stated that the guidelines

> are intended to assist local municipalities, counties, or regions in planning for agriculture in the preparation of official plans or amendments which may affect rural land. The Guidelines also relate to land use or zoning by-laws, and severances and subdivision policies ...
>
> The Food Land Guidelines provide a method to incorporate agricultural considerations into local plans ...[38]

Their application was limited, however: 'It should be noted that the Guidelines are intended only to assist in planning for agriculture, and are not intended to address all of the issues related to planning in rural areas.'[39] Also, the FLG made it clear that the guidelines are not to be applied independently of official plans. The implementation provisions stated that

The Treatment of Provincial Policy 167

The Food Land Guidelines will be implemented over the next few years as new official plans are introduced, and old plans are updated ... Municipalities with official plans not in conformity with the Guidelines are encouraged to review and update their plans. Over the next three to five years, with plans now under review, and the regular amendment of plans, it is expected that official plans will be brought into conformity with the Guidelines.[40]

The board appears to have adopted an approach to the application of this provincial policy which extends its application beyond that envisioned in the policy itself.

The OMB had little opportunity to address provincial policy in this area during the 1971–78 review period as the first statement, A Strategy for Ontario Farmland was not released until 1976. As table 5.4 shows, the OMAF Strategy, Green Paper, and FLG were addressed in only eight reported decisions. The owners supported the applications in each case. As with decisions involving UDIRA, opposition was largely from public agencies, not neighbouring owners. Despite the fact that provincial policy was at issue, the province played a minor role, appearing as a party on only a single hearing. Municipalities were in opposition in the other seven. The public agencies were largely successful, as the board refused approval in 75 per cent of its decisions.

The board considered the application of the FLG in forty-three decisions during the 1987–94 period and eleven during the 1995–2000 period. During the earlier period, 77 per cent of these involved severance applications, mostly for non-farm residential development in rural areas. Many of the severances involved farm retirement lots, and addressed the impact of these on the continuation of agricultural uses. This changed during the later period, as the majority of these decisions involved the application of the FLG to official plan and zoning by-law amendment applications. One-fifth of the decisions in each period dealt with applications related to agricultural uses and addressed the continuing viability of the agricultural use of both the severed and remaining parcels. These decisions exhibited also a different pattern of party involvement than occurred with respect to other policy areas, where neighbours have regularly appeared in opposition to applications, and the province has rarely played a role. The municipal position was divided in both periods between support and opposition. Unlike the 1971–78 review period, however, the province played a very significant

TABLE 5.4
Food Land Guidelines Decisions
(1971–1978 data include decisions in which the Food Land Strategy and the Green Paper are considered)

	1971–78		1987–94		1995–2000	
	No.	%	No.	%	No.	%
Total FLG decisions	8	100	43	100	11	100
Application types						
Official plan	1	13	8	19	4	36
Zoning by-law	1	13	9	21	4	36
Plan of subdivision	2	25	1	2	1	9
Severance	5	63	33	77	5	45
Land use						
Residential	7	88	31	72	6	55
Agricultural	2	25	9	21	2	18
Other	1	13	3	7	3	27
Supporters						
Province	–	–	1	2	1	9
Municipality	2	25	16	37	3	27
Owner	8	100	43	100	11	100
Neighbour	–	–	2	5	–	–
Opponents						
Province	1	13	24	56	7	64
Municipality	7	88	23	53	5	45
Owner	–	–	–	–	–	–
Neighbour	2	25	9	21	3	27
Decision						
Approve	2	25	12	28	6	55
Refuse	6	75	31	72	5	45

role, appearing in opposition in 56 per cent of the hearings during 1987–94 and 64 per cent during 1995–2000. Neighbours appeared in opposition much less frequently. The pattern of these hearings has therefore been primarily one in which the province or municipalities have sought to have the policies expressed in the FLG applied to prevent development. They were largely successful during the 1987–94 period, as the board refused to approve applications in 72 per cent of these decisions. Its post-1994 approval rate was much higher, reflecting the increased overall approval rate during this period.

Although the OMB was dealing in the latter part of the 1971–78 period with ministry statements, not formally adopted provincial policy, it accepted these statements as significant matters to be addressed in considering applications affected by them. It refused to permit cottage development in an area designated agricultural in an official plan primarily because the applicant failed to meet the Green Paper requirement that applicants demonstrate a need to use prime agricultural land for other purposes, or show why the use cannot be located on poor lands or within non-agricultural designations.[41] It refused to approve the creation of residential lots on high-quality agricultural lands on the ground that the application was contrary to the principle set out in the Green Paper, which it stated 'is present government policy that good farm land is to be preserved, not only for the future residents of Richmond Hill but for the whole Province.'[42] While in the above decisions the application of provincial policy was paramount, the board generally treated it as only one among other considerations, primarily interest evaluation, good planning, and prematurity. It appears in these other decisions that it decided on the basis of the application of its own policy approaches in these areas, with the application of provincial policy serving largely as reinforcement for its conclusions.[43]

All of the decisions noted above involved applications to permit residential development in rural areas, and in all instances the applications were refused. In dealing with severance applications pertaining to agricultural operations, however, the OMB exhibited an independence of interpretation reflecting its basic policy position with respect to provincial policy, namely that its role is to interpret and apply such policy in a specific set of facts. It refused to accept OMAF's interpretation of the Green Paper that a twenty-acre parcel was too large to be retained as a retirement lot or that the remaining eighty-acre parcel was inadequate for farming.[44] Similarly, it refused to accept the OMAF argument, based on its interpretation of the Green Paper, that the severance of a 100–acre farm into two fifty-acre parcels would reduce their viability for farming.[45]

By 1987 the FLG had become well-established government policy, and the board had become accustomed to interpreting and applying them in a wide variety of situations. An analysis of its decisions during this period shows it to have extended the application of the FLG beyond that envisaged in the policy itself. Since the policy was expressly intended as a guide to the preparation of official plans, the board could have had regard to the government policy by limiting itself to the interpretation of official plan policies only. Yet it consistently examined the FLG as well as official plan policies, and treated them on a par with each other in determining whether the proposals contravene either or both sets of policies. Where contravention occurred, the applications were not approved. In virtually all of these decisions, the board did not see a conflict between the two sets of policies and therefore was not required to balance one against the other. We cannot be certain why it accorded this status to the FLG, but its approach appears to have been driven by the parties, who regularly argued for or against development proposals on the ground of conformity with both the FLG and official plan policies. The FLG have thus, with the board's concurrence, been interpreted as policy to be applied independently in its own right, rather than, as their introductory language suggests, as a tool to be applied in developing official plan policies. In the few instances when the OMB has clearly had to have regard to the FLG directly, where an official plan amendment has been in issue, it has done so. As it noted in the *Ottawa-Carleton* decision: '... neither the official plan, the *Planning Act, 1983*, nor the Food Land Guidelines prohibit the consideration of an amendment to the official plan in respect of agricultural land. If such change is contemplated, however, it must be justified along the lines of the four tests of s. 3.14 of the Food Land Guidelines.'[46]

Despite the board's acceptance of the FLG as government policy, it has balanced the guidelines with other interests and occasionally overruled them where it concluded that other interests outweighed them. It has permitted severances contravening them so as to protect two historic houses on the ground that the public benefit resulting from the preservation of the homes outweighs the broader and more general public interest expressed in the FLG.[47] While the board has had to have regard to government policy as expressed in the FLG, it has not considered itself bound to accept the interpretations of them offered by ministry officials. In several decisions it has approved development proposals, even though opposed by OMAF on the ground of nonconformity with the FLG, on the basis of its interpretation that the proposals in question did not contravene them.[48]

Agricultural Code of Practice

The Agricultural Code of Practice (the Code) differs greatly from UDIRA and the FLG. It is a technical policy guideline prepared by

OMAF, while the latter are general statements of provincial policy directed to a wide range of measures to achieve certain planning goals considered desirable by the government. Its purpose is to protect agricultural uses, particularly offensive uses such as piggeries and feed mills, from demands from residential and other non-farm related uses for their curtailment or discontinuance as being nuisances by providing guidelines for a minimum distance separation between them. As such it represents an attempt by government, acting through the relevant ministry, to regulate the common law concept of nuisance with respect to specific combinations of land use so as to give a degree of protection in advance to a particular use which it wishes to protect.

The OMB has addressed the Code in too few analysed decisions to make statistical analysis meaningful, or to be able to distinguish differences in its approach to applying the policy over the review period. The decisions do show, however, that the board has applied this technical expression of agricultural land protection policy in much the same manner as it has the more general and inclusive UDIRA and FLG. It has recognized that they must be heeded as provincial policy, yet has shown the same ambivalence establishing the degree of significance to be accorded to them. At the most immediate level, the clear failure of non-farm development proposals to meet the minimum separation distance requirements of the Code has given the board sufficient grounds for refusing to approve them.[49] However, where there has been a degree of uncertainty with respect to the application of the Code, it has held that the criteria for calculating the minimum separation distance is open to interpretation, and has applied its own interpretation.[50] This is consistent with its overall approach to its role of applying government policy in particular situations.

The ambivalence of the board's approach is shown in its assessment of the status to be accorded to this expression of provincial policy. It has noted that, where there is a conflict, the more comprehensive policies of the FLG will take precedence over the more limited policies of the Code.[51] Yet the board has accepted that the Code has a life of its own and does not depend for its application on being embodied in a zoning by-law,[52] and that where there is a conflict between a zoning by-law and the Code, the latter is to apply.[53] It has also subordinated the application of the Code to its own impact and interest evaluation policies, refusing to approve non-farm residential severances which complied with the minimum distance separation formula of the Code on the ground that, in addition to such compliance, severances must not create conflicts or potential conflicts with surrounding farm operations.[54]

Statements of Provincial Policy

The OMB's treatment of policy statements adopted under the Planning Act provides a clear example of how a tribunal has applied expressions of general policy to the specific circumstances of individual cases. Because of the differing nature of policy statements, it has shown some inconsistency in their application. Despite this, two main policy-related themes have emerged from the decisions. The board has treated provincial policy statements as the evidentiary equivalent of municipal official plans, and it has frequently subordinated these statements to its own policies with respect to impact and good planning.

The enactment of the Planning Act, 1983, created the potential for provincial policy, and a form of adherence to such policy, to become a central element in the planning process. Section 3 stated that

> (1) The Minister, or the Minister together with any other minister of the Crown, may from time to time issue policy statements that have been approved by the Lieutenant-Governor-in-Council on matters relating to municipal planning that in the opinion of the Minister are of provincial interest.
>
> (5) In exercising any authority that affects any planning matter, the council of every municipality, every local board, every minister of the Crown and every ministry, board, commission or agency of the government, *including the Municipal Board* and Ontario Hydro, *shall have regard* to policy statements issued under subsection (1). [emphasis mine]

Four section 3 statements were formally approved: Mineral Aggregate Resources (9 May 1986), Flood Plain Planning (11 August 1988), Land Use Planning for Housing (13 July 1989), and Wetlands (14 May 1992). These four policy statements were thus the only expressions of provincial policy to which the OMB was statutorily required to have regard during much of the two later review periods. Despite this, there is no evidence that it treated them differently from other expressions of provincial policy.

The policy statements fell into two categories. The purpose of the Housing Statement was to provide general guidelines for local planning. Its objectives were to foster municipal land use planning practices which were responsive to housing needs throughout the province. Municipalities were required, in order to meet these objectives, to pro-

The Treatment of Provincial Policy 173

vide a sufficient supply of residential land, a range of housing types, and residential intensification policies, but were given no direction as to how or where within the municipality these policies were to be implemented. The other policy statements were spatially focused, as they applied to the identification and protection of specific lands: areas comprising flood plains or wetlands or containing supplies of aggregate materials. These policies were similar in their level of technical detail to official plan policies, leaving the designation of the specific lands to which they applied to the municipal planning process. The differences affected the manner in which the board had regard to them.

The Comprehensive Set of Policy Statements (CSPS), which came into effect in March 1995, consolidated these previous statements, along with the FLG, into a single document focused much more than hitherto on the protection of the province's environmental and natural resources and on the provision of affordable housing. These policies were given enhanced status. They were to override local planning policies, except where municipalities chose to adopt more stringent standards. They received enhanced statutory status also. Whereas the Planning Act had previously required parties to the planning process, including the board, to have regard to section 3 policy statements, the act was now amended to require that decisions of ministers, provincial agencies such as the board, and municipalities, be consistent with statements of provincial policy.[55] This combination of statutory and policy amendments could have had a considerable impact on how planning was undertaken in the province, but they were short-lived. The newly elected government moved quickly to replace the CSPS with the Provincial Policy Statement (PPS), a document which sought to achieve a balance between promoting economic development, protecting resources, and directing development away from locations where there was a risk to public health or safety. At the same time the Planning Act was again amended to, inter alia, require planning decision makers to once again have regard to statements of provincial policy.[56] The latter was no longer accorded priority over local planning policies, but sought to achieve a balance between provincial and local policy initiatives. Given the inevitable time lag between the adoption of new provincial policies and their appearance in new local policies and official plans, the CSPS was not in effect long enough to have much impact on the planning process. There were only two reported decisions in which it was addressed. The PPS remains in effect, and has been applied in twenty-three reported decisions during recent years.

TABLE 5.5
Provincial Policy Statement Decisions

	1987–1994		1995–2000	
	No.	%	No.	%
Total policy statement decisions	37	100	36	100
Application types				
Official plan	12	32	10	28
Zoning by-law	19	51	19	53
Plan of subdivision	4	11	2	6
Minor variance	4	11	2	6
Severance	2	5	14	39
Land use				
Residential	32	86	21	58
Commercial	2	5	5	14
Agricultural	–	–	6	17
Aggregates pit	2	5	4	11
Other	4	11	5	14
Supporters				
Province	3	8	2	6
Municipality	16	43	17	47
Owner	31	84	25	69
Neighbour	2	5	1	3
Opponents				
Province	3	8	3	8
Municipality	12	32	12	33
Owner	1	3	9	25
Neighbour	27	73	19	53
Decision				
Approve	21	57	19	53
Refuse	16	43	17	47

Table 5.5 gives particulars of the decisions in which the OMB addressed these statements. What is most noteworthy, given the significance of provincial adoption of them, is the infrequency with which the province appeared as a party when they were being addressed. The table does not reveal that the province's pattern of involvement was even more distorted than the overall figures suggest. Four of the eleven

direct provincial interventions as a party during the two recent periods were in hearings in which the wetlands policy was being addressed. Three occurred when the application of the PPS was under consideration. The province did not appear on any occasion when the application of the housing policy was under consideration. There can be little doubt that this lack of direct provincial involvement has had some bearing on the significance, described below, which the board has attached to these statements.

While policy statements were designed to direct the planning activities of municipalities and planning boards, the OMB accepted that it was equally obligated to consider them.[57] It has been inconsistent, however, in the importance it has attached to proposed statements. It has concluded both that it was not necessary to have regard to guidelines preceding policy statements,[58] and that a proposed policy statement should be considered because the designation of a wetland area was, by virtue of the policy statement, a matter of public interest.[59] The board has not treated adopted policy statements as the courts do legislation, as documents which must be interpreted and applied to the facts to reach a decision. Rather, it has treated them, as it has other expressions of provincial policy, as evidence that must be evaluated in the context of other considerations and which may or not be followed, depending on these other considerations. It explained its interpretation of 'have regard to' in the *Ottawa-Carleton* decision:

> Statements of provincial policy ... must be regarded by the board. The board is not bound to follow them; however, the board is required to have regard to them, in other words, to consider them carefully in relation to the circumstances at hand, their objectives and the statements as a whole, and what they seek to protect. The board is then to determine whether and how the matter before it is affected by, and complies with, such objectives and policies, with a sense of responsible consistency in principle.[60]

This statement illustrates the two most important aspects of the board's treatment of policy statements: their function as evidence, and the balancing of policy statements with other matters of concern to it.

Policy Statements as Evidence

The OMB has accepted policy statements as part of the package of evidence, encompassing both fact and policy, placed before it for consideration, but it has not generally accorded them greater status or given them greater weight than it gives to other evidence. It has first had to determine whether a policy was applicable at all. In the case of the Aggregates, Flood Plain, and Wetlands statements, this was a technical matter; that is, whether the lands at issue contained aggregate material or were flood plains or wetlands as defined in the policy statement.[61] Once the board had established that a policy statement did apply to the lands, it had to determine its applicability to the facts in the case.[62] In doing this, however, it was taking the same approach as it did when interpreting and applying policies in official plans, and it was, in effect, treating the policy statement as the equivalent of an official plan policy.

The board has shown a degree of ambivalence in its dealings with provincial ministries and their officials with respect to policy statements. Just as it has received the evidence of planning experts as to the interpretation and application of official plan policies, it has received the evidence of ministry experts as to whether policy statements are applicable, and, if they are, what it must do to have regard to them in the circumstances.[63] It has expressed the view that ministries have important roles to play in ensuring that policy statements are followed. It has stated, for example, that ministries dealing with environmental policy should be involved in the environmental monitoring programs agreed to by developers and municipalities.[64] The board has not, however, accorded any special status to the evidence of government experts regarding the interpretation or application of policy statements. It has rejected evidence regarding the location of wetlands tendered by ministry experts in favour of that of municipal and owners' experts.[65] It has shown a degree of consistency in the face of inconsistent Ministry of Housing positions regarding the area over which a key element of the housing policy statement, the requirement that 25 per cent affordable housing be provided, is to be determined. It has accepted the position of ministry staff that the 25 per cent requirement was to be applied over the entire municipality, not to each project.[66] Yet in another decision it overruled the ministry experts' then interpretation that the 25 per cent affordable housing requirement applied to the projects in issue and accepted the city's interpretation of the statement that it applied to the larger planning area of which the projects formed only a part.[67]

Equivalency with Official Plans

The OMB has been consistent in equating the importance of provincial policy and of local policy as expressed in approved official plans. It has frequently spoken of them in the same breath, approving or refusing to approve development applications on the ground that they did or did not comply with both provincial policy and official plans. This has been particularly evident during the post-1994 period. In every instance in which the board has considered the application of the PPS it has approved or refused to approve an application on the ground of compliance or otherwise with the PPS and official plans.[68] Its ability to find a commonality between the two sets of documents has certainly been enhanced by the fact that it has not, in any reported decision, found the two to be inconsistent. The furthest it has gone in this regard has been to treat the PPS provisions as, in effect, a baseline, and to hold that more stringent local policies are not inconsistent with provincial policy.[69]

Balancing Policy Statements with Other Issues

The OMB has recognized that the public interest is expressed through provincial policy statements.[70] Despite this it has regularly engaged in a balancing act, as described in *Ottawa-Carleton*,[71] in which the public policies expressed through these statements were weighed against other matters of concern to it, and were often rejected in favour of the latter. Its approach can itself be regarded as a matter of policy. This policy was revealed in its treatment, for example, of the Aggregates Policy Statement, whose purpose was to ensure the protection of lands containing sand, gravel, or other aggregates from uses such as residential development, which would prevent their extraction. The need to balance the protection of these resources with other land use demands was evident, and the board responded to this need. It refused severances for residential purposes within an area of superior sand and gravel deposits on the ground, inter alia, that approving them would violate that portion of the statement dealing with the protection of aggregate resources to the extent that such protection was practically or realistically possible.[72] It stated that 'The policy of the province seems clear that unless there is an undue social impact in the planning sense, supply of aggregate resources where it may be found in reasonable proximity to the sources of demand should, within reason, be implemented and not hindered.'[73]

It was the board's treatment of the housing statement, which did not itself address the need to balance the provision of housing with other planning concerns, that clearly revealed one element of its policy with respect to the application of provincial policy statements. It subordinated the application of the latter to the application of its own adverse impact test and its own views as to what constituted good planning. In doing so it revealed its own hierarchy of planning values, in which it subordinated a provincial interest to one of its own areas of policy, and it did this without any provincial directive to do so. In the 'impact' variant of the test, the board's position was that it would weigh the impact of the proposed development, as defined in planning terms, against the housing statement's goal of providing housing, particularly affordable housing. If that impact was determined to be greater than the benefit of obtaining the additional housing, it would not approve the development.[74] In the 'good planning' variant of the test the board made it clear that where it saw conflict between the promotion of housing, even of affordable housing, as provided for in the housing statement, and good planning, the latter would prevail. Its position was well expressed in the *Social Housing Coalition* decision:

> Given that the proposal is entirely made up of 'social' and 'alternative' housing, it clearly complies with and is supported by the Provincial Land Use Policy for Housing ... and it is deserving of very careful consideration. Does that, however, by itself, override what may be 'good planning' in favour of having the lands designated and zoned for Industrial Use even if of a very limited nature? Clearly not!
> The provincial policy requires that the board and all other planning agencies 'have regard to' those policies when considering residential applications. It does not require that those policies be applied regardless of valid planning considerations favouring a different use.[75]

In this decision the board concluded that a design modification would sufficiently ameliorate the impact on neighbouring properties to permit the development to be approved. In other decisions, it refused to approve planning changes required to permit projects containing affordable housing on the ground that they failed to meet the tests of good planning that it normally applied, such as the existence of approved planning policies in the municipality, the suitability of the site, the compatibility of existing and proposed uses, and the existence of municipal services and infrastructure.[76] The obverse of this, of course, is that where the board was satisfied that projects did represent good planning it would give its approval.[77]

There was a complex amalgam of policies under consideration in these decisions. The board weighed what it recognized as a broad public

The Treatment of Provincial Policy 179

interest in providing housing against what it perceived to be a public interest in avoiding adverse impact and in promoting good planning. Its decision-making process could be considered also an exercise in the evaluation of differing interests. Where it was considering impact it was weighing a general public interest in the provision of affordable housing against the interests of neighbours who would be most directly affected. Where it was weighing affordable housing against good planning, the latter appeared to represent an amalgam of the immediate interests of neighbours in not being subject to adverse impacts from the proposed development, and a broader public interest in ensuring that the rules of good planning, as it saw them, were also taken into consideration.

The board gave little overt consideration to impact when dealing with the application of the PPS. It did see a link between the two, however, as in the few occasions when it did refer to impact in this context it determined that development proposals would not contravene the PPS because they would have little if any impact on neighbouring properties.[78]

Matters of Provincial Interest

The province greatly strengthened its potential for playing a direct role in the planning process by introducing the statutory concept of matters of provincial interest. Section 2 of the act, added in 1989, stated:

2. The Minister, in carrying out his responsibilities under this act, will have regard to, among other matters, matters of provincial interest such as [for example]

(a) the protection of the natural environment, including the agricultural resource base of the Province, and the management of natural resources; ...
(d) the provision of major communication, servicing and transportation facilities; ...
(f) the co-ordination of planning activities of municipalities and other public bodies; ...
(j) the provision of a range of housing types.[79]

On its face, section 2 placed no direct onus on the OMB to have regard to these matters, either explicitly or by implication.[80] The only specific statutory requirement was that it and other parties involved in plan of subdivision and severance applications were to have regard to, inter alia, 'the effect of development of the proposed subdivision on matters of provincial interest referred to in section 2' (clause 51(4)(a), subsection 53(2)).

Declarations of Provincial Interest

The Planning Act, 1983, provided that if the minister declared that an official plan or zoning by-law or any part thereof before the board had or may have an effect on a matter of provincial interest, its jurisdiction with respect to that document was limited to making a recommendation which would not come into force until confirmed by the Lieutenant Governor in Council (subsections 17(18)–(20), 34(27)–(29)). Despite the only occasionally imposed statutory requirement to consider matters of provincial interest when hearing official plan or zoning by-law applications, the board has treated them in the same manner as other expressions of provincial policy, and has given them the same weight.

The board was called upon to consider the implications of a minister's declaration of provincial interest in 1992 in what is known as the Etobicoke motel strip decision, in which a large area of waterfront land was redesignated for public open space and high-density residential uses.[81] The Minister of Municipal Affairs had, well before the hearing commenced, made a declaration of provincial interest under subsection 17(19) of the act, but had given no particulars until the hearing as to where the provincial interest lay or how it was affected by the proposed official plan. The board heard the referrals of two substantial official plan amendments, and, as it was standing in the shoes of the minister in hearing the referrals, it concluded that it was required to consider the matters under section 2. It concluded also that, as the minister had not identified the parts of the official plan affecting matters of provincial interest, the whole plan was to be taken as possibly affecting such matters, with the result that the entire decision would be subject to confirmation by the Lieutenant Governor in Council. Having said this, it proceeded to distinguish by implication between the statutory, procedural effect of the minister's declaration, which removed its jurisdiction to make a final decision, and the practical implications of such a declaration to its decision making. Although the government was here presenting its positions with respect to matters of provincial interest, the board accorded no higher status to these positions than to the positions of the other parties.[82] It was, in effect, distinguishing between the declaration of matters as being of provincial interest, which established a context within which to evaluate the evidence, and the evidence and the positions put forward by the various parties. In dealing with the latter, it did not appear to accord any greater weight to the evidence and arguments of the government than to those of other parties.

Provincial Guidelines

As we have noted, the cabinet adopted the Growth and Settlement Policy Guidelines and the Oak Ridges Moraine Area Implementation Guidelines as matters of provincial interest under section 2 of the Planning Act, but has not adopted them formally under section 3. The OMB has recognized that these guidelines represent a provincial interest that it must have regard to.[83] It has applied them as provincial policy in a manner similar to, but not identical with, its treatment of section 3 statements of policy. It made this distinction clear in a decision to approve a cemetery proposal to which both of the guidelines were applicable, stating that '... it is important to keep in mind that these [the two sets of guidelines] are what they say they are: *guidelines*. Despite the mandatory wording of many sections, they do not have the force of either Provincial Policy Statements under S. 3 of the *Planning Act* ... or policies in Official Plans. Accordingly, the weight that attaches to them must be carefully considered in the context of the overall planning document framework that applies in a particular application.'[84]

The last comment is in keeping with the board's policy of treating government policy as evidence to be evaluated along with all of the other evidence placed before it. The board has generally approved development applications which have been in compliance with the Growth and Settlement Policy Guidelines, and refused to approve applications which have not. In keeping with its general approach, however, the application of provincial guidelines has never been the sole reason for its decision. As we have already noted, the board has regularly concluded that a development proposal is or is not in compliance with both the guidelines and the official plan. In doing this it has acted in a manner consistent with its policy pertaining to good planning, as it has characterized the guidelines as being the codification of good planning principles.[85]

182   A Law unto Itself

Environmental Protection Policies

The OMB's treatment of environmental protection policies, including Ministry of Environment guidelines and Niagara Escarpment protection provisions, provides further examples of its policy of treating provincial policy not as an absolute to be applied regardless of other considerations, but as one of several interests to be considered. The latter provisions are not environmental protection policies per se, but they are associated directly with an important provincial planning initiative, the Niagara Escarpment Area of Development Control, whose goal is primarily a form of environmental protection. In any event, Niagara Escarpment decisions have often addressed other environmental protection policies also.

Despite the importance of environmental protection concerns in the planning process, table 5.1 shows that these policies have been addressed infrequently by the board: in only 16 per cent of the 1971–78 decisions, 18 per cent of the 1987–94 decisions, and 16 per cent of the 1995–2000 decisions in which it considered provincial policy at all. The numbers have been too small in both periods to permit significant analysis of the decisions, but they can be taken as indicators of its approach to dealing with such expressions of policy. Moreover, while these numbers appear to suggest that the board has given little consideration to environmental protection, they significantly underestimate the true influence of this matter on its decision making, as it has frequently considered environmental impact – the effect of air, water, and soil pollution – in deciding whether to approve development proposals.[86]

The Relationship between Provincial and Municipal/Board Policy

The OMB treated this relationship as a narrow jurisdictional issue during the 1971–78 review period. It stated that, even in the face of ministry approval authority, there remained an important role for both municipalities and itself. It approved a zoning by-law, in the face of an objection that approval would conflict with the right of the Minister of Mines to approve a pit or quarry permit, on the grounds that the roles of the ministry and the municipality were complementary and that the local council was required to decide what restrictions and regulations were most appropriate for the general good of the municipality.[87] It refused to approve a waste disposal site, even though the site had received a provisional certificate of approval from the Ministry of the Environment, on the ground that while it could not impose its direction upon the minister as to the operation of the site, it could enquire into the planning aspects of the operation.[88] Its position was thus that the interests of municipalities seeking to respond to concerns of their residents, and of itself in seeking to ensure that 'good planning' matters were taken into account, were best expressed in terms of the obligations laid on each body in the exercise of its jurisdiction. During the later review periods the board continued to follow its policy of addressing these policies within a larger context. This did not always lead to the dismissal of the provincial policy. The board has approved a minor variance permitting a smaller lot than required by the zoning by-law on the ground that, inter alia, the sewage system for the lot had been approved by the Health Unit.[89] On the other hand, it has refused to apply Ministry of Environment policy that no plan of subdivision be permitted on individual sewage disposal systems on the ground that such a policy would, in the absence of plans to install sewers, effectively freeze development.[90]

The OMB's treatment of the Niagara Escarpment Plan (NEP), which is a formal expression of government policy, is consistent with its approach to balancing provincial interests with other matters it considers important. It has refused to approve applications for development on the ground, inter alia, that they contravene the NEP.[91] Yet it has also overruled the NEP by approving subdivisions located within the Niagara Escarpment Area of Development Control, which could in itself have been a ground for refusal, where satisfied that they have met its 'impact' and 'prematurity' tests.[92]

Ministry of the Environment Guidelines

Unlike policy statements, which have an established statutory authority, ministry guidelines have variable status, such as 'a statement of principles by a person or group having authority over an activity' and as 'nothing more than a preferred position by an authority, under appropriate circumstances.'[93] This variability has been reflected in the weight accorded to them by the board. Guidelines issued by the Ministry of the Environment and other ministries, such as those dealing with noise or stormwater runoff,[94] are highly technical in nature. It has treated them as standards which must be met if a proposed development is to be approved. The only issues are whether they are applicable to the case, and, if so, does the evidence establish that the proposed development will meet them.[95] In keeping with its view that guidelines and policies are to be treated as evidence whose weight is to be assessed in the context of each situation it has given temporary support to a pollution-based, residential-industrial separation policy, pending further study,[96] and has refused to apply, as being unrealistic in the circumstances, a ministry policy that development in a rural municipality should take place only on full municipal services.[97]

Conclusions

The Integration of Provincial Policy into the Planning Process

The OMB has, since 1987, more frequently addressed provincial policy than it did during the 1970s, although it continued to do so in only a minority of its decisions. This reflects the inclusion of such policy in the planning process by way of sections 2 and 3 of the Planning Act, 1983, the increasing need for municipalities to take provincial agricultural land and environmental protection policies into consideration in making planning decisions, and the greater willingness of provincial ministries to appear at board hearings to support their policies and guidelines. During the earlier period, provincial policies were largely independent of the land use planning process established under the Planning Act, although they influenced decision making under that process. At one extreme, the government's regional land use planning initiatives were so general in nature that they bore little relation to day-to-day planning decisions, a situation reflected in the infrequency with which the board was called upon to address them. Ministry policies directed to the control of non-farm-related development in rural areas were more clearly applicable to individual applications, and the board considered them more frequently. Provincial policy had become a formal part of the planning process by the later review period through the statutory provisions allowing the declaration of matters as being of provincial interest and the issuance of provincial policy statements to which the board was required to have regard. At the same time, the ministries played a direct and often unrecognized role through developing an expanding range of guidelines and standards, and applying these in reviewing official plans and commenting on individual development applications.

The OMB's Limited Involvement with Provincial Policy

The OMB has come to address provincial policy more frequently over time, but, as noted above, in only a small minority of its decisions. Yet it is a provincial tribunal, whose ostensible role is to ensure that provincial policies and concerns are addressed in deciding whether local planning decisions should be upheld. There appear to be two main reasons why has it so infrequently considered such matters. The first is to be found in the nature and comprehensiveness of provincial policy throughout the overall review period. Such policy is, of necessity, general in nature. During the earlier review period, the province's regional planning policies, in particular, were drawn with such a broad brush that they had little relevance to individual development applications. The macro-planning they typified simply did not relate to the micro-planning activities expressed in by-law amendments, development proposals, and minor variances. The TCR Plan proposed, for example, that the bulk of urban development be located in a solid band along the shore of Lake Ontario. With rare exceptions, this had no bearing on whether the proposed rezoning of a specific parcel of land within this band should be approved. Only policies dealing with agricultural land protection and environmental protection, both of which arose primarily in considering applications in rural areas, had direct application to the matters considered by the board.

This had changed to some extent by the later review periods. The Food Land Guidelines were well established by 1987, and were regularly addressed in considering development applications for rural areas. The policy statements had direct application to applications in defined physical areas, such as wetlands, or to the provision of housing. Yet this highlights the second reason for the infrequency of provincial policy consideration, the limited coverage of such policy. For most matters the board has had to address, there has been no provincial policy at all, and it has thus had to make its decisions without the benefit of any provincial guidance. In any event, the application of provincial policy has played only a marginal role in the board's decision making. Its prime function as a planning review agency has been to reconsider local planning decisions at the behest of those who are dissatisfied with them. These parties have frequently seen provincial policy as having little relevance because of its generalized nature or because there was no policy which appeared to them to be applicable. Moreover, the board has operated as a court-like tribunal receiving such evidence and argument as the parties choose to present rather than as an investigative agency in its own right, and it has therefore been unlikely to raise questions as to the applicability of provincial policy to the matters before it if the parties choose not to do so.

The Uneasy Balance between Provincial Policy and Board Policies

The OMB is a provincial agency whose mandate requires that it decide matters primarily on policy rather than legal grounds, and it might therefore be expected to ensure that its decisions are based on applicable provincial policy. It has not done this, but it has sought throughout the review period, with varying results, to balance provincial policy with its own policies.

While the board has given consideration to provincial policy, its hearings commonly involve other issues as well. This is unexceptional in itself, but what is significant is that provincial policy has rarely been the sole determinant even where it was addressed. The decisions show that the board's own policies, which reflect its own philosophy in many ways that provincial policies cannot, also proved to be important. This leads to two conclusions. Firstly, it is not possible to accurately assess, with few exceptions, the relative importance the board has accorded to provincial policy and to its own policies in its decision-making activity. Secondly, a matter of greater significance when considering the board's role as a provincial agency is that it has regularly sought to weigh both provincial policy and its own policies in its decision making, rather than giving preponderance to the former.

The board has correctly noted that there is a hierarchy of policy pronouncements. Formal decisions of cabinet, including policy statements made under section 3 of the Planning Act, were the most important. Published guidelines were less so and were, as their name implied, to be treated as guides for assessing applications rather than as policies that must be adhered to. Ministry staff guidelines and standards, or 'concerns,' were to be addressed along with other policy considerations. The board's generally expressed view was that as one descended the hierarchy the importance to be granted to provincial policy decreased and board policy increased. Yet the evidence makes clear that the board has shown little variation in the relative importance it has accorded to provincial policies and to its own, regardless of the importance of the former.

The OMB has throughout the entire review period followed a consistent policy of 'having regard to' provincial policy, regardless of legislative requirements, in such a manner that it subordinates provincial policy to its own policies. It was required by 1987 to have regard to provincial policy statements, but was faced with no such statutory requirement during the earlier period. Despite this difference, its approach to provincial policy appears to have been established by the latter period, and to have been carried forward in its interpretation of 'have regard to.' This generally consistent approach to interpreting and applying provincial policy can be described as a policy of the board. The framework of this policy was clearly spelled out in the *Caledon Official Plan* decision in which, in keeping with its understanding of its role, it adopted a judicial model in which all facts, including expressions of provincial policy, were to be placed before it. In that decision it treated policy statements as being legislative in nature: they were of general application and its role was to apply them in specific fact situations 'without assistance from the Government or any member.' This decision can be treated as almost a declaration of independence on the part of the board, and, as the other reviewed decisions indicate, it adhered to this position with a high degree of consistency throughout the entire review period.

It is ironic that *Barrie Annexation*, the best-known decision of the 1971–78 period with respect to provincial policy, was a policy aberration. The board stated that it was bound by such policy as expressed in a minister's letter, and proceeded to structure the annexation before it in accordance with that policy. Yet it was at the same time granting provincial policy a lower but still significant priority in other decisions. It was generally supportive of such policy, and applied regional planning policies and UDIRA when called upon to do so. In every decision in which it addressed the latter it refused to approve the proposed development on the ground, inter alia, that it did not conform to that policy. Yet two elements displayed in the decisions illustrated the limitations in the board's application of provincial policy during this period. Firstly, and most obviously, such policy rarely provided the only ground for its decision making, thereby making it difficult to assess how much importance the board accorded to it. It often appeared that the board was using conformity with provincial policy, or the lack thereof, as support for decisions based largely on other grounds, such as the evaluation of interests, good planning, or prematurity. Secondly, underlying these decisions was the board's own policy of balancing the public interest inherent in such statements of policy with the interests of other more local 'publics.' This position was most clearly expressed when it noted that, depending on the circumstances, either the provincial or the municipal 'public interest' might have to prevail.

The Planning Act, 1983, appeared to enhance the application of government policy in the planning process, as it required decision makers, including the board, to have regard to policy statements made under section 3 of the act. Yet even in applying these statements it exhibited a degree of independence from the provincial priorities expressed in them by stating that it was 'to use its *independent* judgment on the merits of the proposal, and to see that planning decisions are made with regard to proper planning principles, while always bearing in mind and having regard to provincial policy.'[98] The phrase 'bearing in mind' falls far short of 'being bound by.' In its application of the phrase 'have regard to' the board has endeavoured to achieve, as it did when dealing with provincial policy in the 1971–78 period, a balance between the public interest as expressed in the policy statements and other matters of concern to it.

Of particular significance, as revealed in its frequent interpretation and application of the Land Use for Housing Policy Statement, has been the its subordination of the public interest as expressed in that statement to its own policies as expressed in its 'impact' and 'good planning' tests. Its understanding of *have regard to* may therefore be paraphrased as: 'We will give serious consideration to statements of provincial policy, but will do so in the context of other policies which we consider to be of equal importance. If the interests of the general public inherent in the policy statements are congruent with the interests of those most directly affected by a proposed development, we will approve it. But if the general public interest is, in our opinion, outweighed by the adverse impact on those most directly affected, or does not constitute what we consider to be good planning or meet certain other tests, the proposed development will not be approved, or will be approved only with modifications designed to ensure that the goals expressed in our policies are met.'

The policy paraphrased above is well illustrated by the congruence the board has regularly found between provincial and local policy. It has regularly, where provincial policy is in issue, stated in its decisions that a development proposal is or is not in conformity with both provincial policy, such as in the FLG or PPS, and local policy as expressed in official plans. This was certainly evident during the 1987–94 period, particularly with respect to the application of the FLG. It became even more noticeable during the 1995–2000 period, as during this period the board treated official plans and the PPS as a joint package of policies to be satisfied, and, remarkably, it never found conflict between them. The farthest it ever went was an obiter statement that, if there was ever a conflict between a provincial policy and an out-of-date official plan, the former would prevail.[99] Hardly a ringing endorsement for the predominance of the former.

Treating Provincial Policy as Nothing More than Evidence

The OMB's manner of dealing with provincial policy in those instances where the province took an active party role provide a clear indication of the significance it has attached to such policy statements. It has treated their application to the matters before it as only one among other considerations. It did not consider itself obligated to accept interpretations of policy proffered by ministry witnesses, and often chose not to do so. It balanced these policies with other interests, and occasionally overruled them where it concluded that other interests outweighed them. The board has thus made its decisions within the context of provincial policy but has limited the application of that context by making the policy subject, to some extent, to its self-generated policies. This is reflected in the decision data. As table 5.3 shows, it was more likely to refuse to approve applications where provincial policies were being addressed and the province was opposed to their approval, but the province's position was not determinative. This suggests that active provincial involvement did have some influence on the board's decision making, but certainly not to the degree that its capacity to render an independent judgment was jeopardized.

The Relationship between the OMB and the Province

The analysis in this chapter has focused on how the OMB has interpreted and applied specific, mostly formal, expressions of provincial policy. These are important, and the manner in which it has responded to them says much about its relationship with the government. Such a focus falls short of revealing the full extent of this informal relationship, which has been more pervasive than the formal one. It has been manifested in a general fashion in the meetings that have occurred throughout the entire review period between OMB members and government officials to consider a wide range of planning matters, and in the board's involvement in discussions leading to the Planning Act, 1983, and to the Sewell Report. It is impossible to assess how this relationship has influenced its decision making, although it has likely made its members generally more aware of the thinking and priorities of government. On a day-to-day basis, ministries have frequently stated their positions through reports and comments which form part of the evidence before the board, and ministry staff have sometimes been called as witnesses. There has frequently been no reference to ministry positions or witnesses in individual decisions, and in these instances the influence of provincial policy on these decisions could only be a matter for conjecture. Where such evidence was referred to, however, the board did not appear to have treated it differently from other evidence, but chose to weigh it in the context of all evidence received. The information available to us suggests, therefore, that it maintained a liaison with government to consider matters of a general nature, but also that it sought to maintain an arm's-length relationship when considering individual applications. This leaves open the question of how the board's relationship with government when dealing with general issues affected its thinking when dealing with individual applications. While this question cannot be answered directly, the evidence of its consideration of specific expressions of provincial policy leads to the conclusion that it would have continued to treat ministry guidelines, standards, and concerns as evidence to be assessed and applied in the same manner as other evidence placed before it, but not to give any special weight to such evidence because of its source.

6
A Tribunal Out of Time

It is now time to complete the circle, to review the pertinent facts and arguments, and show how the findings arising from our analysis of the Ontario Municipal Board's decisions lead to the conclusion that, given the nature of its policy development and application, the board has outlived its usefulness as a planning appeal tribunal.

This analysis is important not just because of what it contributes to our understanding of regulatory activity, but because of the importance of the OMB itself. The board is unique in Canada in the breadth of its land use planning appellate jurisdiction. Other provinces have established tribunals to exercise jurisdiction over some elements of planning, but none has given a single body the power to review *all* municipal planning decisions. Some examples will illustrate the differences. British Columbia has no tribunal to which local planning decisions may be appealed. The Planning Appeals Committee of the Saskatchewan Municipal Board may hear appeal of decisions of local development appeal boards with respect to the application of zoning by-laws in specific instances (although it cannot hear appeals arising from the initial passing of the by-laws), and appeals of decisions with respect to subdivision applications. The Manitoba Municipal Board similarly may hear appeals and make orders with respect to zoning by-laws and plans of subdivision only. That board may hold public hearings on development (official) plans, but has jurisdiction only to make recommendations to the Minister of Municipal Affairs, who then decides whether or not to approve them. A property owner in New Brunswick may appeal to that province's planning appeal board against a municipal refusal to issue a development permit or the conditions attached to its approval, but may not appeal against the underlying development plan or zoning by-law.

In Nova Scotia an amendment to or a refusal to amend a zoning by-law may be appealed to that province's municipal board, but the initial zoning by-law may not be appealed. Similarly, few states in the United States make use of a state agency to review local planning decisions, and those agencies which have been created have limited roles, not the all-encompassing jurisdiction of Ontario's board. The question therefore arises: Why employ a tribunal exercising the range of powers given to the OMB when other provinces and states whose planning systems are similar to Ontario's have not done so?

Theory v. Practice

The ideal model of regulatory activity is one in which the federal or provincial governments create tribunals to further the achievement of important public policies which are clearly spelled out in legislation, regulations, or other forms of policy statements, and the role of the tribunals is to apply these policies in making decisions with respect to matters brought before them. What happens, however, if tribunals are given little or no policy direction? What happens if they seek to develop their own policies to fill that void? The reality of regulatory activity, as commentators have fully recognized, is complex and ambiguous, and this study of the OMB's decision making certainly reveals a pattern far removed from the theoretical ideal. It illustrates a real world situation in which a tribunal is created, given a general mandate, then left largely on its own to determine what policy, if any, it is to apply. Expressions of provincial land use planning policy have certainly been limited in Ontario, and the options available to the board have thus been to make its decisions on a totally ad hoc basis or to develop its own policy as it goes along so as to provide at least some element of continuity in its decision making. While these two options are theoretically available, my analyses strongly suggest that, in practice, a tribunal which receives little or no policy guidance will be drawn immutably to filling that vacuum by developing policies to give direction to its members, and, of equal importance, to provide stability and continuity to the process it is regulating. Also of importance has been the finding that, even where the board has addressed provincial planning policy, it has treated this as just another piece of evidence and has frequently subordinated its application to that of its own internally developed policies. We are thus confronted with a free-standing tribunal, one which pays lip service to public policy but which makes its decisions, in a manner largely independent of such considerations, by applying its own policies.

The OMB has denied that it engages in policy development. It has occasionally referred to the 'principles' it follows, and in its internal deliberations has certainly considered what approach it should take in dealing with various issues. Yet at the same time it has regularly stated that it decides each matter on its own merits. This is true on the surface. There is no question that the board has proceeded by considering the facts of each application before it. Yet it has not analysed these facts in an ad hoc, isolated manner, but in each hearing has filtered them through the medium of its own policies.

The OMB and the Province

The decision-making activities of the OMB reveal a tribunal which not only relies largely on its own rather than on received public policy, but which has often subordinated both provincial and local expressions of public policy to its own internally developed policies when it has perceived a conflict between the two. It has been a tribunal which, on its face, has operated largely without interference from the province. This independence is seen in the context of the board's overt policy development activities, as successive provincial governments appear to have shown a benign neglect with respect to these activities. Yet this apparent independence masks a deeper interdependence between the board and the province, resulting from the convenience of having an independent agency through which provincial governments can continue to exert an influence on municipal decision making, and from having a shared philosophical outlook with respect to real property rights and planning.

The board has been left free to develop and apply specific planning policies and to treat provincial planning policy as it has – without overt provincial government interference – because it has played a central role in the more fundamental policy espoused by successive governments of overseeing municipal activities without direct provincial involvement. This was made apparent in 1906 when the Ontario Railway and Municipal Board was created for the purpose of providing a forum for the regulation of municipal street railways, gas and electricity supplies, and municipal financial activities, without the need for the direct involvement of the provincial government or politicians in dealing with each specific issue or application. There were sound reasons for this.

Provincial politicians and staff would be swamped by the need to make a myriad of local decisions and would be unable to devote adequate attention to matters of provincial concern. Provincial politicians would run severe political risks if they were directly involved in making decisions with respect to what were often contentious local matters. Both of these problems were avoided, while retaining provincial oversight of municipal decision making, by delegating the review function to a provincially appointed tribunal. Successive provincial governments have continued to exercise a supervisory role over the activities of municipalities, but have rarely intervened directly.

This provincial commitment to subjecting local decision making to review quickly became apparent when planning legislation was first introduced, and it has remained a central element of planning in Ontario. As we have seen, the province has never believed that municipalities should be free to make planning decisions without the opportunity for 'sober second thought' by a tribunal consisting of its appointees. When municipalities were initially given zoning powers the coming into force of their zoning by-laws was made conditional on board approval. Its approval was similarly required for municipal (official) plans. This theme of control by means of a provincial tribunal has run unaltered through numerous changes to planning legislation. The board has been left free to develop and apply its own policies to the specific matters before it, even when those policies have overridden specific provincial policy statements, because it has throughout its history been carrying out the fundamental provincial policy of overseeing municipal decision making. It is apparent also – because successive provincial governments of all political persuasions have not intervened to change or reduce its mandate – that the board has conducted its policy development and decision-making activities in a manner which these governments have not considered a threat to their vital political interests. Thus, while it has often chosen not to apply specific provincial planning policies in specific instances, the board has met the province's underlying public policy goal of exerting indirect control over planning and other types of municipal decision making.

Much of the discussion of regulatory theory has focused on the independence of tribunals from the governments which created them. There has been a considerable difference in outlook between American and Canadian commentators arising from the differing constitutional structures of each nation. The position expressed in Canadian writings is that the sovereignty of Parliament or the provincial legislatures in

Canada precludes the emergence of tribunals which are truly independent of their creators. Their existence can be terminated at any time by the repeal of the legislation under which they were created, and the government of the day can establish the policies which they are to apply. This is undeniably true in law, yet the analyses described herein point to a very different relationship. They reveal the existence of a tribunal which has over a long period of time openly developed and applied its own policies and has on occasion openly subordinated provincial policy to its own policies, all without any apparent retribution.

Successive provincial governments have played only a limited role in those decisions involving areas within which the OMB has developed and applied its own substantive planning policies. Apart from ministry comments on proposed official plans and plans of subdivision, they have treated land use planning as primarily a matter of process. While the province has always had an underlying policy influence through its review of official plans and amendments and its formal or informal adoption of provincial policy statements, it has left the interpretation and application of these expressions of provincial policy almost entirely to the board. Most board hearings have dealt with applications for specific development proposals, and the province has been content to let substantive issues be worked out at the local level. This is clearly reflected in the infrequency with which the province has appeared as a party in hearings, even hearings in which the board has been considering the application of provincial planning policies. It is reflected also in the fact that successive provincial governments have seen fit not to interfere with the basic structure, jurisdiction, or mode of operation of the board, even though the planning process, and its role therein, has been addressed in a number of important studies.

This relationship between the province and the OMB appears to have held firm regardless of the political and doctrinal leanings of the party in power. During the 1971–78 review period, and for many years previously, the then right-of-centre Progressive Conservative party was in power. Yet the relationships between the board and the government of the day appeared to be no different during the 1987–94 review period, when the province was governed successively by the centrist Liberal party and then by the distinctly left-leaning New Democratic Party. The latter was replaced in 1995 by a strongly right-wing Progressive Conservative government dedicated to encouraging economic growth and development activity, yet the board continued to apply its policies as it had earlier. The only significant difference, which is probably not coincidental, is that the board's overall rate of approving applications during the initial Conservative 1971–78 review period was 44 per cent, and during the Liberal and NDP dominated 1987–94 period was 47 per cent, while for the largely new-style Conservative 1995–2000 period this rate increased to 59 per cent. It strongly suggests that the board members recognized the pro-development priorities of the new government and sought to put them into effect.

Documentary evidence of meetings and correspondence suggests that there has been a close working relationship between provincial governments and the board. It is likely that direct provincial intervention was not required for several reasons. A lack of provincial policy for the board to apply is an obvious one. Another is that the local nature of most matters considered by it, and the consequently limited political impacts of its decisions, meant that it was rarely dealing with matters of sufficient provincial interest that the government felt a need to intervene. It is probable also that during the earlier review period the members of the board, because they had been appointed by Progressive Conservative governments over a long period of time, shared with members of the government many beliefs with respect to the role of planning, the importance of protecting private property interests, and the need for an increasing degree of public participation in the planning process. The Liberal and NDP governments did not have the advantage of longevity in office – the former being in power from 1985 to 1990, and the latter from 1990 to 1995 – but because new board members were now appointed for a three-year term it was possible for them to appoint members in sympathy with their policies, which they did. It was equally possible for the Progressive Conservative government elected in 1995 to do the same, and it did so. Finally there is the possibility, which would certainly warrant further study, that provincial governments have generally not considered their own planning policies to be of sufficient political importance to require the board to hew closely to them.

The role of the NDP government is of particular interest. It showed a much stronger bias than its predecessors in favour of a more direct provincial role in planning. It developed more stringent provincial land use policies – the Comprehensive Set of Policy Statements, along with 600 pages of guidelines for their application – and amended the Planning Act to require that board, municipal, and public agency decision making be consistent with these policies rather than merely have regard to them. Despite these changes, there is no evidence that the government sought to alter the relationship between itself and the board, or to transfer any of the latter's decision-making authority to itself. Moreover, there is no evidence that the board behaved any differently vis-à-vis the government in developing and applying its own policies or that it attached greater importance to provincial policy statements during this period, although it might have done so had these policy statements not remained in force for less than a year. The logical conclusion is that the OMB has continued, regardless of the political positions of different provincial governments, to function largely independently of them and to apply its own policies without any degree of interference from them.

How has the board been able to maintain this degree of independence? It is not unrealistic to expect it to bring its own policies to bear in interpreting received provincial policies and applying them to the specific facts of the matters before it. Yet the board has gone beyond this to the extent that it has generally failed to accord priority of status to provincial policies and has often applied its own policies in preference to the former. The legitimacy of its actions in this regard is dubious at best. As we have seen, it has interpreted the Planning Act requirement that it have regard to formally adopted statements of provincial policy as permitting it to override such policy, and has applied other expressions of policy not subject to this requirement in the same manner. Its actions in this regard are a far cry from those anticipated by regulatory theory, namely those of a tribunal which seeks to apply the policies of its senior level of government. How has it been able to do this?

Two possible reasons come to mind, both rooted in the subtle ongoing relationship between the OMB and the province. The first lies in the astuteness and sensitivity of the board to the nature of that relationship. It has identified with the general commitment of successive conservative-minded provincial governments of all political persuasions to the institution of private property and its protection from adverse impact. It has consistently supported this fundamental provincial policy and has consistently developed and applied its own policies to this end. While it has freely and openly subordinated the imposition of specific provincial policies to its own policies, it has not crossed the invisible line by adopting and applying policies which threaten the province's ongoing commitment to private property or the functioning of a planning system dedicated to a considerable degree to protecting property rights.

The second reason the board has retained this degree of freedom is largely negative. It was created by the province, and is technically subject to political accountability and control. It has, however, been able to exercise a considerable degree of independence in developing and applying the policies analysed herein because successive provincial governments have been content to let it do so. Despite its apparent independence, the board's authority has rested ultimately on its accountability to the governments of the day. The latter have chosen, probably because the board has recognized its limits and has not therefore been perceived as a threat to their interests, to allow it the flexibility it deems necessary in dealing with appeals and referrals. The board has responded to this ongoing opportunity by developing and applying the wide range of policies reviewed herein, but never in a fashion which governments would see as compromising this relationship.

The OMB's decision making has received remarkably few judicial challenges. One important reason is that its decisions have rarely presented a target. While evidence of policy development can be discerned through the analysis of a large number of its decisions, it has regularly professed that it does not develop or apply policy, but decides each application on its own merits. This is true in a formal sense. The board has not, other than in the instance overturned by the court in *Hopedale*, set down policies and stated its intention to be bound by them. There have thus rarely been grounds, in the context of individual applications, for arguing that it has exceeded its jurisdiction. Another reason lies in the nature of the interests represented before the board, which have been largely economic or policy-oriented. The fundamental legal rights considered by the courts have not been at issue. Municipalities have supported their planning policies and been generally interested in encouraging development in accordance with them. Developers have wanted to build. Neighbours have wanted protection from adverse impacts. Municipalities and developers have appeared regularly before the board and have preferred to have a harmonious relationship with it. They have generally understood the planning process and factored the possibility of board hearings into their financial and temporal calculations. Neither group has normally been interested in the lengthy, costly, and uncertain process of challenging the board's decisions on legal grounds. Neighbours have had diffuse interests and often fewer resources, and have thus been even more likely to be deterred by the costs and uncertainty of judicial challenges. Parties have been aware, moreover, or could easily become aware, that the courts are loath to overturn decisions of administrative tribunals on any but clearly legal grounds, and challenges based on the board's application and interpretation of policy, whatever its source, are unlikely to be successful.

The Implications of Applying a Private Law Ideology

Why retain the OMB when we have the courts? The board's policy development has reflected a strongly held private law ideology. Its application of an adverse impact test has been determinative not only of disputes between private parties, but of those in which public interests have been in opposition to private ones. This has clearly been the case with its treatment of substantive planning policy issues. This test has been applied also in its dealings with procedural policy issues, in which the adequacy of the assessment of adverse impact has often been the determining factor in deciding whether an application had been dealt with in a procedurally adequate manner. The board has thus functioned in a court-like manner in both its operational procedures – treating applications as *lis inter partes* to be resolved in an adversarial setting and basing its decisions on the evidence placed before it by the parties – and in its policy development, which has focused on the law of nuisance. In doing so, it has called into question its reason for being as a tribunal, which, in theory, applies public policy to regulatory decision making. The uncertainty of its role is magnified by the policy approach it has espoused.

The board's pattern of decision making has turned on its head the theoretical view of tribunals as being public policy-oriented entities whose existence is justified by that orientation. Property owners have appeared as parties before it at almost every hearing, and municipalities have frequently appeared also. Because the board limits itself to the evidence placed before it, those parties who cannot afford lawyers and expert witnesses to shape the issues and submit evidence and argument to support their positions have generally been at a distinct disadvantage to those who can afford such support. Because of the private property bias inherent in the board's policies, there has been a hidden onus built into its entire process. It is the position of these private property interests that has provided the norm, and the onus has by implication been placed on those pursuing public policy goals to satisfy the board that this norm should be overruled. This has been illustrated in several areas of the board's decision making, and, of equal interest, lack of decision making. It has been demonstrated in the differing degrees of protection given to owners in single-family or low-density residential areas and to owners in other types of areas. The board has treated the amenities enjoyed by the former with great solicitude in protecting their neighbourhoods, yet has expected the latter to put up with land use changes.

Moreover, because it has tended to deal primarily with property owners it has shown little evidence of addressing concerns of less favoured socio-economic categories, such as residential tenants.[1] This has been clearly demonstrated in its treatment of social housing, including the provision of assisted housing as a matter of articulated public policy. The interests of the current owners of private property have regularly been given precedence over the general public interest in the provision of such types of housing and over the interests of those members of the public, not specifically identified or appearing as parties, who would benefit from the increased availability of such housing. Because these persons are not parties before the board, their interests, which should also be considered a legitimate public concern, simply do not register on its policy radar unless one of the parties present chooses to raise them.

The retention of the OMB as a planning tribunal is therefore open to question. Consider two of the main reasons for using tribunals rather than courts: the ability to apply public policy to matters to be decided and the provision of a quick and inexpensive system of hearings. The board has to some degree vitiated the former by basing its decisions largely on policies derived from the common law rather than on public policy considerations. Its utility with respect to the latter, while not examined herein, is also doubtful. One of major complaints that has been expressed over the years in reviews of the board's role and manner of operation has been the cost, in both time and financial resources, of taking part in its hearing process.[2]

If we assume that a forum for reviewing local planning decisions is required at all, which is highly debatable, it would be inadvisable to remove the OMB and rely on the courts to resolve land use disputes. The matters to consider are three-fold: the retrospectivity of harm, the inclusivity of the concerns addressed, and the application of policy.

The legal process before the courts is designed to deal with alleged breaches of common or statute law, and with allegations of harm. Generally speaking, an act must have occurred – a contravention of the law or an act creating a measurable harm – for an action to be sustainable in the courts. Claims of prospective harm should an act occur in the future are extremely difficult to sustain, except occasionally as the basis for obtaining a temporary injunction. Yet a major purpose of planning controls is to enable disputes regarding the impacts of proposed developments and land use changes to be resolved before, not after, they come into being. An administrative tribunal can do this. It is not limited to the judicial tests. Proof of an actual, measurable impact is not required. The board has developed what might be termed a credible perception test. It has accepted reasoned concerns about the potential impact of proposed developments as grounds for refusal, concerns which are subjective and often immeasurable, such as a desire to preserve a particular environment or set of amenities. It has accepted concerns with respect to prospective economic impact, such as the concerns expressed by industries and farmers that the approval of residential development in their vicinity might lead to future pressure on them to curtail or cease their operations. It has even given weight to the expectations of property owners that they will not be subject to changes that would have an adverse impact on their enjoyment of their properties. These are matters which extend beyond the tests of nuisance that can be addressed by the courts.

The courts cannot deal with the public policy concerns which are often at issue in planning decision making. Even though the OMB has, as a matter of its own policy, frequently subordinated these to private concerns, it has also addressed broader policy issues. This is seen in its development of a policy with respect to commercial competition, where it has considered the impact of proposed commercial development on the functioning of a municipality's planned commercial structure. It is seen in the board's acceptance, at least for a time, that the public interest underlying the adoption of interim control by-laws outweighs the adverse impact of a temporary development limitation or freeze. It is seen in the board's treatment of residential development in agricultural areas, where it has regularly applied the provincial Food Land Guidelines in tandem with cognate policies in official plans when deciding whether or not to approve severances. The board has been able to consider the public policy implications of approving comprehensive official plans and zoning by-laws, which frequently change permitted land uses in such a manner as to lessen the development potential of individual properties. The courts can address none of these matters.

While a tribunal can thus address policy issues in a way that the courts cannot, it must be kept in mind that the OMB's manner of proceeding mirrors that of the courts in many respects. It follows an adversarial process and bases its decisions on the cross-examined evidence and the arguments of opposing parties. As any person familiar with its operations is aware, its hearing time is frequently devoted to such legal, court-orientated matters as motions for adjournment, dismissal, or review, procedural disputes, challenges to its jurisdiction, and the determination of entitlement to awards of costs. These matters are ancillary to the board's primary role of evaluating and applying planning policy per se, and, to the extent that it devotes its time to them, its superiority over the courts as a planning review tribunal is not apparent.

A Forum for Sober Second Thought

Yet, a clear conclusion arising from this study is that the Ontario Municipal Board has outlived its usefulness as a planning review tribunal. Underlying the conclusion that the review of local planning decisions is preferably carried out by a tribunal is the assumption that a review is required at all. It appears evident from this analysis of the OMB's decision making, however, that it no longer performs a necessary role in Ontario's planning system; that, if anything, it makes the planning process more complex, time-consuming, and expensive. Most importantly, it places the ultimate decision-making authority for land use planning, which is in its essence a political process, in the hands of appointed, non-accountable officials.

The OMB occupies an anomalous position in regulatory theory. In what might be called the standard model of regulation, a tribunal oversees the activity which is subject to regulation. In the area of planning and land development, however, the primary activity of land development is regulated locally, mostly by elected municipal councils but also by municipally appointed committees of adjustment and land division committees. There are several arguments of a political and administrative nature for providing a provincially appointed planning review tribunal. These relate to the ability to bring greater expertise to bear on making planning decisions than local municipalities are often able to do, ensuring that adequate consideration is given to provincial planning policy, avoiding local political pressures, and addressing inter-municipal concerns. In other words, the 'value-added' political and administrative arguments for retention of the board's role in planning review is that it provides something in the process which local decision makers cannot, or, at least, are unlikely to provide. Evidence drawn from its actual decision making casts doubt on these arguments. It has consistently subjected provincial policy to the test of its own locally oriented policy. It has accorded considerable weight to municipal council decisions and to local interests represented by councils and property owners. It has shown little evidence of considering broader inter-municipal implications of matters before it.

The OMB is a product of history. It is salutary to remember that it is almost a century old, and that, while it has expanded both in size and in the breadth of jurisdiction, its structure and mode of operation have changed little over that period. The board reflects a continuing relationship between the province and its creatures, the municipalities, a relationship based on the belief that municipalities cannot be fully trusted to manage their own affairs. The province's initial concern was with municipal financial management. There was once justification for this, particularly during the 1930s, as municipalities often found themselves in financial difficulties, some becoming bankrupt. Yet while municipal borrowing still requires board approval, this has become a largely pro forma exercise. As long as proposed borrowing does not exceed limits based on the board's maximum debt load formulae, approval is virtually automatic. The reviewing of municipal planning decisions, including the decisions of committees of adjustment and land division committees, is now by far the most important area of the board's discretionary control over local decision making.[3] Apart from the claim that the board, not depending on local political support, has been a more impartial decision maker than municipal councils could be, it is difficult to see what value it adds to the planning process.

Given the nature of the OMB's policy development, it does little that could not be done by local decision makers. The latter can also determine adverse impact, and in reviewing local decisions the board is merely substituting its opinion on this matter for theirs. The only rationale for retaining its jurisdiction in this area is the essentially unprovable argument that local councils or committees might not make this assessment with the same degree of impartiality. There have been very few instances in which the board has overturned council or committee decisions on the ground that they were made solely for political reasons, to satisfy a particular group, without consideration being given to planning issues. In any event, this might not have mattered if the board had been injecting a strong public policy component into its decision making, but, as the evidence of its actual decision making makes clear, it has done so in only a limited manner. This is not entirely its own doing. It has been given little policy direction and has thus been left on its own to develop principles to ensure some consistency in its decision making. But in doing so it has failed to take the opportunity presented to it, as a regulatory tribunal, to give primacy to public policy considerations, and, where they have existed, to expressions of provincial planning policy.

The approach the OMB has taken to determining who constitutes the 'public' whose interests are to be protected also militates against the retention of its planning review role. It has adopted the group public interest theory, and has generally held up decisions of municipal councils as the highest expression of the public interest. Following from this, it has often stated that it does not lightly overrule council decisions. Its conclusion that development proposals are in conformity with approved official plans has always been a powerful reason for approving them. Yet the board has frequently reversed council and committee decisions. If it had done so on the ground that these local decisions had contravened more broadly based public interests or stated provincial policies, it would have justified its role as a provincial review tribunal. It has done so, however, primarily by substituting its opinion as to adverse impact for that of locally elected or appointed decision makers.

Regulatory theory speaks of the life cycle of agencies. This is seen as a process in which agencies originally created to regulate, in the public interest, the activities of certain industries develop close links with and adopt the values of those industries, and regularly make decisions favourable to them rather than to the interests of those affected by them. The frequency with which the board has refused to approve planning applications, both overall and in the face of municipal and owner support, suggests that it has not been captured, in the sense suggested by regulatory theory, by interests regularly appearing before it and whose behaviour it is supposed to be regulating. But capture can be more subtle. If a tribunal is constantly subjected to the world view of particular groups to the exclusion of the views of others, it is likely to accept the arguments and positions expressed by the former as representing the real world. The board has functioned largely as a forum for property owners, as both developers and opponents of development, and for municipalities which are generally allied with one or the other groups of owners. This fact, plus the paucity of public policy support it has received, help to explain its adoption of its largely private law-oriented policies.

The OMB did have a role to play in earlier years. The use of official plans and of land use controls developed gradually throughout Ontario. In a province of mostly small municipalities with few resources to undertake planning and little understanding of the rationale for or the mechanics of land use controls, the board could play a stabilizing and educating role, and could subject local decisions to review by an agency which had developed considerable experience in this area. Those conditions have now largely disappeared. Most of the province's population, and certainly the great bulk of its planning and development activity, are now found in large municipalities whose councils are regularly dealing with planning policies and development proposals and with the conflicts these can generate. These municipalities have considerable planning expertise available to them. Nor is this experience and expertise limited to larger municipalities, as the administration of planning controls has become customary throughout the province. As the board has not been contributing something beyond this, such as ensuring that provincial policies are being followed, resolving inter-municipal disputes, or considering the implications of major planning or development initiatives on inter-municipal or regional development patterns, it is making decisions that many municipalities are equally well equipped to make.

The province's gradual shift in recent years of official plan approval responsibilities from the Minister of Municipal Affairs and Housing to upper-tier municipalities is indicative of the continuing evolution of planning controls and the maturing of the municipal role in planning. As this trend continues, and the province's direct approval or regulatory role in planning and other areas diminishes, the need for its alter ego, a provincially appointed review tribunal, also diminishes.

The experience of other Canadian provinces shows that a tribunal exercising an all-encompassing planning review function is not required to ensure that the interests of all parties receive an equitable hearing. Alberta, Saskatchewan, Manitoba, and Nova Scotia, for example, have provincially appointed boards exercising some planning appeal functions, but their jurisdiction is limited compared with that of Ontario's. The planning jurisdiction of the Alberta Municipal Government Board, for example, is limited to statutory (official) plan, zoning by-law, and development permit matters involving licenses issued by other provincial boards, such as the Natural Resources Conservation Board or the Alberta Energy and Utilities Board, and to resolving inter-municipal disputes. It does not consider municipal planning decisions otherwise. The Manitoba Municipal Board considers all official plans, but can only make recommendations to the Minister of Municipal Affairs. The Saskatchewan and Nova Scotia boards have no jurisdiction over official plans. This common situation is reflective of the fact that official plans are first and foremost policy documents, giving expression to the local public interests as determined by municipal councils, not documents directly affecting the rights of property owners.

Even in dealing with planning approvals having a direct effect on property rights such as zoning, minor variances, development control, and severances, the record of other provinces is variable. In Saskatchewan a zoning by-law is adopted by council, and there is no right of appeal from this decision. An initial zoning by-law may not be appealed to the Nova Scotia Municipal Board, but an amendment may be. In these provinces it is only when planning controls affect the details of development proposals – that is, minor variances and development permits or review, thus having a direct impact on the rights of property owners to develop as they see fit – that the right to appeal to a provincial tribunal becomes more common. Yet even in these instances an appeal right may not always be direct. In Saskatchewan, for example, council decisions on these matters must first be appealed to a development appeals board, a local tribunal consisting of council appointees (although councillors and municipal staff cannot be members). It is only the decision of this board, not of council, that may be appealed to the provincial municipal board. Then there is British Columbia, which functions without a provincial planning appeal tribunal at all. That province and, to a lesser extent, those named above, rely on other mechanisms than an appeal tribunal to ensure that interested parties are given a full and fair right to be heard and that elements of the public interest are addressed.

This leads us to consider a legal rationale, frequently given for retaining the OMB's planning review function, namely that a tribunal operating in a quasi-judicial manner is required to ensure that the rules of natural justice are applied in determining the rights of property owners. This rationale was sustained by the *Zadravec* decision in which the Ontario Court of Appeal established that the existence of a right to appeal from a municipal decision to a tribunal whose hearings are conducted in accordance with the rules of natural justice makes it unnecessary for municipal councils to meet this standard. It is supported also by the Statutory Powers Procedure Act, which requires that persons be afforded a hearing by a decision-making body, with rights to present evidence in support of their position, engage in cross-examination, and be represented by counsel when decisions affecting their rights are being made. Yet the experience of other provinces having similar procedural requirements shows that the requirement can be met without resorting to an all-encompassing provincial appeal tribunal. Other provinces have achieved the same result by establishing public hearing requirements prior to the adoption of official plans and zoning by-laws which are considerably more stringent that those found in Ontario's Planning Act. In British Columbia, for example, municipal councils must hold a public hearing at which 'all persons who believe their interest in the proposed by-law may be affected must be afforded a reasonable opportunity to be heard or present written submissions respecting matters contained in the by-law' and a 'written report of each public hearing, containing a summary of the representations respecting the by-law that were made at the hearing must be prepared and maintained as a public record.'[4] Alberta has a similar public hearing provision. In both Alberta and Saskatchewan, where such site-specific matters as development permits and minor variances are approved or refused by municipal officials, municipal councils are required to establish local boards to hear appeals from those decisions. An Alberta subdivision and appeal board may 'accept any oral or written evidence that it considers proper, whether admissible in a court of law or not, and is not bound by the laws of evidence applicable to judicial proceedings,' and it 'must make and keep a record of its proceedings which may be in the form of a summary of the evidence presented at a hearing.'[5] In Saskatchewan all parties to a development appeals board hearing must file all written material upon which they intend to rely several days prior to the hearing so that it may be available for public inspection. The board must also permit all parties and all affected persons to be heard and must maintain a written record of the proceedings.

These various examples have been presented, not to suggest that Ontario should adopt any of them specifically, but to show that it is possible to provide for full and fair public participation in planning decision making without relying totally on a provincially appointed planning review tribunal. Moreover, even where such tribunals exist, their role is generally limited to hearing appeals affecting site-specific development rights. They are not called upon to determine public policy issues associated with the preparation and adoption of official plans or zoning by-laws, which are considered to be primarily matters of local public interest to be dealt with by locally elected representatives. Given the experience of other provinces, why must Ontario retain a quasi-judicial tribunal to second-guess all municipal planning decisions? Given the manner in which the board has and continues to make its decisions, such retention is no longer necessary.

While there is little planning or legal justification for the OMB to retain its planning review function, there are strong political interests favouring such a retention. The board is a long-established tribunal of the provincial government. Without it, there might well be greater pressure placed on provincial politicians to become involved in resolving local planning disputes.[6] The board provides security for municipal politicians, who know that making decisions with respect to politically contentious land use disputes will ultimately be the responsibility of someone other than themselves. Members of what might be called the OMB industry – those lawyers, planning consultants and other experts who appear regularly before the board – have a strong economic interest in its retention. Looked at more generally, the board provides a sounding board for the public, a tribunal removed from the political arena which it believes will make unbiased decisions, although this is always a subjective conclusion which is impossible to measure. Institutional inertia is also a consideration, as the board has long been an accepted part of the political landscape, satisfying the needs of the provincial government and of major municipal and private interests participating in the planning process. Nevertheless, the OMB is indeed a tribunal out of time. Its role in the planning process has become an anachronism. One can but hope that the political impetus will be forthcoming to either greatly reduce or abolish its planning review mandate.

APPENDIX

Methodology

As this is a study of decision making by an administrative tribunal, the focus must be on the decisions themselves. The Ontario Municipal Board has regularly generated huge numbers of decisions. During the 1989–90 reporting year, for example, it held 1,912 hearings, all of which resulted in a decision being issued. Moreover, the board has not been bound by precedent and has not issued, as do the courts, recognizably leading decisions from which a legal trail can be followed. It has therefore been necessary to select, from a huge 'anonymous' decision base, those decisions dealing with the policy matters selected for review and to subject them to meaningful analysis. The approach taken in this book has involved selecting an appropriate period within which to examine board decisions, selecting decisions within that period which dealt with the application and development of planning policy, and subjecting the decisions chosen to numerical and textual analysis.

Selection of a Review Period

Three periods permit an examination of the board's policy development activities in differing planning contexts. The first period – 1971 to 1978 – was one in which the Planning Act provided little procedural and less substantive direction, and in which the province was engaged in developing and starting to apply broadly based planning policies. The second period – 1987 to 1994 – was one in which the major procedural reforms embodied in the 1983 re-enactment of the Planning Act had become established practice and were being considered and applied by the board. By this time the province was also formally adopting planning policy statements under section 3 of the Planning Act, 1983. The third period – 1995 to 2000 – was one of limited legislative change with respect to planning, but one whose analysis brings the study up to the present.

Selection of Policy Areas for Review

There are certain themes which have appeared regularly in the board's decisions throughout the review periods. These have included adverse impact, good planning, prematurity, matters that are or are not in the public interest, opportunities for public participation in making planning decisions, the protection of neighbourhoods, and the treatment of interim control by-laws. They and similar matters became the basis for deciding which cases to select for analysing the board's own policy development. The selection of decisions dealing with its treatment of provincial policy was straightforward, as all decisions within the chosen database in which it made reference to provincial policy were selected for analysis.

Selection of a Decision Database

The OMB's heavy involvement in planning and other municipal-related matters has provided a huge database of decisions. It would not have been feasible, nor statistically necessary, to review and analyse all of these. Selection was therefore limited, in all but one of the years during the review periods, to decisions released during those periods which were published in the Ontario Municipal Board Reports (OMBRs). Data for 1971 was selected differently. The OMBRs were first published in 1972, and before then decisions were only occasionally and intermittently published. The staff of the Law Society of Upper Canada's Great Library had, however, been collecting many of the board's decisions for a number of years previously, and these provided a database similar to that found in the OMBRs. It was thus possible to select these in much the same manner as for the post-1971 published decisions.

Coding and Analysis of Decisions

The selected OMB decisions were coded in accordance with a wide range of categories, and of fields within each, in order to record the information they contained that was considered necessary for the analyses. It was then possible to sort these decisions to obtain subsets of decisions dealing with specific matters or combinations thereof, which provided the raw material for the subsequent detailed analyses. This provided the basis, for example, for the numerical analysis of decisions illustrating such matters as the different rates of approval for different types of applications. It provided also the basis for selecting decisions exhibiting common characteristics so that they could be individually reviewed to determine what light, if any, they cast on the board's thinking with respect to the matters under study. Examples of such subsets include all decisions in which the board considered the application of the province's Food Land Guidelines, those decisions in which it addressed the adequacy of approval procedures under the Planning Act, and those in which it approved or refused to approve interim control bylaws.

Following the review process outlined above, I selected a total of 870 decisions for analysis, 348 from the 1971–78 review period, 321 from the 1987–94 review period, and 201 from the 1995–2000 review period.

A Note Regarding Parties

Because of the nature of the analysis, the aim has been to identify the parties supporting or opposing planning applications referred or appealed to the board. We have not therefore used the normal terms – applicants, appellants, respondents – by which parties are identified in decisions, but have identified them as supporters, or opponents only. For example, parties supporting the approval of a zoning by-law that has been appealed are referred to as supporters, although they are identified in the decision as respondents. Where a municipal council has refused to approve a requested zoning amendment, however, the parties seeking its approval by the board are referred to as supporters although they are identified as appellants in the decision. The same comments apply to parties seeking approval of official plans or of amendments to official plans. In the case of minor variances and severances, the party seeking approval of the variance or severance is always identified as the supporter, although it may be either the appellant, if the application was refused by a committee of adjustment, or the respondent, if it was approved and is being appealed by another party. Where a subdivision application is being heard, the subdivider is identified as the supporter even though it is appealing the municipality's conditions of draft plan approval.

Notes

Introduction

1 Lamer, 'Administrative Tribunals,' 108.
2 See Ontario Economic Council, *Subject to Approval*; Planning Act Review Committee, *Report*; Government of Ontario, White Paper; Commission on Planning and Development Reform in Ontario, *New Planning for Ontario*.
3 The one provincial study dealing directly with the board was the 1972 Select Committee on the Ontario Municipal Board, *Report*. In recent years the House Standing Committee on General Government has addressed the role of the board on occasion.
4 Hutchinson, 'Rise and Fall,' 293.
5 Sossin, 'The Politics of Discretion,' 380.
6 Ibid.
7 McAuslan, *Ideologies of Planning Law*, 2.
8 Ibid.
9 Ibid., 4.
10 The position has been more complex at the provincial level, where, subject to referral or appeal to the OMB, the minister has been responsible for approving official plans and plans of subdivision. This has meant in practice that ministry staff have had a substantial decision-making role. This role has lessened in recent years, however, with the delegation of official plan and subdivision approval authority to both regional and larger local municipalities.

1: The Genesis, Evolution, and Operation of the OMB

1 Armstrong and Nelles, *Monopoly's Moment*, 192.

2 W.C. Bickel, clerk-solicitor of Belleville, addressing the 1906 convention of the Ontario Municipal Association. Quoted in Brief of the Ontario Municipal Association to the Select Committee of the Legislature on the Ontario Municipal Board, 1972, at 5.
3 Humphries, *Honest Enough*, 141.
4 R.S.O. 1990, c. O.28.
5 Prior to 1983 all board decisions could be petitioned to the provincial cabinet, and its planning decisions frequently were. While some of these were with respect to matters of public importance, the majority involved local applications, such as site-specific rezonings or minor variances, which had no significant public policy implications that would warrant the cabinet's attention. The right to submit petitions to the cabinet with respect to decisions arising from appeals or referrals under the Planning Act was terminated in 1983.
6 The referral and appeal provisions are described here in a simplified manner. For example, no reference is made to the circumstances under which an approval authority could refuse to refer an official plan to the board. For more detail, see the specific provisions in the Planning Act.
7 R.S.O. 1990, c. A.8.
8 City and Suburbs Plans Act, 2 Geo. V (S.O. 1912) c. 43, s. 2, 3.
9 Planning and Development Act, 7 Geo. V (S.O. 1917) c. 44, s. 4.
10 Municipal Amendment Act, 1921, 11 Geo. V. (S.O. 1921) c. 63, s. 10.
11 Planning Act, 1946, S.O. 1946, c. 71.
12 Planning Amendment Act, 1959, S.O. 1959, c. 71.
13 Brief of the Ontario Municipal Association to the Select Committee of the Legislature on the Ontario Municipal Board, 1972, 4.
14 Select Committee, *Report*, 4.
15 The one exception has been plans of subdivision, where the matters to be addressed prior to giving approval have been spelled out in detail. See Planning Act, s. 51(24). The act gives very little direction, however, in the subdivision area in which the board is most frequently involved: appeals of conditions imposed by municipalities for approval of plans of subdivision.
16 *Supra* note 10, s. 10.
17 *Re City of Toronto By-law No. 10129* (6 November 1924), No. 9536 (O.R.M.B.).
18 [1934] O.R. 421 at 428 (C.A.).
19 Bureau of Municipal Research, *Urban Development*, 9.
20 Cushman, *The Independent Regulatory Commission*; Fainsod, 'Some Reflections on the Nature of the Regulatory Process,' in Friedrich and Mason, *Public Policy*, 297–323; Herring, *Public Administration*; Leiserson, *Administrative Regulation*.

21 Bernstein, *Regulating Business*; Downs, *Inside Bureaucracy*; Stigler, 'Theory of Economic Regulation'; Posner, 'Theories of Economic Regulation.'
22 Mitnick, *Political Economy of Regulation*; Peltzman, 'Toward a General Theory'; Wilson, *Politics of Regulation*; Niskanen, 'Bureaucrats and Politicians.'
23 Corry, *Growth of Government Activities*; Willis, *Canadian Boards at Work*.
24 Baggaley, *Emergence of Regulatory State*; Breton, *Regulation*; Brown-John, *Canadian Regulatory Agencies*; Economic Council of Canada, *Responsible Regulation*; Janisch, 'Independent Regulatory Agency'; Stanbury, *Studies on Regulation*; Trebilcock, 'Markets for Regulation,' in Ontario Economic Council, *Government Regulation*.
25 Ontario Municipal Board, *55th Annual Report* (Toronto: Queen's Printer, 1958) at 3.
26 *IPCF Properties v. City of Windsor* (1993), 29 O.M.B.R. 184 at 188.
27 The transcript for Mr J.A. Kennedy is contained in Select Committee on the Ontario Municipal Board, *Proceedings*, 63.
28 Select Committee on the Ontario Municipal Board, *Report*, 3.
29 Ontario Economic Council, *Subject to Approval*, 102.
30 Planning Act Review Committee, *Report*, 91.
31 Jaffary and Makuch, *Local Decision-Making and Administration*, 82.
32 [1966] 2 O.R. 439. For a more recent expression of this position, see *Re Corporation of the Township of Oro and BAFMA Inc.* (1995), 21 O.R. (3d) 483.
33 [1965] 1 O.R. 259 at 263 (C.A.). See also *Re Township of Westminster and City of London* (1975), 5 O.R. (2d) 401 (H.C.).
34 MacFarlane, *Land Use Planning*, 6-3.
35 (1974), 5 O.R. (2d) 763 (Div. Ct.).

2: The Evaluation of Interests

1 Cullingworth, *Ontario Planning*, 27.
2 *Chedoke Terrace Inc. v. City of Hamilton* (1993), 29 O.M.B.R. 430 at 494.
3 There is considerable literature pertaining to the concept of the public interest. See Schubert, *The Public Interest*; Friedrich, *Nomos V*; Flathman, *The Public Interest*; Held, *The Public Interest*; Meyer, *Public Good*; Lewin, *Self-Interest*.
4 See Held, *The Public Interest*, 196; Lewin, *Self-Interest*, 23.
5 Planning Act Review Committee, *Report*, 23. It should be noted that the committee identified what it admitted were recognized and often well organized interest groups, and that it 'acknowledged from the outset that the way in which the review was structured would not give us access to the views, interests or concerns of the individual residents of the Province' (paragraph 2.10).

6 *Matakovic* v. *Township of Sandwich West Committee of Adjustment* (1994), 30 O.M.B.R. 299 at 307.
7 *Ministry of Agriculture and Food* v. *County of Elgin Land Division Committee* (1994), 30 O.M.B.R. 432 at 440.
8 *Maxine Holdings Ltd.* v. *Barrie,* (1974), 3 O.M.B.R. 56 at 63.
9 For the earlier review period, see *Re Newmarket Planning Area Official Plan* (1979), 8 O.M.B.R. 319 at 327; *Re Oakville Planning Area Official Plan Amendments 28, 31 and 32* (1979), 9 O.M.B.R. 412 at 429. For the later review period, see *Nicholson* v. *Town of Markham* (1987) 20 O.M.B.R. 102; *Di Nardo* v. *Town of Vaughan* (1993), 29 O.M.B.R. 245.
10 *Oxford Official Plan Amendment 100* (1993), 27 O.M.B.R. 385. *Re City of Brampton Official Plan Amendment 208* (1994), 30 O.M.B.R. 1.
11 *Petch* v. *City of Cambridge* (1993), 28 O.M.B.R. 117.
12 *Planning Act*, R.S.O. 1990, c. P.13, cl. 51(24)(b).
13 *Re Town of Caledon East and Lawson Subdivision* (1979), 9 O.M.B.R. 188 at 203–4.
14 *Oakville, supra* note 9 at 429; *Re Hamacher* (1973), 1 O.M.B.R. 59.
15 *Supra* note 8, 64.
16 *Re Ottawa-Carleton Planning Area Official Plan* (1979), 9 O.M.B.R. 332 at 337-38.
17 *1099184 Ontario Limited* v. *City of London* (1997) 34 O.M.B.R. 150.
18 *Malahide Developments Ltd.* v. *City of London* (1973), 1 O.M.B.R. 334 at 337.
19 *Price Club* v. *City of Scarborough* (1995), 31 O.M.B.R. 264 at 272-3.
20 *McDonald* v. *City of London* (1978), 7 O.M.B.R. 182 at 184.
21 W.T. Lane, 'Public and Private Rights in Land,' quoted in R.L. Barsh, 'Comparative Styles of Administering Land Use Planning,' in Morris, *Public and Private*, 119.
22 The one exception is the *quia timet* injunction, granted to temporarily prohibit a prospective and irreversible harm to a property. It is extremely difficult in most situations of potential land use conflict to prove that the harm would be irreversible. See *Palmer* v. *Nova Scotia Forest Industries* (1983), 29 C.E.L.R. 157 at 229 (N.S.S.C., Trial Div.).
23 See *Re City of Oshawa Zoning By-laws 108-89 and 125-89* (1992), 26 O.M.B.R. 336 at 351.
24 *Re Town of Richmond Hill Interim Control By-law 110-88 and Zoning By-law 126-88* (1989), 22 O.M.B.R. 150 at 156. The board approved the day nursery, but at a greatly reduced scale than proposed.
25 *Re City of Waterloo Temporary Use By-law 86-86* (1987), 20 O.M.B.R. 69 at 74.
26 *Supra* note 2, 442.
27 Ontario Municipal Board, *64th Annual Report* (Toronto: Queen's Printer, 1969), 13.

28 *Re Spadina Expressway* (1971), 1 O.M.B.R. 1 at 24.
29 *Re Toronto-Metro Centre* (1974), 2 O.M.B.R. 5 at 7–8.
30 *Re City of Toronto Official Plan Amendment 25 and Restricted Area By-law 348-73*. This was known as the '45-foot height by-law decision' because it concerned an official plan and zoning by-law designed to put an indirect freeze on development in the central area of the city, while new planning policies and by-laws were put into effect by limiting all new development to a height of 45 feet. (1975), 4 O.M.B.R. 221 at 235.
31 Ontario Economic Council, *Subject to Approval*, 24.
32 *Chedoke, supra* note 2, 494.
33 *Municipal Amendment Act, 1921* 11 Geo. V, c. 63, s. 10, adding zoning provisions, s. 399a.2(b) to the Municipal Act.
34 *West Hill Redevelopment Co. v. City of Scarborough* (1995), 31 O.M.B.R. 218 at 229.
35 *Morris v. Township of Brock* (1997) 34 O.M.B.R. 374 at 378.
36 *Re City of Toronto Zoning By-law 1997-0273* (2000) 39 O.M.B.R. 174.
37 *Traher v. Township of Middlesex Centre* (2000) 39 O.M.B.R. 235.
38 *Re Township of Nepean Restricted Area By-law 73-76* (1978) 9 O.M.B.R. 36 at 55.
39 *Mooradian Ltd. v. Town of Burlington* (1973), 1 O.M.B.R. 344; *Re City of London New Official Plan (No. 2)* (1974), 3 O.M.B.R. 238; *Tollefson v. Township of Gloucester* (1977), 6 O.M.B.R. 206; *Re City of Ottawa Zoning By-law 80-87* (1988), 21 O.M.B.R. 426.
40 *Russell v. City of Toronto* (1998) 36 O.M.B.R. 169.
41 *Dickinson v. City of Toronto* (1999) 37 O.M.B.R. 362. This decision by a review panel was appealed to the Divisional Court, which reversed it. The latter's decision was appealed to the Court of Appeal, which reversed the lower court decision on the ground of the board's broad jurisdiction under s. 43 and upheld the decision of the review panel. (2001), 53 O.R. (3d) 9 (C. of A.).
42 *Ibid.*, 366.
43 *Ministry of Natural Resources v. County of Haliburton Land Division Committee* (1995), 31 O.M.B.R. 69 at 69.
44 *Shala v. City of Toronto* (1999) 39 O.M.B.R. 54.
45 *Von Zuben v. Herman* (1990), 23 O.M.B.R. 441 at 444.
46 See *Re Township of Westmeath Interim Control By-law 89-18* (1991), 24 O.M.B.R. 442 at 448.
47 *Re City of Oshawa Interim Control By-laws 134-89 and 105-90* (1992), 26 O.M.B.R. 71 at 79.
48 See *Motosi v. Bernardi* (1987), 20 O.M.B.R. 129.
49 See *Dalfen v. City of Ottawa Committee of Adjustment* (1994), 30 O.M.B.R. 235.

218   Notes to pages 50–64

50 *Cott* v. *City of Toronto Committee of Adjustment* (1987), 19 O.M.B.R. 410 at 412; *Waisberg* v. *City of Toronto Committee of Adjustment* (1987), 20 O.M.B.R. 179 at 187.
51 *Rebelo* v. *City of Toronto Committee of Adjustment* (1991), 25 O.M.B.R. 477 at 481.
52 *Supra* note 19, 274
53 The classic exposition of this model is found in Bernstein, *Regulating Business*. Variants of the theory are found in Cary, *Politics*, 67; Downs, *Inside Bureaucracy*, 13; Shepherd, *Treatment of Market Power*, 227–33.
54 Each decision was reviewed to determine, if possible, the character of the owner supporting the application. These were most often companies which, from their names or from descriptions of their activities, were clearly engaged in the business of land development. A few others were individuals who, from the decisions, appeared to be engaged in the business of land development, as opposed to merely seeking approval to put their properties to new or expanded residential, commercial, or other uses. The number of developers must therefore be taken as approximate.
55 The industry was well represented through its associations, as were municipalities through the Association of Municipalities of Ontario, at the hearings of the Select Committee on the Ontario Municipal Board, the Planning Act Review Committee and the Committee on Planning Development Reform in Ontario. It is the author's understanding that the industry has more recently had a major role in discussions with the Minister of Municipal Affairs and Housing leading in 1996 to Bill 20, another major revision to the Planning Act.
56 See also Chipman, *Planning and Pollution*, for a limited discussion of this aspect of the Board's operation.

3: Policy Development in a Statutory/Judicial Context

1 Select Committee on the Ontario Municipal Board, *Report*, 3.
2 Subsection 34(12) was repealed and replaced by S.O. 1989, c. 5, s. 14(1).
3 S.O. 1971, c. 47. Now R.S.O. 1990, c. S.22.
4 [1965] S.C.R. 512.
5 (1973), 37 D.L.R. (3d) 326 (Ont. C.A.).
6 (1979), 24 O.R. (2d) 532.
7 *Re Borough of North York Official Plan Amendment 257* (1975), 4 O.M.B.R. 294.
8 *Re Township of Kingston Official Plan Amendment 3* (26 May 1971), No. R 2903-70 (O.M.B.). The board did refuse to approve the amendment on substantive planning grounds.
9 *Re City of Toronto Restricted Area By-law 375-75* (1977), 6 O.M.B.R. 82 at 85.

10 *Re City of Hamilton Development Control By-law 74-39* (1975), 4 O.M.B.R. 383.
11 *Supra* note 7.
12 *Re City of Cornwall Restricted Area By-law 1894–1975* (1977), 6 O.M.B.R. 125 at 126.
13 (1985), 16 O.M.B.R. 172 (H.C.).
14 *Ibid.*, 197.
15 *Ibid.*, 196.
16 (1985), 17 O.M.B.R. 389 (C.A.).
17 *Re Town of Wasaga Beach Zoning By-law 99-65* (2000) 40 O.M.B.R. 338; *Re Township of Elizabethtown Official Plan* (2001) 41 O.M.B.R. 55.
18 *Re Town of Niagara-on-the-Lake Zoning By-law 500EX-88* (1990), 23 O.M.B.R. 444. See also *St. Jude Homes* v. *City of Toronto* (1989), 22 O.M.B.R. 460; *Re Township of Muskoka Lakes Zoning By-law 86-80* (1988), 21 O.M.B.R. 141.
19 *Re Township of Albemarle Official Plan Amendment 7 and By-law 25-86* (1988), 21 O.M.B.R. 210.
20 *Re Village of Thornbury Zoning By-law 4-91* (1992), 26 O.M.B.R. 481 at 486.
21 *Re Village of Casselman Zoning By-law 91-498* (1994), 30 O.M.B.R. 379.
22 *Re City of Ottawa Zoning By-law 13-88* (1989), 22 O.M.B.R. 300.
23 *Ibid.*
24 *500176 Ontario Ltd.* v. *City of London* (1993), 27 O.M.B.R. 118 at 123.
25 *Re City of Brampton Official Plan Amendment 208* (1994), 30 O.M.B.R. 1 at 24–6.
26 *Re City of Vanier Zoning By-law 3069* (1992), 26 O.M.B.R. 63. See also *Henderson* v. *County of Simcoe Land Division Committee* (1994), 30 O.M.B.R. 200.
27 *Re Township of North Elmsley Zoning By-law 89-35* (1991), 25 O.M.B.R. 202.
28 *Re Township of West Carleton Zoning By-law 36-89* (1990), 23 O.M.B.R. 257.
29 *Brampton, supra* note 25.
30 *Haughie* v. *DeRubeis* (1977), 6 O.M.B.R. 127. See also *Chokan* v. *Legault* (1977), 6 O.M.B.R. 303.
31 *Kilby* v. *Regional Municipality of Waterloo* (1975), 4 O.M.B.R. 51; *D'Antimo* v. *Town of Richmond Hill* (1977), 6 O.M.B.R. 94.
32 *McGill* v. *City of Orillia Committee of Adjustment* (1987), 20 O.M.B.R. 235. See also *Cott* v. *City of Toronto Committee of Adjustment* (1987), 19 O.M.B.R. 410 and *Gautreau* v. *City of Etobicoke* (1997), 34 O.M.B.R. 292.
33 *Lawless* v. *City of Peterborough Committee of Adjustment* (1991), 25 O.M.B.R. 287 at 288.
34 *Re City of Cambridge Restricted Area By-law 228* (1976), 5 O.M.B.R. 21.
35 *Re Town of Goderich Official Plan Amendment 11* (1987), 20 O.M.B.R. 464.
36 *Re Town of Listowel Zoning By-law 88-15* (1990), 23 O.M.B.R. 450 at 454.
37 See *Tan-Mark Holdings Ltd.* v. *Town of Vaughan* (1987), 19 O.M.B.R. 385 at 390.

38 *Franco* v. *Town of Innisfil Committee of Adjustment* (1997), 34 O.M.B.R. 184; *Toronto Lawn Tennis Club* v. *City of Toronto* (1998), 36 O.M.B.R. 102.
39 *Geautreau, supra* note 32.
40 McRuer, *Royal Commission Inquiry*.
41 It is probably not coincidental that this expression of board policy began in 1960, as this was the year in which A.J. Kennedy was appointed chair. His views on the role of the board, and its relationship with government, municipalities, and citizens, were clearly expressed in its annual reports, his submissions to various committees, and in board decisions throughout his 12-year tenure as chair.
42 Ontario Municipal Board, *56th Annual Report*, 11.
43 *Etobicoke Board of Education* v. *Highbury Developments Ltd.* [1958] S.C.R. 196 at 200 [hereinafter *Highbury* cited in S.C.R.].
44 *Re Spadina Expressway* (1971), 1 O.M.B.R. 1 at 4.
45 *Re City of Pembroke Restricted Area By-law 77-85* (1979), 9 O.M.B.R. 496 at 500.
46 See, for example, *City of Toronto Restricted Area By-law 258-71* (1974), 2 O.M.B.R. 243 at 244; *City of London Official Plan Amendment and Restricted Area By-law C.P.-306(eg)-641* (1975), 4 O.M.B.R. 152 at 155; *Hamilton, supra* note 10, 385.
47 *Re Township of Pickering Restricted Area By-law 3978-71* (8 September 1971), No. R 5776-71 (O.M.B.).
48 *Re City of London Restricted Area By-law CP-315(dv)-539* (1973), 1 O.M.B.R. 551 at 553–4.
49 *Toronto, supra* note 46 at 250; *Re Town of Vaughan Official Plan Amendment 74 and Restricted Area By-laws 156-77 and 180-77* (1978), 7 O.M.B.R. 369 at 387.
50 *Re City of Brockville Restricted Area By-law 44-72* (1974), 2 O.M.B.R. 343 at 347.
51 *Re City of Sudbury Official Plan Amendment and Restricted Area By-law 73-186* (1974), 3 O.M.B.R. 296 at 297. See also *Brampton, supra* note 25.
52 *Hamilton, supra* note 10, 384.
53 *Re Municipality of Metropolitan Toronto Official Plan Amendment No. 4* (2000), 40 O.M.B.R. 1.
54 *Re Township of London Restricted Area By-law 3700-118* (1978), 7 O.M.B.R. 124 at 127.
55 *Re City of Toronto Restricted Area By-law 280-69* (7 January 1971), No. R3805-70 (O.M.B.).
56 *London, supra* note 46.
57 *Re Township of Amaranth Official Plan Amendment* (1977), 6 O.M.B.R. 39.
58 *Re Township of Eramosa Restricted Area By-law 12-1975* (1977), 6 O.M.B.R. 64.
59 *Re City of London Restricted Area By-law C.P.374(hf)524* (1978), 7 O.M.B.R. 91.
60 *Re Borough of Scarborough Restricted Area By-law 17100* (1978), 7 O.M.B.R. 305.

Notes to pages 77–86   221

61 For zoning appeals see the Planning Amendment Act, 1959, S.O. 1959, c. 71, s. 27a(19). A similar provision was previously found in the Municipal Act.
62 Planning Act, 1983, S.O. 1983, c. 1. See s. 22(4) for very similar wording with respect to referrals of proposed official plan amendments.
63 [1963] 2 O.R. 625 at 630.
64 *Re Hopedale Developments Ltd. and Town of Oakville*, [1965] 1 O.R. 259 at 264, quoting from unreported O.M.B. decision *Re Highway Developments Ltd. v. Township of Etobicoke.*
65 *Ibid.*, 264–5.
66 *Tollefson v. Township of Gloucester* (1977), 6 O.M.B.R. 206 at 213. See also *Vaughan, supra* note 49, 388.
67 *Tollefson, ibid.*
68 *Ptak Construction Ltd. v. City of Hamilton* (10 February 1971), No. R.2897-70 (O.M.B.).
69 *Claverley Investments Ltd. v. Borough of East York* (1974), 3 O.M.B.R. 356 at 356.
70 *Oriental Investments Ltd. v. City of Toronto* (1977), 6 O.M.B.R. 432.
71 *Rush v. Township of Scugog* (1979), 8 O.M.B.R. 370. See also *Valtrent Developments Ltd. v. City of Peterborough* (1987), 7 O.M.B.R. 327.
72 *Hardix Developments Ltd. v. City of London* (13 October 1971), No. R. 3743-70 (O.M.B.); *Arkbo Holdings v. City of Kitchener* (1973), 1 O.M.B.R. 470.
73 *Crofton Developments Ltd. v. Borough of Scarborough* (1975), 4 O.M.B.R. 303 at 304.
74 *Sarnia and District Association for the Mentally Retarded v. City of Sarnia* (1974), 2 O.M.B.R. 396 at 399. See also *Re Preston Sand and Gravel Co. Ltd.* (1976), 5 O.M.B.R. 209 at 216.
75 *Toronto Airways Ltd. v. Town of Markham* (1975), 4 O.M.B.R. 372 at 379.
76 *Regional Municipality of Sudbury Official Plan Amendment* (1976), 5 O.M.B.R. 462.
77 *Nicholson v. Town of Markham* (1987), 20 O.M.B.R. 102 at 108–9.
78 *Maiocco v. City of Guelph* (1991), 25 O.M.B.R. 211.
79 *Re Town of Meaford Restricted Area By-law 537 A.D. 1972* (1974), 2 O.M.B.R. 257 (lack of study establishing need to locate funeral home in residential area); *Re City of Niagara Falls Official Plan and Restricted Area By-law 70-211* (1973) 1 O.M.B.R. 433 (no study of amount of land needed for shopping centre use).
80 *Re City of Thunder Bay Official Plan Amendment 9* (1988), 21 O.M.B.R. 78. See also *Re City of Scarborough Interim Control By-law 22169-81* (1989), 22 O.M.B.R. 129.
81 *Lavigne v. City of Cornwall* (1973) 1 O.M.B.R. 391 at 392.
82 *Meaford, supra* note 79, 260.
83 *Lavigne, supra* note 81, 392.

84 *Re City of Oshawa Zoning By-laws 108-89 and 125-89* (1992), 26 O.M.B.R. 336 at 351.
85 *Re Town of Fort Frances Official Plan Amendment No. 18 and Restricted Area By-law 35/70* (18 May 1971), No. R 2680-70 (O.M.B.), (enlargement of pulp mill near residential area); *Martin v. Township of North Dorchester* (1977), 6 O.M.B.R. 363 (commercial use of building in residential area); *Re Moore Planning Area Official Plan Amendment 10 and Township of Moore Restricted Area By-law 47 of 1977* (1978), 7 O.M.B.R. 390 (proposed senior citizen's home near existing industry).
86 *Re Township of Pittsburgh Zoning By-law 36-87* (1988), 21 O.M.B.R. 455 at 458; *Wendland v. City of Kitchener Committee of Adjustment* (1992), 26 O.M.B.R. 364; *Re Township of Kingston Official Plan Amendment 77* (1991), 24 O.M.B.R. 385.
87 *Regional Municipality of Niagara v. City of Niagara Falls* (1978), 7 O.M.B.R. 412.
88 *Re City of Welland Official Plan Amendment 66* (1992), 26 O.M.B.R. 311.
89 *Re Township of Stanley Zoning By-law 11-1991* (1993), 28 O.M.B.R. 1; *Hamblin v. Township of Douro* (1996), 32 O.M.B.R. 98.
90 *Re Town of Lindsay Restricted Area By-law 22-73* (1974), 3 O.M.B.R. 384 at 388.
91 *Re City of North York Official Plan Amendments 269, 277 and 280 (No. 2)* (1989), 22 O.M.B.R. 63 at 80.
92 *Re Township of Hamilton Interim Control By-law 92-65* (1993), 29 O.M.B.R. 129 at 137.
93 *Re City of Ottawa Interim Control By-law 283-86* (1987), 20 O.M.B.R. 435; *Re City of Toronto Interim Control By-law 4-2000* (2000), 40 O.M.B.R. 226.
94 *Tan-Mark, supra* note 37.
95 *Oshawa, supra* note 84, 351.
96 *Re Regional Municipality of Ottawa-Carleton Official Plan Amendment 8, et al.* (1992), 26 O.M.B.R. 129.
97 *Toronto, supra* note 55.
98 *Lapointe v. Minister of Municipal Affairs* (1995), 31 O.M.B.R. 495; *Robinson v. Minister of Municipal Affairs* (1995), 31 O.M.B.R. 489.
99 *Re City of Toronto Official Plan Amendment 25 and Restricted Area By-law 348-73* (1975), 4 O.M.B.R. 221.
100 *Minister of Municipal Affairs v. Township of Innisfil* (28 October 1971), No. R 4642-70 (O.M.B.); *Township of Lake of Bays v. Borecki* (1977), 6 O.M.B.R. 305.
101 *Re Stroobant* (1974), 2 O.M.B.R. 55; *Re Stewart* (1974), 2 O.M.B.R. 335.
102 *Re City of Windsor Official Plan Amendment 44 and Restricted Area By-law 3934* (3 May 1971), No. R 3928-70 (O.M.B.); *Re Township of Mono Restricted Area By-law 875* (17 May 1971), No. R96-69 (O.M.B.); *Morrison v. 251555 Projects*

Notes to pages 89–96 223

Ltd. (1975), 4 O.M.B.R. 33; *Re Village of Morrisburg Restricted Area By-law 26-74* (1976), 5 O.M.B.R. 184.
103 *Re Township of Sydenham By-law 1989-26* (1992), 26 O.M.B.R. 317.
104 There were, in addition, 3 reported decisions in 1986. One of these, *Gilbert*, contained a significant statement of the board's policy, and is quoted in this chapter. However, none of these decisions are included in the data, which is limited to 1987–94 and 1995–2000 decisions.
105 *Gilbert v. Town of Oakville* (1987), 19 O.M.B.R. 168.
106 *Tan-Mark, supra* note 37, 389.
107 *Ottawa, supra* note 93; *Re City of Scarborough Interim Control By-law 22169-81* (1989), 22 O.M.B.R. 129; *Re Town of Newmarket Interim Control By-law 1991-136* (1993), 27 O.M.B.R. 323; *Re City of Mississauga Interim Control By-law 551-92* (1993), 29 O.M.B.R. 300.
108 *Tan-Mark, supra* note 37; *Newmarket, ibid.*
109 *Gilbert, supra* note 105.
110 See *Re Town of Markham Interim Control By-law 160-86* (1987) 20 O.M.B.R. 51; *Ottawa, supra* note 93.
111 *Re Township of the Archipelago Interim Control By-law 89-48* (1991), 25 O.M.B.R. 43.
112 (1998), 35 O.R. (3d) 321 at 338.
113 *Supra* note 111. See also *Re Township of Radcliffe Interim Control By-law* (1993), 28 O.M.B.R. 141.
114 *Re Town of Caledon Interim Control By-law 89-88* (1991), 24 O.M.B.R. 26.
115 *Re Township of Westmeath Interim Control By-law 89-18* (1991), 24 O.M.B.R. 442.
116 *Hamilton, supra* note 92.
117 *Re Township of Shuniah Interim Control By-law 1601* (1990), 24 O.M.B.R. 377; *Re Township of Westmeath Interim Control By-law 89-18* (1991), 24 O.M.B.R. 442; *Re City of Ottawa Interim Control By-law 72-91* (1993), 28 O.M.B.R. 72. Other examples include *Markham, supra* note 110; *Re City of Burlington Interim Control By-law 4000-589* (1989), 23 O.M.B.R. 233; *Caledon, supra* note 114.
118 (1988), 63 O.R. (2d) 102 at 106.
119 *Supra* note 112, 337.
120 *Russell v. City of Toronto* (1998), 36 O.M.B.R. 169, reversed by *Dickinson v. City of Toronto* (1999), 37 O.M.B.R. 362.
121 See, for example, *Re Township of Wolford Interim Control By-law 1273* (1998), 37 O.M.B.R. 24 (overreaction, prejudice to owner); *Re City of Toronto Zoning By-law 1997–0321* (1998), 37 O.M.B.R. 239 (abuse of process); *Re Town of Bracebridge Zoning By-law 98-80* (1999), 38 O.M.B.R. 327 (lack of planning

rationale, delay); *Re Township of North Frontenac Interim Control By-law No. 20-99* (2000) 40 O.M.B.R. 476 (inadequate planning rationale, delay).
122 (1977), 15 O.R. (2d) 718 at 721 (Div. Ct.).
123 [1971] 3 O.R. 666 at 668 (HC.).
124 (1974), 5 O.R. (2d) 763 at 766 (Div. Ct.).
125 *Supra* note 122, 721.
126 *Waisberg* v. *City of Toronto Committee of Adjustment* (1987), 20 O.M.B.R. 179 at 186.
127 Examples in which this position is clearly stated include *Hoppe* v. *Borough of North York* (1978), 7 O.M.B.R. 102 at 102; *Macaulay* v. *Prime Equities Inc.* (1979), 8 O.M.B.R. 358 at 362; *Chung* v. *City of North York Committee of Adjustment* (1988), 21 O.M.B.R. 421 at 426; *Thomas* v. *Toronto Committee of Adjustment* (1993), 27 O.M.B.R. 262 at 264.
128 See *Foster* v. *City of Toronto Committee of Adjustment* (1996), 33 O.M.B.R. 280; *Spence* v. *City of Toronto Committee of Adjustment* (1998), 37 O.M.B.R. 113.
129 *Grant* v. *Art Construction Ltd.* (1973), 1 O.M.B.R. 241 at 242.
130 *McLean* v. *City of Toronto Committee of Adjustment* (1990), 23 O.M.B.R. 27 at 30-31. See also *Rebelo* v. *City of Toronto Committee of Adjustment* (1991), 25 O.M.B.R. 477 at 489.
131 *Glinert* v. *Toronto* (1990), 23 O.M.B.R. 427 at 436.
132 *Woodgreen Community Housing Inc.* v. *City of Toronto Committee of Adjustment* (1993), 27 O.M.B.R. 1 at 24. See also *Alexander* v. *Reusse Construction Co. Ltd.* (1973), 1 O.M.B.R. 207; *Marocco* v. *Genovese* (1977), 6 O.M.B.R. 245 at 247; *Darling* v. *Brockville Committee of Adjustment* (1995), 31 O.M.B.R. 285 at 291.
133 *Cassidy* v. *Infante Brothers General Contractors Ltd.* (1978), 7 O.M.B.R. 149 at 152. See also *Monpetit* v. *City of Ottawa Committee of Adjustment* (1999), 38 O.M.B.R. 92, where the board considered a variance to be minor because it did not impact on the character of the neighbourhood.
134 *Fairgrounds Shopping Centre Ltd.* v. *Town of Orangeville* (2000), 39 O.M.B.R. 313.
135 *Zupancic* v. *City of London* (2000), 40 O.M.B.R. 211.
136 *Margolis* v. *City of London Committee of Adjustment* (1994), 30 O.M.B.R. 296 at 298.

4: Policy Development in a Public Policy Vacuum

1 Planning Act Review Committee, *Report*, 30.
2 Jaffary and Makuch, *Local Decision-Making*, 84.
3 *Re Ottawa-Carleton Planning Area Official Plan* (1979), 9 O.M.B.R. 332 at 337-8.

4 The following are other matters the board has held to be determinants of good planning: adequacy of land use control by-law; adequacy of planning reports; buffering of incompatible uses; building and site design features – adequate setbacks, parking; compatibility with existing development in vicinity; establishing clear urban-rural boundaries; environmental protection provisions; Health Unit approval; meeting of housing needs; prevention of strip development; separation from single-family residential areas; subdivision design matters.
5 *Hope v. Township of Wilmot* (2000), 40 O.M.B.R. 122.
6 *Supra* note 3, 338.
7 *Ibid.*, 338.
8 *Re City of Oshawa Zoning By-laws 108-89 and 125-89* (1992), 26 O.M.B.R. 336 at 351.
9 *South and Metcalfe Non-Profit Housing Corp.* v. *Town of Simcoe* (1992), 26 O.M.B.R. 369 at 375.
10 *Re City of Niagara Falls Restricted Area By-law 72-107* (1973), 1 O.M.B.R. 547.
11 *Regional Municipality of Halton* v. *Chudleigh* (1977), 6 O.M.B.R. 64.
12 *South and Metcalfe, supra* note 9.
13 *Alfrin Enterprises Corp.* v. *City of Hamilton* (1993), 28 O.M.B.R. 328.
14 *Re Township of Uxbridge Zoning By-law 96-106* (1997), 35 O.M.B.R. 221.
15 *1098748 Ontario Ltd.* v. *City of Toronto* (1998), 37 O.M.B.R. 68.
16 *Nurmi* v. *Town of Oakville* (1977), 6 O.M.B.R. 226.
17 *Broatch* v. *Town of Haldimand* (1989), 22 O.M.B.R. 126.
18 *Arkbo Holdings Ltd.* v. *City of Kitchener* (1973), 1 O.M.B.R. 470; *Regional Municipality of Halton* v. *Regional Municipality of Halton Land Division Committee* (1992), 26 O.M.B.R. 474; *Re Township of Brantford Official Plan Amendment 16* (1992), 26 O.M.B.R. 491.
19 *Deschamps and Lafontaine* (1974), 2 O.M.B.R. 368 at 369 (apparent reference to UDIRA); *Re Seven Links Planning Area Official Plan* (1979), 9 O.M.B.R. 483 at 485 ('policy' of requiring waterfront lots to have frontage on public roads also).
20 *Ministry of Natural Resources* v. *Young* (1987), 20 O.M.B.R. 156 (mineral aggregates resources policy); *Ontario Ministry of Agriculture and Food* v. *County of Elgin Land Division Committee* (1994), 30 O.M.B.R. 432 at 441.
21 In one instance the board accepted provincially approved guidelines for minimizing scattered rural residential development as statements of good planning principles: *Re Town of Bradford West Gwillimbury Official Plan Amendment No. 17* (1997), 34 O.M.B.R. 176. In other instances good planning appeared to be a matter in addition to such conformity: *Re Township of North Marysburgh Zoning By-law 96-P-02* (1997), 34 O.M.B.R. 416; *Re Township of*

Goderich Zoning By-law 26-1997 (1998), 37 O.M.B.R. 95; *Holan* v. *Township of Carling* (1998), 37 O.M.B.R. 170.
22 *Brantford, supra* note 18, 496.
23 *Sarnia and District Association for the Mentally Retarded* v. *City of Sarnia* (1974), 2 O.M.B.R. 396.
24 *Edison Centre Inc.* v. *City of Toronto* (1991), 24 O.M.B.R. 489; *Woodtree Co-operative Inc.* v. *City of Toronto Committee of Adjustment* (1991), 25 O.M.B.R. 312; *Re City of Toronto Official Plan Amendment 579 and Zoning By-law 678-91* (1993), 28 O.M.B.R. 32.
25 *South and Metcalfe, supra* note 9.
26 *Dolbear* v. *Town of Strathroy* (1988), 21 O.M.B.R. 235; *South and Metcalfe, ibid.*; *Brensylvania Properties Ltd.* v. *Town of Markham Committee of Adjustment* (1990), 23 O.M.B.R. 253; *O'Hara* v. *Township of Rochester* (1998), 36 O.M.B.R. 265; *Re County of Bruce Official plan Amendment No. 4* (2000), 39 O.M.B.R. 40; *Re Township of Hamilton Zoning By-law 99-45* (2000), 40 O.M.B.R. 316.
27 *Sevendon Holdings Ltd.* v. *City of Scarborough* (1987), 20 O.M.B.R. 1; *Nicholson* v. *Town of Markham* (1987), 20 O.M.B.R. 102; *Martin* v. *Township of North Dorchester* (1977), 6 O.M.B.R. 363.
28 *Woodtree, supra* note 24; *Miljan Bros. Inc.* v. *Town of Grimsby* (1998), 37 O.M.B.R. 177.
29 *Rickaby* v. *City of Toronto Committee of Adjustment* (1992), 26 O.M.B.R. 285.
30 *Oshawa, supra* note 8; *Re City of Brampton Official Plan Amendment No. 292* (1998), 36 O.M.B.R. 230.
31 *Tahanen Non-Profit Homes Corp.* v. *City of Toronto* (1993), 27 O.M.B.R. 62.
32 *Robinson* v. *Town of Halton Hills Committee of Adjustment* (1988), 21 O.M.B.R. 1 at 5.
33 Clause 2(b) para. 1 of s. 399a of the Municipal Act, added by the Municipal Amendment Act, 1921, 11 Geo. V, (S.O. 1921), s. 63, s. 10.
34 Ontario Municipal Board, minutes of meeting, 15 October 1962.
35 *Ibid.*, 29 May 1964.
36 *Ibid.*, 21 September 1964. This and the preceding quotations are of particular interest as indicators of the close relationship between the board and the government. The reference to 'uphold these decisions' refers to the right of a party to petition the cabinet to reverse or amend a decision of the board. This right was taken away with respect to planning matters when the Planning Act, 1983 was enacted.
37 D.R. Steele, 'Planning and the Municipal Board, December 1963.
38 *Canmer Investments Ltd.* v. *Borough of Etobicoke* (1973), 1 O.M.B.R. 46 at 48.
39 *Re Town of Lindsay Restricted Area By-law 22-73* (1974), 3 O.M.B.R. 384 at 388.

40 *Re Borough of North York Restricted Area By-law 22887* (21 January 1971), No. R 3781-70 (O.M.B.). This looks suspiciously like a policy statement. See also *Re Town of Oakville Restricted Area By-law 1970-157* (10 June 1971), No. R 4893-71 (O.M.B.).
41 See, for example, *Project 90 Limited* v. *City of Toronto* (30 July 1971), No. R3272-70 (9 O.M.B.); *North Bound Construction Ltd.* v. *City of Mississauga* (1977), 6 O.M.B.R. 243; *Rupkal* v. *Facey* (1977), 6 O.M.B.R. 387; *Re City of Thunder Bay Restricted Area By-law 40-1977* (1978), 7 O.M.B.R. 436; *Cavallin* v. *Township of Mono* (1991), 24 O.M.B.R. 108.
42 See, for example, *Tri-Met Developments Ltd.* v. *Scarland* (1975), 4 O.M.B.R. 336; *Cott* v. *City of Toronto Committee of Adjustment* (1987), 19 O.M.B.R. 410; *DeMarsico* v. *North York Committee of Adjustment* (1991), 24 O.M.B.R. 324; *Laurie* v. *City of North York Committee of Adjustment* (1991), 25 O.M.B.R. 442; *Korkontzilas* v. *Borough of East York Committee of Adjustment* (1993), 28 O.M.B.R. 186.
43 See, for example, *Re City of Woodstock Restricted Area By-law 4538-70* (20 April 1971), No. R 4231-70 (O.M.B.) (row houses in single-family area); *City of Welland Restricted Area By-law 5442* (1973), 1 O.M.B.R. 427 (semi-detached houses facing single-family houses); *Re Town of Walkerton Restricted Area By-law 74-29* (1975), 4 O.M.B.R. 259 (row houses in residential area); *Tishman* v. *Sault Ste. Marie* (1990), 23 O.M.B.R. 119 (townhouses in single-family residential area); *Re Village of Casselman Zoning By-law 91-498* (1994), 30 O.M.B.R. 379 (townhouses in single-family residential area).
44 *Hevey* v. *Maynard* (1997), 35 O.M.B.R. 311.
45 See *Wheeler* v. *City of Sarnia Committee of Adjustment* (1996), 32 O..B.R. 427; *Pilon* v. *Township of Russell* (1997), 34 O.M.B.R. 243; *Ruffolo* v. *City of Etobicoke* (1997), 35 O.M.B.R. 215; *Jacobs* v. *City of Hamilton* (1999), 39 O.M.B.R. 1; *Lucente* v. *City of Toronto* (2000), 40 O.M.B.R. 489.
46 These terms are commonly applied in zoning by-laws as minimum figures. Lot area means the total area of an individual building lot. Frontage is the length of the lot line abutting a public street. Setback is the distance a building or other structure on a lot must be set back from the front, side, or rear lot lines. See *Porter* v. *Gatto Construction Ltd.* (1978), 7 O.M.B.R. 451; *Derbyshire and Jones* v. *Portscheller* (1979), 9 O.M.B.R. 341; *Motosi* v. *Bernardi* (1987), 20 O.M.B.R. 129; *Dalfen* v. *City of Ottawa Committee of Adjustment* (1994), 30 O.M.B.R. 235.
47 *Town of Richmond Hill* v. *Taylor* (1976), 5 O.M.B.R. 158 at 162.
48 *Strome* v. *Regional Municipality of Peel* (1978), 7 O.M.B.R. 174 at 175.
49 *Project 90*, *supra* note 41.
50 *Tri-Met*, *supra* note 42; *Hobbs* v. *Snowden* (1977), 6 O.M.B.R. 273; *Bickell Estate* v. *County of Oxford Land Division Committee* (1990), 23 O.M.B.R. 371.

51 *Supra* note 44, 316.
52 *Re Hamilton-Wentworth Official Plan Amendment 126* (1979), 9 O.M.B.R. 162, headnote at 163.
53 The board is clearly, even if not specifically, referring to property owners in most of its decisions. It rarely makes reference to tenants, or to the interest and expectations of tenants in preserving the character of their environment. See *Erem* v. *Richmond Hill* (1995), 31 O.M.B.R. 186. See also *Chedoke Terrace Inc.* v. *City of Hamilton* (1993), 29 O.M.B.R. 430 at 492 for a discussion of 'experience of place.'
54 *Re Town of Meaford Restricted Area By-law 537 A.D. 1972* (1974), 2 O.M.B.R. 257 (funeral home); *Lindsay, supra* note 39 (commercial parking); *City of Barrie* v. *Brookdale Park Inns Ltd.* (1976), 5 O.M.B.R. 199 (motel expansion).
55 *Vallentgoed* v. *Kingston* (1973), 1 O.M.B.R. 505 (nursing home); *South and Metcalfe, supra* note 9 (shelter for battered women); *Eickmeier* v. *Town of Pickering* (1987), 20 O.M.B.R. 219 (daycare centre).
56 *Town of Markham* v. *Luftman* (1979), 8 O.M.B.R. 422 at 423. See also *Richards* v. *Weldon* (1978), 7 O.M.B.R. 121; *McDonald* v. *City of London* (1978), 7 O.M.B.R. 182.
57 *Lafferty* v. *Lennox and Addington Land Division Committee* (1990), 23 O.M.B.R. 395 at 401.
58 *Cassidy* v. *Infante Brothers General Contractors Ltd.* (1978), 7 O.M.B.R. 149 at 152. See also *Perry* v. *Borough of North York* (14 April 1971), No. R 4204-70 (O.M.B.) for an earlier expression of this view.
59 *Re City of London Restricted Area By-law CP-315(dv)-539* (1973), 1 O.M.B.R. 551; *Perry, ibid*; *Re City of Welland Restricted Area By-law 5300* (1973), 1 O.M.B.R. 236; *Re Township of Moore Restricted Area By-law 27 of 1972* (1974), 2 O.M.B.R. 324.
60 *Martin* v. *Cumberland* (1988), 21 O.M.B.R. 487 at 499.
61 *Marimpietri* v. *County of Victoria* (1976), 5 O.M.B.R. 498 at 500.
62 *Re Town of Keewatin Zoning By-law 94–613* (1996), 33 O.M.B.R. 293.
63 *Brookvalley Holdings Ltd.* v. *Town of Whitby* (1998), 35 O.M.B.R. 394.
64 *Oakville, supra* note 40, 10.
65 *Re City of St Catharines Restricted Area By-law 73-337* (1975), 4 O.M.B.R. 97 at 100. See also *Walkerton, supra* note 43.
66 *Re City of Windsor Restricted Area By-law 4887* (1976), 5 O.M.B.R. 353 (apartment buildings); *Re City of Sault Ste Marie Restricted Area By-law 76-351* (1987), 7 O.M.B.R. 117 (apartment buildings); *Nettie* v. *Quinlan* (1991), 24 O.M.B.R. 68 (two-family dwelling).
67 *Chan* v. *City of Toronto* (2000), 39 O.M.B.R. 342.
68 *Ashland Oil Ltd.* v. *City of Thunder Bay* (1976), 5 O.M.B.R. 54 at 58.

69 *Darte v. City of St Catharines* (1974), 2 O.M.B.R. 417.
70 Palmer and Erkkila, *The Ontario Municipal Board*, 9.
71 *Re Township of Pickering Restricted Area By-law 3978-71* (8 September 1971), No. R5776-71 (O.M.B.). See also *Re Town of Gananoque Restricted Area By-law 1971-29* (1973), 1 O.M.B.R. 454 at 455; *Revere Motors Limited v. Texaco Canada Limited* (1975), 4 O.M.B.R. 117 at 118; *Re Borough of Scarborough Restricted Area By-law 15909* (1975), 4 O.M.B.R. 434 at 436; *Tannenbaum v. City of Toronto* (1992), 26 O.M.B.R. 257 at 259.
72 *Re Town of Georgina Official Plan Amendment 62* (1993), 29 O.M.B.R. 250 at 256.
73 See *Re City of Thunder Bay Parking Structure* (1974), 2 O.M.B.R. 162 at 168. For a more recent expression of this position, see *Re City of Brampton Official Plan Amendment 208* (1994), 30 O.M.B.R. 1 at 9.
74 See *Re Town of Kincardine Restricted Area By-law 3022* (1975), 4 O.M.B.R. 15; *Re City of Niagara Falls Official Plan and Restricted Area By-law 70-211* (1973), 1 O.M.B.R. 433; *Re City of Timmins Official Plan Amendment 27 and Restricted Area By-law 1974-284* (1975), 4 O.M.B.R. 322; *Regional Municipality of Sudbury Official Plan Amendment* (1976), 5 O.M.B.R. 462.
75 *Re City of Belleville Restricted Area By-law 10000* (1977), 6 O.M.B.R. 217; *Morsyd Investments Limited v. Town of St. Mary's* (1979), 9 O.M.B.R. 80.
76 *Southwick Investments Limited v. Town of Orangeville* (1979), 8 O.M.B.R. 341; *Re Township of Sarnia Restricted Area By-law 73 of 1976* (1979), 9 O.M.B.R. 219.
77 *Oxford Official Plan Amendment 100* (1993), 27 O.M.B.R. 385 at 429. See also *757258 Ontario limited and Town of Orangeville* (1989), 22 O.M.B.R. 385; *Heritage Glen West Ltd. v. City of Barrie* (1993), 28 O.M.B.R. 332.
78 *Sevendon, supra* note 27 at 8. See also *Maywelle Properties Limited v. City of Mississauga* (1987), 21 O.M.B.R. 32; *Re City of Peterborough Official Plan Amendment 90* (1997), 34 O.M.B.R. 191; *Loblaw Properties Ltd. v. Town of Ancaster* (1998), 36 O.M.B.R. 149.
79 *Re Town of Ajax Official Plan Amendment 1* (1987), 20 O.M.B.R. 418 at 431. See also *Re City of Etobicoke Official Plan Amendments C-65-86 and C-82-88 (No. 2)* (1993), 27 O.M.B.R. 129.
80 *Brampton, supra* note 73, 9.
81 The board approved commercial developments in *Re City of Barrie Official Plan Amendment 23* (1993), 27 O.M.B.R. 303; *Orlando Corporation v. City of London* (1993), 29 O.M.B.R. 66; *Kargakos v. City of Ottawa Committee of Adjustment* (1993), 27 O.M.B.R. 32. It refused approvals, on the ground of undue impact on planned commercial functions, in *Re Town of Vaughan Official Plan Amendment 249 and Zoning By-law 90-88* (1990), 23 O.M.B.R. 160; *Jurian Investments Limited v. City of Mississauga* (1990), 23 O.M.B.R. 219.

82 *Re Town of Orangeville Official Plan Amendment 39 and Zoning By-law 22-90* (1996), 33 O.M.B.R. 55; *Penex Property VI Ltd. (Highland Farms)* v. *City of Mississauga* (1997), 35 O.M.B.R. 85; *Re Town of Collingwood Official Plan Amendment Nos. 23, 27 & 28* (1998), 36 O.M.B.R. 1.
83 *Loblaw Property Ltd.* v. *Town of Hawkesbury* (2000), 39 O.M.B.R. 334.
84 *Re Town of Leamington Zoning By-law 4407-98* (1999), 38 O.M.B.R. 506; *Meadowbank Investments Ltd.* v. *City of Waterloo* (2000), 40 O.M.B.R. 42.
85 *Re City of Toronto Restricted Area By-laws 377-74 and 58-75* (1976), 5 O.M.B.R. 385.
86 *Re City of Toronto Restricted Area By-law 23-75* (1976), 5 O.M.B.R. 301.
87 *Sarnia, supra* note 23.
88 *Walkerton, supra* note 43.
89 See, for example, *Nettie, supra* note 66; *Tisdale Whitney Housing Co-operative Inc.* v. *City of Timmins* (1992), 26 O.M.B.R. 101; *Re City of York Zoning By-law 2596-92* (1993), 29 O.M.B.R. 283.
90 *Re City of Vanier Zoning By-law 3069* (1992), 26 O.M.B.R. 63.
91 *Re City of Hamilton Zoning By-law 86-206* (1987), 19 O.M.B.R. 437 (city policy to encourage provision of low-income housing); *Toronto, supra* note 24 (city'sprivate social housing legislation).
92 *St Jude Homes* v. *City of Toronto (No.2)* (1989), 22 O.M.B.R. 465 (group home).
93 *Wilson* v. *City of Toronto Committee of Adjustment* (1992), 26 O.M.B.R. 438; *York, supra* note 89.
94 *Oshawa, supra* note 8. See also *Wendland* v. *City of Kitchener Committee of Adjustment* (1992), 26 O.M.B.R. 364; *Kalsatos* v. *City of Toronto Committee of Adjustment* (1990), 23 O.M.B.R. 321; *Von Zuben* v. *Herman* (1990) 23 O.M.B.R. 441; *Martins* v. *City of York Committee of Adjustment* (1993), 27 O.M.B.R. 268.
95 *DeMarsico, supra* note 42. In any event, the board refused to approve the proposed dwelling because of its negative impact on the character of the neighbourhood.
96 *Re Highbury Estates* (1957), 8 D.L.R. (2d) 694 at 699, per Aylesworth J.A., affd.; *Etobicoke Board of Education* v. *Highbury Developments Ltd.* [1958] S.C.R. 196. The Planning Act was subsequently amended to include the adequacy of school sites as a matter to be addressed (clause 51(24)(j)).
97 *Clutterbuck* v. *Township of Hamilton* (1979), 9 O.M.B.R. 227 at 236.
98 The board has made the consideration of prematurity a matter of policy in hearing zoning appeals. See *Re Township of West Nissouri Zoning By-law 63-91* (1993), 29 O.M.B.R. 357 at 366.
99 *Re Stewart* (1974), 2 O.M.B.R. 335.

Notes to pages 140–2 231

100 *Clutterbuck, supra* note 97.
101 *Re City of Windsor Restricted Area By-law 4138* (1973), 1 O.M.B.R. 167.
102 *Re Bezemer and Regional Municipality of Hamilton-Wentworth* (1975), 4 O.M.B.R. 149. See also *Davies* v. *Township of South Dumfries* (1 February 1971), No. R 3325-70 (O.M.B.).
103 *Re Stroobant* (1974), 2 O.M.B.R. 55. See also *Regional Municipality of Ottawa-Carleton* v. *Patterson* (1976), 5 O.M.B.R. 201; *West Nissouri, supra* note 98; *Re Village of Morrisburg Restricted Area By-law 26-74* (1976), 5 O.M.B.R. 184; *Gray* v. *Township of March* (1977), 6 O.M.B.R. 380.
104 *JNS Developments Limited* v. *City of Stoney Creek* (1989), 22 O.M.B.R. 292.
105 *Re City of North York Official Plan Amendments 269, 277 and 280 (No. 2)* (1989), 22 O.M.B.R. 63; *Home Depot Canada* v. *City of Toronto* (2000), 39 O.M.B.R. 411.
106 *Walden Point Ltd.* v. *Town of Burlington* (1974), 2 O.M.B.R. 389. See also *Bezemer, supra* note 102.
107 *Re Township of Humphrey Zoning By-law Z148-92* (1996), 32 O.M.B.R. 441.
108 *Re Town of East Gwillimbury Official Plan Amendment No. 89* (1998), 36 O.M.B.R. 307.
109 *Re Scarborough Transportation Corridor (No. 1)* (1979), 8 O.M.B.R. 500 at 506.
110 *Re Township of Mono Restricted Area By-law 875* (17 May 1971), No. R96-69 (O.M.B.).
111 *Wuthering Heights Limited* v. *Town of Oakville* (1973), 1 O.M.B.R. 292.
112 *Walden Point, supra* note 106.
113 *Re Township of Amaranth Official Plan Amendment* (1977), 6 O.M.B.R. 39; *Beaver Road Builders Ltd.* v. *Township of Rideau* (2000), 40 O.M.B.R. 193.
114 *Rowlan and City of Peterborough* (1990), 23 O.M.B.R. 81.
115 *Boucher* v. *City of Ottawa* (1991), 24 O.M.B.R. 20.
116 *Alexandra* v. *Township of Sombra* (25 November 1971), No. R 4360-70 (O.M.B.).
117 *Lapointe* v. *Minister of Municipal Affairs* (1995), 31 O.M.B.R. 495 at 499.
118 *Darwon Investments Limited* v. *Borough of Scarborough* (20 December 1971), No. R 3518 (O.M.B.).
119 *Re City of Niagara Falls Official Plan and Restricted Area By-law 70-211* (1973), 1 O.M.B.R. 433. See also *Re Borough of Scarborough Official Plan Amendment 304* (1976), 5 O.M.B.R. 1.
120 *Re Township of Hamilton Restricted Area By-law 3192* (1976), 5 O.M.B.R. 435. See also *Re Town of Kincardine Restricted Area By-law 2242* (1974), 2 O.M.B.R. 207; *Re Township of Albemarle Official Plan Amendment 7 and By-law 25-86* (1988), 21 O.M.B.R. 210.

Notes to pages 142–3

121 *Whitby Estates Ltd.* v. *Town of Whitby* (1993), 27 O.M.B.R. 276; *Re Town of Newcastle Zoning By-law 89-103* (1993), 29 O.M.B.R. 26.
122 *Re Borough of York Official Plan* (1975), 4 O.M.B.R. 143.
123 *Re Regional Municipality of Durham Official Plan Amendment 233* (1993), 28 O.M.B.R. 90 (area subject to Oak Ridges Moraine Area Implementation Guidelines).
124 *Re City of Etobicoke Official Plan Amendments C-65-86 and C-82-88 (No. 2)* (1993), 27 O.M.B.R. 129.
125 *Minister of Municipal Affairs* v. *Township of Innisfil* (28 October 1971), No. R4642-70 (O.M.B.). See also *Township of Cardiff* v. *Thompsett* (1977), 6 O.M.B.R. 496.
126 *Crandall* v. *Town of Caledon* (1974), 3 O.M.B.R. 455.
127 Development control provisions had in fact been introduced into the act by the Planning Amendment Act, 1973 S.O. 1973, c. 168, s. 10.
128 *Re Town of Goderich Official Plan Amendment 11* (1987), 20 O.M.B.R. 464; *Re Township of Stanley By-law 11-1991* (1993), 28 O.M.B.R. 1.
129 *Supra* note 97.
130 *Windsor, supra* note 101; *Town of Niagara-on-the-Lake* v. *Stremlaw* (1990), 23 O.M.B.R. 485; *Re City of Stoney Creek Zoning By-law 3383-91* (1993), 29 O.M.B.R. 335.
131 *Re Town of Trenton Restricted Area By-law 71-2521* (30 August 1971), No. R 6096-71 (O.M.B.) (inadequate water, sewers, parks, traffic problems); *Town of Richmond Hill* v. *O'Hara* (1974), 3 O.M.B.R. 162 (drainage problems); *Township of Gloucester – Licence to Operate Quarry* (1974), 3 O.M.B.R. 249 (traffic problems on existing access road).
132 *D'Antimo* v. *Town of Richmond Hill* (1977), 6 O.M.B.R. 94 (provision of sewers); *Fabbri* v. *Town of Vaughan* (1988), 21 O.M.B.R. 260 (provision of connecting road); *Walden Point, supra* note 106 (possibility of acquiring part of subject property for open space as yet unresolved); *Re Township of Cumberland Restricted Area By-law 2222* (1979), 9 O.M.B.R. 363 (possibility of acquiring subject property for park use to be explored).
133 *Re Village of Cookstown Restricted Area By-law 135* (1977), 6 O.M.B.R. 197. See also *Re Town of Caledon East and Lawson Subdivision* (1979), 9 O.M.B.R. 188.
134 *Krah* v. *Minister of Municipal Affairs* (1995), 31 O.M.B.R. 213.
135 *Pattison* v. *Township of Amaranth Committee of Adjustment* (1990), 23 O.M.B.R. 500; *Kroesbergen* v. *Township of South Dumfries Committee of Adjustment* (1995), 31 O.M.B.R. 250.
136 *Re City of Thorold Restricted Area By-laws 18(75) and 34(75)* (1979), 8 O.M.B.R. 290.

Notes to pages 145–56   233

5: The Treatment of Provincial Policy

1 Select Committee on the Ontario Municipal Board, *Report*, 3.
2 Ontario Municipal Board, *Annual Report* (Toronto: Queen's Printer, 1976) at 1.
3 Ministry nomenclature can be confusing. Over the review period land use planning has been variously the responsibility of the Ministry of Treasury, Economics and Intergovernmental Affairs, the Ministry of Municipal Affairs, and the Ministry of Municipal Affairs and Housing. The ministry responsible for agricultural land use matters was identified as the Ministry of Agriculture, then the Ministry of Agriculture and Food, before receiving its current name. The ministry responsible for transportation matters was identified as the Ministry of Highways, then as the Ministry of Transportation and Communications, and is now the Ministry of Transportation. The Ministry of the Environment is now the Ministry of Energy and the Environment. Generally speaking, ministry references throughout will refer to the ministry as it was named at the time of the reference.
4 For a discussion of why the TCR concept was largely unsuccessful, see Frankena and Scheffman, *Economic Analysis*, 44, 127; Frisken, *Planning and Servicing*, 153.
5 *White Paper on the Planning Act* (Toronto: Queen's Printer, May 1979) at 38.
6 Frankena and Scheffman, *Economic Analysis*, 143.
7 *Guidelines Directory* lists 43 guidelines issued by these ministries pertaining to land development.
8 Reporting on a regular basis commenced with the 1972 decisions. Those for 1971 were selected from the decisions compiled by the library of the Law Society of Upper Canada.
9 Minutes of board members' meetings, 2 February 1979 and 30 March 1979. The author was given access to the minutes of the members' meetings on condition that, in order to comply with the protection of personal information provisions of the Freedom of Information and Protection of Privacy Act, no personal information, i.e., names of individuals, be revealed.
10 Minutes of members' meeting, 18 September 1992.
11 Letter dated 6 September 1990.
12 *Re Township of Caledon Official Plan* (1974), 2 O.M.B.R. 1. While the board does not give leading decisions in the sense that a significant decision of a court will be openly followed, if not binding, through the operation of stare decisis, there have been some board decisions which give clear expression to its position on various matters. These positions are reflected, if not always clearly articulated, in other decisions.

13 *Ibid.*, 3.
14 *Ibid.*, 3.
15 *Re Town of Grimsby Official Plan and Certain Implementing Restricted Area (Land Use) By-laws* (1975), 4 O.M.B.R. 158 at 161.
16 *Re Barrie Annexation* (1978), 7 O.M.B.R. 225; *Re Township of Innisfil and City of Barrie* (1978), 17 O.R. (2d) 277, (1978), 80 D.L.R. (3d) 85 (Div. Ct.); *Re Barrie Annexation* (1978), 7 O.M.B.R. 233 (Div. Ct.), rev. *Re Township of Innisfil and Township of Vespra* (1979), 95 D.L.R. (3d) 298 (Div. Ct.), *Re Township of Innisfil* v. *Township of Vespra*, [1981] 2 S.C.R. 145 (S.C.C.) [hereinafter *Innisfil* cited to S.C.R.].
17 *Innisfil* cited to S.C.R., *ibid.*, 164.
18 *Re Regional Municipality of Ottawa-Carleton Official Plan Amendment 8, et al.* (1992), 26 O.M.B.R. 129 at 181.
19 *IPCF Properties* v. *City of Windsor* (1993), 29 O.M.B.R. 184 at 188–89.
20 Frankena and Scheffman, *Economic Analysis*, 156.
21 *Barrie Annexation, supra* note 16. More accurately stated, government policy with respect to the population target for Barrie of 125,000, which was developed by the Simcoe-Georgian Area Task Force, a refinement of the TCR planning process, was the reason for the decision as to the amount of land to be annexed. Other considerations determined what lands were to be included and where the new boundary was to be drawn. This was not, technically, a planning decision. Nevertheless, the hearing dealt to a substantial degree with land use planning issues (as the author can testify from personal knowledge) such as the amount of land required for residential, industrial, and commercial development, and the most appropriate locations for such land uses. The board's decision, once it had accepted the need to accommodate a population of 125,000, turned primarily on these planning matters.
22 *Maxine Holdings Ltd.* v. *Barrie* (1974), 3 O.M.B.R. 56 at 63-4.
23 *Re Vaughan Planning Area Official Plan Amendment 1* (1977), 6 O.M.B.R. 327. The main determinant of the amount of permissible growth here appeared, however, to be the regional municipality's interim policy paper on rural residential development.
24 *Re Town of Vaughan Official Plan Amendment 74 and Restricted Area By-laws 156-77 and 180-77* (1978), 7 O.M.B.R. 369.
25 *Toronto Airways Ltd.* v. *Town of Markham* (1975), 4 O.M.B.R. 372.
26 *Barrie Annexation, supra* note 16 (Div. Ct.).
27 *Re Oakville Planning Area Official Plan Amendments 28, 31 and 32* (1979), 9 O.M.B.R. 363 at 427.
28 Ministry of Agriculture and Food, *A Strategy*.

Notes to pages 164–71   235

29 Government of Ontario, *Green Paper.*
30 Government of Ontario, *Food Land Guidelines.*
31 Spooner, Hon. J.W., 27 June 1966. Later refined in an address by the Hon. D.W. McKeough, 12 February 1968.
32 J.A. Kennedy, memorandum to board members, 29 May 1969.
33 *Rodrigues* v. *Township of Erin* (25 May 1971), No. R–3982-70 (O.M.B.) at 2.
34 See, for example, *Laevens* v. *Township of Dover* (1974), 3 O.M.B.R. 129; *Mau* v. *Township of Alice* (1974), 3 O.M.B.R. 226; *Bruce County South Planning Board* v. *Emke* (1977) 6 O.M.B.R. 27.
35 *Ontario* v. *Freeman* (1974), 2 O.M.B.R. 172; *Horton* v. *Fekete* (1974), 3 O.M.B.R. 325; *Rush* v. *Regional Municipality of Durham* (1979), 8 O.M.B.R. 257.
36 *Re Slater* (1974), 2 O.M.B.R. 48; *Horton* v. *Fekete, ibid.*
37 *Hudson* v. *County of Leeds and Grenville Land Division Committee* (1988), 21 O.M.B.R. 414 at 418; *Shoemaker* v. *Regional Municipality of Niagara Land Division Committee* (1991), 25 O.M.B.R. 366 at 375; *Ontario Ministry of Agriculture and Food* v. *County of Elgin Land Division Committee* (1994), 30 O.M.B.R. 432 at 433.
38 Government of Ontario, *Food Land Guidelines* s. 1.6, 1.7.
39 *Ibid.*, s. 1.8.
40 *Ibid.*, s. 5.5.
41 *Lakeshore Developments Ltd.* v. *County of Huron* (1978), 7 O.M.B.R. 24.
42 *Re Parshan Subdivision and Richmond Hill* (1979), 9 O.M.B.R. 119 at 122. See also *Rush, supra* note 35.
43 See *Re City of Thorold Restricted Area By-laws 18(75) and 34(75)* (1979), 8 O.M.B.R. 290; *Laviolette* v. *Town of Rockland* (1979), 8 O.M.B.R. 297; *Re Township of Zorra Restricted Area By-law 92-76* (1979), 8 O.M.B.R. 317.
44 *Heathcote* v. *Regional Municipality of Hamilton-Wentworth* (1979), 8 O.M.B.R. 303.
45 *Ginou* v. *Regional Municipality of York* (1979), 8 O.M.B.R. 332.
46 *Ottawa-Carleton, supra* note 18, 172.
47 *Roamin' Stables Ltd.* v. *Town of Markham Committee of Adjustment* (1988), 21 O.M.B.R. 482.
48 See, for example, *Witteveen Meats Ltd.* v. *Township of South Dumfries Committee of Adjustment* (1993), 27 O.M.B.R. 102; *MacMillan* v. *County of Prescott and Russell Land Division Committee* (1993), 28 O.M.B.R. 141.
49 *Cameron* v. *County of Bruce* (1978), 7 O.M.B.R. 460; *Re Township of South Dumfries Restricted Area By-law 17-77* (1979), 9 O.M.B.R. 109.
50 *Re Township of Nichol Restricted Area By-law 897* (1977), 6 O.M.B.R. 489; *Re Newmarket Planning Area Official Plan* (1979), 8 O.M.B.R. 319.
51 *982136 Ontario Ltd.* v. *Township of Essa* (1998), 35 O.M.B.R. 497.

52 *Re Township of Nepean Restricted Area By-law 73-76* (1979), 9 O.M.B.R. 36.
53 *Re Township of Haldimand Zoning By-law 1-H-86* (1987), 20 O.M.B.R. 170.
54 *Reid* v. *Essa* (1988), 21 O.M.B.R. 189.
55 *Planning and Municipal Statute law Amendment Act, 1994,* S.O. 1994, c. 23, s. 3(5), (6).
56 *Land Use Planning and Protection Act, 1996,* S.O. 1996, c. 4, s. 3.
57 *Concorde Square Ltd.* v. *City of North York* (1991), 24 O.M.B.R. 82.
58 *Re Township of Front of Yonge By-law 7-88* (1990), 23 O.M.B.R. 235.
59 *Re Township of West Carleton Zoning By-law 36-89* (1990), 23 O.M.B.R. 257. There was no discussion here of 'have regard to'; rather, it was implied by the public interest rationale cited.
60 *Ottawa-Carleton, supra* note 18, 181–2.
61 *Re Township of Burleigh and Anstruther Zoning By-law 114-1991* (1993), 28 O.M.B.R. 417.
62 See, for example: *Re Town of Flamborough Official Plan Amendment 31* (1994), 30 O.M.B.R. 411 at 418; *Remer Holdings Ltd.* v. *Regional Municipality of Ottawa-Carleton* (1994), 30 O.M.B.R. 466; *Re Township of Dummer Official Plan* (1995), 31 O.M.B.R. 36.
63 See *Landco Developments Inc.* v. *Regional Municipality of Niagara* (1993), 29 O.M.B.R. 140 at 142.
64 *Township of Oro-Medonte Official Plan Amendment 39* (1995), 31 O.M.B.R. 15.
65 *Remer, supra* note 62.
66 *Daniels Lakeshore Corporation* v. *City of Etobicoke* (1992), 26 O.M.B.R. 208 at 226.
67 *Re City of Etobicoke Official Plan Amendments C-65-86 and C-82-88* (1993), 27 O.M.B.R. 129 at 204-6 [commonly referred to as the Etobicoke motel strip decision].
68 *Re Township of Uxbridge Zoning By-law 96-106* (1997), 35 O.M.B.R. 221; *Re County of Bruce Official Plan Amendment No. 4* (1999), 39 O.M.B.R. 40; *Re Township of Hamilton Zoning By-law 99-45* (2000), 40 O.M.B.R. 316.
69 *Reid* v. *County of Bruce* (1999), 38 O.M.B.R. 440.
70 See *West Carleton, supra* note 59 at 260; *Standard Aggregates Inc.* v. *County of Grey Planning Approval Committee* (1993), 27 O.M.B.R. 378 at 382.
71 *Ottawa-Carleton, supra* note 18.
72 *Ministry of Natural Resources* v. *Young* (1987), 20 O.M.B.R. 156.
73 *Re Harold Sutherland Construction Ltd. and Township of Keppel* (1990), 23 O.M.B.R. 129 at 137. See also *Young, ibid.* at 160; *Standard Aggregates, supra* note 70, 382.
74 *Woodgreen Community Housing Inc.* v. *City of Toronto Committee of Adjustment* (1993), 27 O.M.B.R. 1; *Serra* v. *Township of Sandwich West Committee of Adjustment* (1991), 24 O.M.B.R. 316; *Bay-Elizabeth Construction Ltd.* v. *City of Toronto*

(1992), 26 O.M.B.R. 422. An unusual aspect of *Serra* is that the board considered the housing policy statement without it being raised by either of the parties.
75 *City of Toronto* v. *Social Housing Coalition* (1994), 30 O.M.B.R. 136 at 138–39. See also *Woodgreen, supra* note 74; *Ram-Land Corporation* v. *City of North York* (8 June 1990), No. O 900011 (O.M.B.).
76 *Woodtree Co-operative Inc.* v. *City of Toronto Committee of Adjustment* (1991), 25 O.M.B.R. 312. This should be contrasted with the decision in *Woodgreen, supra* note 74 as an illustration that, while the board has been consistent in the application of this balancing policy, it may tip the balance either way, depending on the facts before it. See also *Van Loenen* v. *County of Lennox and Addington Land Division Committee* (1992), 26 O.M.B.R. 85; *Tahanen Non-profit Homes Corp.* v. *City of Toronto* (1993), 27 O.M.B.R. 62; *Re City of Oshawa Zoning By-law 108-89 and 125-89* (1992), 26 O.M.B.R. 336; *Wheeler* v. *City of Sarnia Committee of Adjustment* (1996), 32 O.M.B.R. 427; *Gallivan* v. *City of Ottawa Committee of Adjustment* (1996), 33 O.M.B.R. 42.
77 *LaPrade* v. *City of Ottawa* (1993), 33 O.M.B.R. 39.
78 *Ministry of Municipal Affairs and Housing* v. *McKee* (1998), 36 O.M.B.R. 115.
79 *Planning Amendment Act, 1989*, S.O. 1989, c. 5, s. 2.
80 Section 2 was amended by the Planning and Municipal Law Statute Amendment Act, 1994, S.O. 1994, c. 23, s. 5 to require that, in addition to the Minister, 'the council of a municipality, a local board, a planning board and the Municipal Board' also had regard to matters of provincial interest. This amendment was made too late in the review period to affect the decisions analysed here. In any event, as described here, the board did not ignore matters of provincial interest prior to 1994.
81 *Etobicoke, supra* note 67.
82 For example, the government declared the secondary plan, dealing with detailed planning issues, to be a matter of provincial interest, and retained a firm of design consultants to prepare specific design guidelines for development proposals. The board considered the design guidelines to be generally acceptable on planning grounds, but subjected them to considerable amendment to meet the many concerns raised by the affected property owners.
83 *Re Regional Municipality of Durham Official Plan Amendment 233* (1993), 28 O.M.B.R. 90.
84 *Memorial Gardens Canada Ltd.* v. *Town of Whitchurch-Stouffville* (1997), 34 O.M.B.R. 424 at 428. See also *Barnhardt* v. *Town of Fort Erie* (1995), 31 O.M.B.R. 76.
85 *Lapointe* v. *Ministry of Municipal Affairs* (1995), 31 O.M.B.R. 495; *Re Town of*

Bradford West Gwillimbury Official Plan Amendment No. 17 (1997), 34 O.M.B.R. 176.
86 For a detailed analysis of how the OMB has dealt with issues of air, water, and soil pollution, see Chipman, *Planning and Pollution*. The author analysed 406 decisions of the board, made between 1984 and 1993, in which significant pollution issues were raised.
87 *Re Township of Mono Restricted Area By-law 875* (17 May 1971), No. R 96-69 (O.M.B.).
88 *Town of Orangeville* v. *Township of East Garafraxa* (1974), 2 O.M.B.R. 326.
89 *Bodnaruk* v. *Township of Amabel Committee of Adjustment* (1993), 29 O.M.B.R. 61. The board's real reason for approving the minor variance appears to have been the application of its own impact policy, and its conclusion that the proposed use would have no impact on the neighbours.
90 *Re Township of Gosfield South Official Plan Amendment 15* (1993), 29 O.M.B.R. 339.
91 *Re Township of Mulmer Planning Area Official Plan* (1976), 5 O.M.B.R. 317; *Mclaughlin* v. *Town of Caledon* (1977), 6 O.M.B.R. 385; *Niagara Escarpment Commission* v. *Regional Municipality of Halton Land Division Committee* (1991), 25 O.M.B.R. 285.
92 *Re Town of Caledon East and Lawson Subdivision* (1979), 9 O.M.B.R. 188.
93 *Chedoke Terrace Inc.* v. *City of Hamilton* (1993), 29 O.M.B.R. 430 at 465.
94 E.g., *Guidelines on Noise and New Residential Development Adjacent to Freeways; Interim Stormwater Quality Control Guidelines for New Development*.
95 For the interpretation of ministry guidelines see *Re Township of Amaranth Zoning By-law 31-86* (1987), 20 O.M.B.R. 385; *Sutherland, supra* note 73; *Re Township of Sydenham By-law 1989-26* (1992), 26 O.M.B.R. 317.
96 *Re City of Nanticoke Official Plan Amendment 16* (1990), 23 O.M.B.R. 391.
97 *Gosfield South, supra* note 90, 349.
98 *Ottawa-Carleton, supra* note 18, 161.
99 *Legentil* v. *Town of LaSalle Committee of Adjustment* (1995), 31 O.M.B.R. 245 at 249.

6: A Tribunal Out of Time

1 One should keep in mind that the board does so partly because the planning process is biased in that direction. Notice is generally required to be given to property owners only, so that tenants are less likely to be aware of applications which might affect them. It is obvious that in virtually all applications the owners of properties subject to them appear as parties. It is often, although not always, clear from decisions that neighbouring objectors are property owners rather than tenants. In any event, whether parties are own-

ers or tenants, it is their local and immediate interests and concerns that are the focus of the board's consideration far more frequently than what can be identified as general public concerns or the concerns of those members of the public who are not represented at the hearings.
2 For a limited discussion of the time and monetary costs of taking part in board hearings, see Chipman, *Planning and Pollution*, 105–112.
3 The board also, until recently, heard a large number of assessment appeals. These are not municipal matters, however, but are quasi-judicial hearings of appeals of decisions of provincially appointed assessment review boards. It does not exercise policy-related discretion in this area, but, like an appeal court, applies the provisions of the Assessment Act to the facts before it.
4 Municipal Act, R.S.B.C. 1996, c. 323, s. 890(3), (6).
5 Municipal Government Act, R.S.A. 1999, c. M-26.1, s. 629(a), (b).
6 The recent history of dealing with proposals for large-scale residential development on the Oak Ridges Moraine, a major open space and ground water recharge area north of Toronto, provides an example of what can happen when political pressures become too great and force the province to take direct responsibility for decisions it had hitherto left to the board. For several years the current Progressive Conservative government relied on the board to deal with the many development applications for this area. Early in 2001, however, when faced with mounting public pressure, it passed legislation placing a temporary development limitation on some of the Moraine lands and a stay of indefinite duration on the board's hearing of any appeals pertaining to these lands. These pressures continued to increase, the government lost a by-election in a previously strongly held riding in the area, and, in late 2001, it introduced legislation placing an ongoing freeze on development on much of the Moraine, effectively precluding the board from playing any role.

Bibliography

Abel, A. 'The Dramatis Personae of Administrative Law' (1972) 10 Osgoode Hall L.J. 61.
Attorney General's Committee on Administrative Procedure, *Administrative Procedure in Government Agencies*. Washington: Senate Document No. 8, 77th Congress, 1st session, 1941. Reprint, Charlottesville: University Press of Virginia, 1968.
Adeyinka, A-J.G. *Telecommunications Reform: Theories, Principles and Policies*. S.J.D. thesis, University of Toronto, 1992.
Adler, G.M. *Land Planning by Administrative Regulation: The Policies of the Ontario Municipal Board*. Toronto: University of Toronto Press, 1971.
Armstrong, C., and H.V. Nelles. *Monopoly's Moment: The Organization and Regulation of Canadian Utilities, 1830–1930*. Philadelphia: Temple University Press, 1986.
Arthurs, H.W. *Law and Learning: Report to the Social Sciences and Humanities Council of Canada by the Consultative Group on Research and Education in Law*. Ottawa: Social Sciences and Humanities Council of Canada, April 1983.
– 'Rethinking Administrative Law: A Slightly Dicey Business.' (April 1979). 17(1) Osgoode Hall L.J. 1
Baggaley, C. *The Emergence of the Regulatory State in Canada, 1867–1939*. Ottawa: Economic Council of Canada, 1981.
Baldwin, J.R. *The Regulatory Agency and the Public Corporation: The Canadian Air Transport Industry*. Cambridge, Mass.: Ballinger, 1975.
Becker, G. 'Comment' (August 1976) 19 J. L. & Econ. 245.
Bernstein, M.H. *Regulating Business by Independent Commission*. Princeton: Princeton University Press, 1955.
Bilson, B. *The Canadian Law of Nuisance*. Toronto: Butterworths, 1990.

Bjork, G.C. *Life, Liberty, and Property: The Economics and Politics of Land Use Planning and Environmental Controls.* Lexington, Mass.: D.C. Heath, 1980.

Blachy, F.E., and M.E. Oatman, *Federal Regulatory Action and Control.* Washington: Brookings Institution, 1940.

Bossons, J. *Reforming Planning in Ontario: Strengthening the Municipal Role.* Toronto: Ontario Economic Council, 1978.

Boyer, M.C. *Dreaming the Rational City: The Myth of American City Planning.* Cambridge, Mass.: MIT Press, 1983.

Breton, A. *The Regulation of Private Economic Activity.* Montreal: C.D. Howe Research Institute, 1976.

Brown-John, C.L. *Canadian Regulatory Agencies: Quis custodiet ipsos custodes?.* Toronto: Butterworths, 1981.

Buckley, R.A. *The Law of Nuisance.* London: Butterworths, 1996.

Bureau of Municipal Research. *Urban Development and the Ontario Municipal Board.* Toronto: Bureau of Municipal Research, 1971.

Cairns, R.D. *Rationales for Regulation.* Technical Report, no. 2, Ottawa: Economic Council of Canada, October 1980.

Cary, W.L. *Politics and the Regulatory Agencies.* New York: McGraw-Hill, 1967.

Caves, R.E. *Air Transport and Its Regulators.* Cambridge, Mass.: Harvard University Press, 1962.

Chipman, J.G. *Planning and Pollution: A Study of the Ontario Municipal Board in Dealing with Pollution Issues, 1984–1993.* Ll.M. thesis, University of Toronto, 1994.

Commission on Planning and Development Reform in Ontario. *New Planning for Ontario: Final Report Summary and Recommendations.* Toronto: Commission on Planning and Development Reform in Ontario, June 1993.

Consultative Group on Research and Education in Law. *Law and Learning: Report to the Social Sciences and Humanities Research Council of Canada by the Consultative Group on Research and Education in Law.* Ed. H.W. Arthurs. Ottawa: Social Sciences and Research Council of Canada, April 1983.

Corry, J.A. *The Growth of Government Activities since Confederation.* Ottawa: King's Printer, 1939.

Crampton, R.C. 'The Why, Where and How of Broadened Public Participation in the Administrative Process' (1972), 60 Georgetown L.R. 525 at 529.

Cullingworth, J.B. *Ontario Planning: Notes on the Comay Report on the Ontario Planning Act.* Paper No. 19, Papers on Planning and Design. Department of Urban and Regional Planning, University of Toronto, October 1978.

Cushman, R.E. *The Independent Regulatory Commission.* New York: Oxford University Press, 1941.

Da Costa, D.M., and R.J. Balfour. *Property Law: Cases, Texts and Materials.* Toronto: Emond-Montgomery, 1982.

de Smith, S.A. *Judicial Review of Administrative Action.* London: Stevens, 1960.

Dakin, J. *Toronto Planning: A Planning Review of the Legal and Jurisdictional Contexts from 1912 to 1970.* Papers on Planning and Design, no. 3. Toronto: University of Toronto Department of Urban and Regional Planning, 1974.

Davis, K.C. *Discretionary Justice: A Preliminary Inquiry.* Baton Rouge: Louisiana State University Press, 1969.

Diver, C. 'Policymaking Paradigms in Administrative Law' (1981) 95 Harvard L. Rev. 393.

Downs, A. *Inside Bureaucracy.* Boston: Little, Brown, 1967.

Dwivedi, O.P., ed., *Resources and the Environment: Policy Perspectives for Canada.* Toronto: McClelland and Stewart, 1980.

Eckert, R.D. 'On the Incentives of Regulators: The Case of Taxicabs' (Spring 1973) 14 Pub. Choice 83.

Economic Council of Canada, *Responsible Regulation: An Interim Report.* Ottawa: Ministry of Supply and Services, 1978.

Ellickson, R.C. 'Alternatives to Zoning: Covenants, Nuisance Rules and Fines as Land Use Controls' (1973) U. Chicago L. Rev. 681.

Farris, M.T., and R.J. Sampson, *Public Utilities: Regulation, Management and Ownership.* Boston: Houghton, Mifflin, 1973.

Fischel, W.A. *The Economics of Zoning Laws: A Property Rights Approach to American Land Use Controls.* Baltimore: Johns Hopkins University Press, 1985.

Flathman, R.E. *The Public Interest: An Essay Concerning the Normative Discourse of Politics.* New York: Wiley, 1966.

Foote, S.B. 'Independent Agencies under Attack: A Sceptical View of the Importance of the Debate' (April/June 1988) Duke L.J. 223.

Frankena, M.W., and D.T. Scheffman, *Economic Analysis of Provincial Land Use Policies in Ontario.* Toronto: Ontario Economic Council, 1980.

Friedrich C.J., ed., *Nomos V: The Public Interest.* New York: Atherton Press, 1962.

Friedrich, C.J., and E.S. Mason. *Public Policy.* Cambridge, Mass.: Harvard University Press, 1940.

Frisken, F. 'Planning and Servicing the Greater Toronto Area: The Interplay of Provincial and Municipal Interests.' In *Metropolitan Governance: American/Canadian Intergovernmental Perspectives,* ed. D.N. Rotblatt and A. Sancton. Berkeley: Institute of Governmental Studies Press, 1993.

Frug, G.E. 'The Ideology of Bureaucracy in American Law' (April 1984) 97(6) Harvard L. Rev. 1276.

Garrett, M.A. *Land Use Regulation: The Impacts of Alternative Land Use Rights.* New York: Praeger, 1987.

Glaeser, M.G. *Public Utilities in American Capitalism.* New York: Macmillan, 1957.

Government of Ontario. *Food Land Guidelines: A Policy Statement of the Government of Ontario on Planning for Agriculture.* Toronto: Queen's Printer, 1978.
– *Foodland Preservation Policy Statement (Draft).* Toronto: Queen's Printer, 1986.
– *Green Paper on Planning for Agriculture: Food Land Guidelines.* Toronto: Queen's Printer, 1977.
– *White Paper on the Planning Act.* Toronto: Queen's Printer, May 1979.
– *Guidelines Directory: A Listing of Provincial Policies and Guidelines Related to Land Development.* Toronto: Queen's Printer, 1993.
Hahn, R.W., and J.A. Hird. 'The Costs and Benefits of Regulation: Review and Synthesis.' Yale J. Reg. 233 (1991).
Hamilton, S.W. *Regulation and Other Forms of Government Intervention Regarding Real Property.* Technical Report No. 13. Ottawa: Economic Council of Canada, July 1981.
Hartle, D.G. *Public Policy Decision Making and Regulation.* Montreal: Institute for Research on Public Policy, 1979.
Harvey, J. *Urban Land Economics.*, 3d ed. (London: MacMillan, 1992).
Hayek, F.A. *The Constitution of Liberty.* Chicago: Henry Regnery, 1960, 1972.
Held, V. *The Public Interest and Individual Interests.* New York: Basic Books, 1970.
Herring, E.P. *Public Administration and the Public Interest.* New York: McGraw-Hill, 1936.
Hibbets, B.J. *A Change of Mind: The Supreme Court of Canada and the Board of Railway Commissioners, 1903–1939.* Ll.M. thesis, University of Toronto, 1986.
Hirschleifer, J. 'Comment' (August 1976) 19 J. L. & Econ. 241.
Hulchanski, J.D. *The Evolution of Ontario's Early Land Use Planning Regulations, 1900–1920.* Toronto: University of Toronto Centre for Urban and Community Studies, 1982.
Humphries, C.W. *'Honest Enough to Be Bold': The Life and Times of Sir James Pliny Whitney.* Toronto: University of Toronto Press, 1985.
Huntington, S.P. 'The Marasmus of the ICC: The Commission, the Railroads, and the Public Interest' (April 1952) 61(4) Yale L.J. 467.
Hutchinson, A.C. 'The Rise and Fall of Administrative Law and Scholarship' (1985) 48 Mod. L. Rev. 293.
Jaffary, K.D., and S.M. Makuch, *Local Decision-Making and Administration: A Study for the Royal Commission on Metropolitan Toronto.* Toronto: Royal Commission on Metropolitan Toronto, June 1977.
Janisch, H.N. 'The Role of the Independent Regulatory Agency in Canada' (1978) 27 U.N.B.L.J. 83.
Jones, T.H. 'Administrative Law, Regulation and Legitimacy' (Winter 1989) 16(4) J. L. & Soc. 410.

Jordan, W.A. 'Producer Protection, Prior Market Structure and the Effects of Government Regulation' (April 1972) 15(1) J.L. & Econ. 151.
Joskow, P.L. 'Inflation and Environmental Concern: Structural Change in the Process of Public Utility Price Regulation' (October 1974) 17 J. L. & Econ. 291.
Jowell, J.L. *Law and Bureaucracy: Administrative Discretion and the Limits of Legal Action.* Port Washington, N.Y.: Dunellen, 1975.
Kaplan, H. *Reform, Planning and City Politics: Montreal, Winnipeg, Toronto.* Toronto: University of Toronto Press, 1982.
Lamer, A. 'Administrative Tribunals: Future Prospects and Possibilities' (1991–92) 5 Cdn. J. of Admin. Law and Pract. 107.
Lefcoe, G. *Land Development Law: Cases and Materials.* New York: Bobbs-Merrill, 1974.
Leiserson, A. *Administrative Regulation: A Study in Representation of Interests.* Chicago: University of Chicago Press, 1942.
Lewin, L. *Self-Interest and Public Interest in Western Politics.* Oxford: Oxford University Press, 1991.
Macaulay, R.W. *Directions: Review of Ontario's Regulatory Agencies.* Toronto: Management Board of Cabinet, September 1989.
MacFarlane, C.B. *Land Use Planning: Procedure, Practice and Policy.* Toronto: Carswell, 1994.
Mandelker, D.R. *The Zoning Dilemma: A Legal Strategy for Urban Change.* New York: Bobbs-Merrill, 1971.
McAuslan, P. *The Ideologies of Planning Law.* Oxford: Pergamon, 1980.
McKeough, Hon. W. Darcy. 'Presentation of Design for Development: Toronto-Centred Region.' 5 May 1970.
McRuer, J.C. Hon. *Royal Commission Inquiry into Civil Rights.* Toronto: Queen's Printer, 1968.
Meyer, W.J. *Public Good and Public Authority: A Pragmatic Proposal.* Port Washington, N.Y.: Kennikat Press, 1975.
Minister of Municipal Affairs and Minister of Housing. Land Use Planning for Housing, 13 July 1989.
Minister of Municipal Affairs and Minister of Natural Resources. *Flood Plain Planning* (11 August 1988).
– *Mineral Aggregate Resources* (9 May 1986).
– *Wetlands* (14 May 1992).
Ministry of Agriculture and Food, *A Strategy for Ontario Farmland.* Toronto: Queen's Printer, March 1976.
Miron, J.R. *House, Home and Community: Progress in Housing Canadians, 1945–1986.* Montreal: McGill-Queens University Press, 1993.

Mitnick, B.M. *The Political Economy of Regulation.* New York: Columbia University Press, 1980.

Morris, A.A., ed., *Public and Private Rights in Land: Regulation vs. Taking.* Seattle: Institute for Environmental Studies, University of Washington, 1976.

Nelson, R.H. *Zoning and Property Rights: An Analysis of the American System of Land-Use Regulation.* Cambridge, Mass.: MIT Press, 1977.

Niskanen, W. 'Bureaucrats and Politicians' (December 1975) 18(3) J. L. & Econ. 645.

Noll, R.G. *Reforming Regulation: An Evaluation of the Ash Council Proposals.* Washington: Brookings Institution, 1971.

Nonet, P. *Administrative Justice: Advocacy and Change in a Government Agency.* New York: Russell Sage Foundation, 1969.

Ontario Economic Council. *Government Regulation: Issues and Alternatives.* Toronto: Ontario Economic Council, 1978.

– *Subject to Approval: A Review of Municipal Planning in Ontario.* Toronto: Ontario Economic Council, 1973.

Ontario Municipal Board, 1st to 84th Annual Reports. Toronto: Ontario Municipal Board, 1907 to 1994.

Owen, B.M., and R. Braeutigam, *The Regulation Game: Strategic Use of the Administrative Process.* Cambridge, Mass.: Ballinger, 1978.

Palmer, J., and J. Erkkila, *The Ontario Municipal Board: A Study in the Resolution of Conflicts between Private and Social Welfare Functions.* Ottawa: Canadian Consumer Council, 1972.

Peltzman, S. 'Toward a More General Theory of Regulation' (August 1976) 19 J. L. & Econ. 211.

Planning Act Review Committee. *Report of the Planning Act Review Committee.* Toronto: Queen's Printer, April 1977.

Posner, R.A. 'Taxation by Regulation' (1971) 2 Bell J. Econ. & Pol. Sci. 22.

– 'Theories of Economic Regulation' (1974) 5 Bell J. Econ. & Manage. Sci. 335.

Reich, C.A. 'The Law of the Planned Society' (1966) 75 Yale L.J. 1227.

– 'The New Property' (1974) 73 Yale L.J. 733.

Schubert, G. *The Public Interest: A Critique of the Theory of a Political Concept.* Glencoe, Ill.: Free Press of Glencoe, 1960.

Schultz, R. 'The Impact of Regulation: Panel Discussion' (Autumn 1979) 4 Can. Pub. Pol. 486.

Scott, M. *American City Planning Since 1890.* Berkeley: University of California Press, 1969.

Select Committee on the Ontario Municipal Board. *Proceedings, Select Committee*

on the Ontario Municipal Board. Toronto: Select Committee on the Ontario Municipal Board, various dates in 1972.
- *Report of the Select Committee on the Ontario Municipal Board.* Toronto: Select Committee on the Ontario Municipal Board, 21 November 1972.

Shepherd, W.G. *The Treatment of Market Power: Antitrust, Regulation and Private Enterprise.* New York: Columbia University Press, 1975.

Siegan, B.H. 'Non-Zoning in Houston' (1970) J. L. & Econ. 71.

Sossin, L. 'The Politics of Discretion: Toward a Critical Theory of Public Administration' (1993) 36 Can. Pub. Admin. 364.

Stanbury, W.T., ed. *Government Regulation: Scope, Growth, Process.* Montreal: Institute for Research on Public Policy, 1980.
- *Studies on Regulation in Canada.* Toronto: Institute for Research on Public Policy, 1987.

Stigler, G.H. 'The Theory of Economic Regulation' (Spring 1971) 2 Bell J. Econ. & Manage. Sci. 3.
- 'Law or Economics' (1992) 35 J. L. & Econ. 455.

Stone, A. *Regulation and Its Alternatives.* Washington: Congressional Quarterly Press, 1982.

Task Force on Regulatory Commissions of the Commission on Organization of the Executive Branch of Government. *Task Force Report on Regulatory Commissions,* 1949.

Tullock, G. *The Politics of Bureaucracy.* Washington: Public Affairs Press, 1965.

United States Senate, Committee on the Judiciary. *Report on Regulatory Agencies to the President-Elect.* 1960.

Weingast, B.R. *A Positive Model of Public Policy Formation: The Case of Regulatory Agency Behaviour.* Working Paper no. 25. St Louis: Centre for the Study of American Business, 1978.

Willis, J.A., ed. *Canadian Boards at Work.* Toronto: Macmillan, 1941.

Wilson, J.Q. *The Politics of Regulation.* New York: Basic Books, 1980.

Index of Cases

1099184 Ontario Ltd. v. City of London, 34
251555 Projects Ltd. and Morrison, 24–5, 100
715113 Ontario Ltd. and City of Ottawa, 95, 96
Archipelago (Township) Interim Control By-law 89-48, 94
Ashby, Re, 19
Ashland Oil Co. v. City of Thunder Bay, 123

Barrie Annexation, Re, 161, 162, 163, 187
Brookvalley Holdings Ltd. v. Town of Whitby, 121

Caledon (Township) Official Plan, 156–7, 159, 162, 187
Caledon East (Town) and Lawson Subdivision, Re, 30
Central Ontario Coalition Concerning Hydro Transmission Systems and Ontario Hydro, Re, 64–5
Chedoke Terrace Inc. v. City of Hamilton, 42, 45
Claverly Investments Ltd. v. Borough of East York, 79

Cloverdale and Township of Etobicoke, Re, 24
Clutterbuck v. Township of Hamilton, 137
Crofton Developments Ltd. v. Borough of Scarborough, 79

Darte v. City of St Catharines, 123

Equity Waste Management of Canada and Corporation of the Town of Halton Hills, Re, 94, 95, 96

Glinert v. Toronto, 101
Grant v. Art Construction Ltd., 101
Grimsby (Town) Official Plan and By-laws, Re, 157–8

Hamilton-Wentworth Official Plan Amendment 126, Re, 119
Highbury Estates, Re, 75, 137
Hopedale Developments Ltd. v. Town of Oakville, 24, 78, 198

IPCF Properties v. City of Windsor, 22, 159
Joint Board and Regional Municipality of Ottawa-Carleton, 65

250   Index of Cases

Keewatin (Town) Zoning By-law 94-613, Re, 121

Lavigne v. City of Cornwall, 86

Maiocco v. City of Guelph, 80
Martin v. Township of North Dorchester, 120
Maxine Holdings Ltd. v. Barrie, 29, 162
McLean v. Toronto Committee of Adjustment, 101
McNamara Corporation and Colekin Investments Ltd., 99–100
Mississauga Golf and Country Club, Re, 78

Nepean (Township) Restricted Area By-law, 46, 47
Nicholson v. Town of Markham, 80

Oakville (Town) Restricted Area By-law 1970-157, 122
Oshawa (City) Interim Control By-laws 134-89 and 105–90, Re, 48
Oshawa (City) Zoning By-laws 108-89 and 125-89, Re, 107
Ottawa-Carleton Official Plan Amendment No. 8, Re, 33, 88, 106, 107, 159, 170, 177

Perry and Taggart, Re, 100
Price Club v. City of Scarborough, 35, 51

Pugliese and Borough of North York, Re, 64

Richmond Hill (Town) v. Taylor, 118
Rodrigues v. Township of Erin, 165

St Catharines Restricted Area By-law 73-337, 122
Sarnia and District Association for the Mentally Retarded v. City of Sarnia, 109–10
Scarborough Transportation Corridor, Re, 141
South and Metcalfe Non-Profit Housing Corp. v. Town of Simcoe, 107
Spadina Expressway, Re, 32, 43, 76

Tollefson v. Township of Gloucester, 78, 79
Toronto (City) v. Social Housing Coalition, 178
Toronto Airways Ltd. v. Town of Markham, 162–3
Toronto-Metro Centre, Re, 43–4

Von Zuben v. Herman, 48

Wiswell v. Metropolitan Corporation of Greater Winnipeg, 63

Zadravec v. Town of Brampton, 63, 64, 67, 206

General Index

administrative agency, 3–4
administrative law, 4
adverse impact test, 19, 36–7, 45; adoption by OMB, 39–40; commercial competition, 127, 129–30; council decision-making adequacy, 86–7; double onus, 50; expectations principle, 41–3; —, neighbourhood character, 119–21; good planning, 104, 109–12; harm, credible perception of, 40–1; interference with council decisions, 71–2, 77; interim control by-laws, 94, 95–6; majority v. minority rights test, 43–5; *minor,* meaning of, 100–2; neighbourhood character, 118–19, 120, 122; OMB application, implications of, 49; provincial policies, subordination to, 6; public interest, subordination to, 45–9, 50–1; social housing, 132, 134, 135; statement of, 46, 50
affordable housing, 31, 32, 47–8
Aggregate Resources Act, 17
Agricultural Code of Practice, 150, 170–1; OMB, application of, 170–1

agricultural land protection, 32, 163–71. *See also* Agricultural Code of Practice; Food Land Guidelines; Foodland Preservation Policy Statement; Strategy for Ontario Farmland; Urban Development in Rural Areas
Alberta, 205, 207; Energy and Utilities Board, 205; Municipal Government Board, 205; Natural Resources Conservation Board, 205
approval procedures, adequacy of, 58, 59–71; application type, selection of, 67–9; decision data, 59–61; enhancement of, 69–70; notice, adequacy of, 66–7; —, requirements, 61–5; OMB policy, 59, 66–7, 70–1; —, 1971–1978, 59, 63–4, 66, 68, 70, 71; —, 1987–1994, 59, 64–5, 66–7, 68–9, 70, 71; —, 1995–2000, 59, 65, 68, 69; province, limited role of, 61; public confidence, ensuring, 65–6; public meetings; adequacy of, 66–7; —, requirements, 61–5; public participation in, 67–9

252 General Index

Barrie annexation application, 158, 161, 163
Board of Railway Commissioners, 10–11
British Columbia, 191, 206–7
British North America Act, 11
Bureau of Municipal Research, 19

Cabinet, Ontario. *See* Lieutenant Governor in Council, Ontario
capture of OMB, developers and municipalities, 55–6; developers and non-developer owners, 52–4; municipalities, 54; theory, 51–2
Central Ontario Lakeshore Urban Complex, 161, 162
commercial competition, 103, 124–31; adverse impact test, application of, 127, 129–30; applications, type of, 124; central business districts, impact on, 127, 128, 129–31; decision data, 124–6; market studies, reliance on, 127–8; OMB policy, 103, 126–7, 130–1; —, 1971–1978, 127–8, 131; —, 1987–1994, 127, 128–30; —, 1995–2000, 127, 130; planned commercial structure, 128–30
common law: OMB, adoption of test by, 39–40; implications of application of, 199–202; remedies, 37–9
Comprehensive Set of Policy Statements, 148, 150, 164, 173, 196
Congress, United States, 10
Consolidated Hearings Act, 1981, 65
council decision making, adequacy of, 58, 81–90; adverse impact test, application of, 86–7; decision data, 82–5; decision-making process, adequacy of, 88–9; deficiencies, correction of, 88; informed decisions, making of, 85–7; interim control by-laws, 87; OMB policy, 82, 85–7, 88, 89, 90; standards, establishment of, 89–90
council decisions, interference with, 58, 71–81; decision data, 72–4; municipal applications, 74–7; OMB policy, 71–2, 76–7, 78–9, 80–1; —, 1971–1978, 79–80; —, 1987–1994, 80; private applications, 77–80
critical legal studies, 7

Department of Municipal Affairs, 64
Design for Development, 160, 161
developers, influence of, 51–4, 55–6
double-onus test, 50, 94–5
Doyle, Sir Arthur Conan, 161

environmental protection policies, 182–4; decision data, 182; OMB policies, relationship with, 182–3. *See also* Ministry of Energy and the Environment guidelines; Niagara Escarpment Plan
Erkkila, J., 123

Flood Plain Planning, 172–3
Food Land Guidelines, 32, 147, 148, 150, 155, 164, 166–70, 173, 185, 188, 201; applications where considered, 167; OMB, application by; —, general, 166–7; —, 1971–1978, 167, 169; —, 1987–2000, 169–70; decision data, 167–9; matter of provincial interest, 166; official plans, equivalency with, 170; purpose of, 166–7
Foodland Preservation Policy Statement, 164

Frankena, M.W., 149, 159–60

general municipal plan, 18
good planning, 103, 104–12; approved official plans, —, conformity with, 104, 107–9, 111; —, distinguished from policies under consideration, 108; collateral issues, 107; decision data, 104, 105; impact and compatibility, 104, 106, 109–10, 111–12; matters representing, 106, 108, 110; OMB policy, 103, 104, 106–7, 107–9, 109–11, 111–12; —, 1971–1978, 108; —, 1987–1994, 108; —, 1995–2000, 108–9; process, adequacy of, 106; property rights, protection of, 110–12; provincial policies, conflict with, 109; public and private interests, tension between, 111–12; public interest, identification with, 33–4, 111–12; social housing, 133, 135; subordination to Land Use Planning for Housing policy statement, 177–9, 188; substantive elements, 106–7
government, Ontario, relationship with OMB, 24, 193–9
Green Paper on Planning for Agriculture, 164, 166, 169
Growth and Settlement Policy Guidelines, 181

Housing and Urban Development Institute of Canada, 52
Humphries, C.W., 12
Hutchinson, A.C., 6

interim control by-laws, 15, 58, 91–7; adverse impact test, modified application of, 94; appeal to OMB, 16; conditions precedent test, 93–4; decision data, 91–2; decision to adopt, adequacy of, 87; OMB policy, 93–4, 97; —, 1987–1994, 95–6; —, 1995–2000, 96; private interests, subordination to public interest, 48–9, 95–6; purpose, 15–16; test developed by OMB, 69, 93–4
interprovincial railways, 10

Jaffary, K.D., 23, 106

Kennedy, J.A., majority v. minority rights test, 43; Select Committee, appearance before, 23

Land Use Planning for Housing, 30, 134, 172–3; purpose, 172; subordination to adverse impact test, 177–9, 188
land use planning, Ontario; limited provincial direction, 22, 23–4; new planning system in 1946, 18; role of OMB, 3
Lane, W.T., 38
legal ideology, 6–8; legal system, most appropriate, 6; private interest, 7; private law, application to planning, 199–202; public interest, 7, 8; public participation, 7, 8, 69–70
legislature, Ontario, 11, 23
Liberal government, Ontario, 195, 196
Lieutenant Governor in Council, Ontario, 146, 148; matters of provincial interest, 180; petitions to, 146; policy statements adopted by, 150

MacBeth Committee. *See* Select Committee of the Legislature on the Ontario Municipal Board

Makuch, S.M., 23, 106

Manitoba, 205; Municipal Board, 191, 205

matters of provincial interest, 179–81; declarations of, 180–1; evidence, treating as, 181; OMB, application of, 180–1; provincial guidelines, 181. *See also* Growth and Settlement Policy Guidelines; Oak Ridges Moraine Area Implementation Guidelines

McAuslan, P., 7–8

methodology, 8, 209–11; decision database, 210; decisions, coding and analysis, 210–11; parties, 8, 211; policy areas for review, 210; review period, 209–10

Mineral Aggregate Resources, 172–3

Minister of Mines, 182

Minister of Municipal Affairs. *See* Minister of Municipal Affairs and Housing

Minister of Municipal Affairs and Housing, agricultural land, protection of, 163–4; matters of provincial interest, 148, 180; official plans, approval of, 15, 29, 74, 84–5, 205; policy statements, approval of, 149

Ministry of Agriculture and Food. *See* Ministry of Agriculture, Food and Rural Affairs

Ministry of Agriculture, Food and Rural Affairs, 147, 164, 166, 170, 171

Ministry of Energy and the Environment, 147, 148, 149; guidelines, 182, 183–4

Ministry of Housing, 148

Ministry of Municipal Affairs. *See* Ministry of Municipal Affairs and Housing

Ministry of Municipal Affairs and Housing, 15, 147, 149, 152, 160; 'fast-track' procedures, 135

Ministry of Natural Resources, 47, 147, 149

Ministry of Transportation, 147, 148

Ministry of Treasury and Intergovernmental Affairs, 160

minor, meaning of, 58, 97–102; cumulative impact test, 101; decision data, 98, 99, 100–1; impact test and statutory interpretation, 100–2; judicial test, application of, 98–101; OMB policy, 97, 100–2

minor variances, 16; adequacy of approval procedures, 68, 70; appeal to OMB, 16; purpose, 16

Municipal Amendment Act, 1921, 18–19, 45

municipal conduct, standards of, 6

municipal councils, 6; adequacy of decision making. *See* council decision making, adequacy of

municipal debentures, 17

municipal interests, equation with, 29–31, 32, 34

municipal planning decisions, review by province, 194

municipal street railways, 11

municipalities, influence of at OMB, 54–6

municipalities, involvement in hearings, 199; approval procedure adequacy, 59–61, 62; commercial competition, 126; council decision interference, 74; good planning,

104; Food Land Guidelines, 167–8; interim control by-laws, 91; *minor,* meaning of, 98; neighbourhood character, 116; social housing, 132

New Brunswick, 191
New Democratic Party government, Ontario, 13, 148, 195, 196–7
neighbourhood character, protection of, 103, 112–24; adverse impact test, application of, 118–19, 120, 122; decision data, 114–16; elements of, 117–19; expectations principle, 119–21; mixed use and marginal neighbourhoods, 121–3; OMB policy, 103, 112, 117–19, 119–21, 121–3, 123–4; —, 1971–1978, 117, 120–1; —, 1987–1994, 117–18, 120–1; —, 1995–2000, 112, 118, 121; OMB policy debate, 1960s, 112–14; planning standards, 117–19; preponderant character test, 118–19; property owners, rights of, 119–20; public interest in retention, 35–6, 120
neighbours, involvement in hearings, approval procedure adequacy, 61; commercial competition, 124, 126; council decision interference, 74; Food Land Guidelines, 168; good planning, 104; *minor,* meaning of, 98; neighbourhood character, 114; social housing, 132
Niagara Escarpment, 182
Niagara Escarpment Plan, 183
non-developer owners, influence of at OMB, 52–4
notice and hearing requirements, 61–5

Nova Scotia, 205; Municipal Board, 192, 205, 206
nuisance, tort of, 37, 39

Oak Ridges Moraine, 148, 150
Oak Ridges Moraine Area Implementation Guidelines, 181
official plans, 15; appeal or referral to OMB, 15, 29; definition, 81; as expressions of public interest, 29, 30, 32; good planning, 104, 107–9; prematurity, 139–41; provincial policy statements, equating with, 176–7, 189; purpose, 15; role of OMB, 48, 74–5, 77
OMB. *See* Ontario Municipal Board
OMB industry, 208
Ontario Economic Council, 23, 44
Ontario Home Builders' Association, 52
Ontario Housing Action Program, 148–9
Ontario Municipal Board
annual reports, 28, 43, 72, 145–6
applications received, 20–1
balance between own policies and provincial policies, 186–9
chairs, 20
composition, 12–13, 20
establishment, 12
group public interest theory, application of, 28–9
hearings: conduct of, 13–15, 20, 199, 201; length and cost of, 14
independence of, 194–5, 197–8; interest evaluation by, 27; private law-oriented approach, 37. *See also* good planning; private interests; provincial policies; public interest

256 General Index

judicial challenges, lack of, 198
jurisdiction: financial, 12, 17; pit licences, 17
jurisdiction, planning: compared with other provinces, 4; interim control by-laws, 16; minor variances, 16, 25; official plans, 15, 17–18, 29–30, 74–5; planning generally, xi, 4, 20; plans of subdivision, 16, 24, 30; severances, 16, 24; site plans, 17; uniqueness, 4; zoning by-laws, 15, 18, 24, 75
members: appointment of, 13; lawyers as, 13, 20
'ombudsman,' as 43
Ontario Railway and Municipal Board, successor to, 12
planning appeal role, 15–17
planning tribunal, retention as, 200, 202–5, 206–8
policy development, 22–5; where no provincial policy, 159–60
policies, substitution of local decisions for own, 5–6
private lands, requiring purchase of, 46
province, relationship with, 159, 189–90, 192, 193–8
staffing, 14
studies of role of, 4–5
'value-added' considerations, 26–7
See also adverse impact test; capture of OMB; legal ideology; private interests; provincial policies
Ontario Municipal Board Act, 13, 46–7, 96
Ontario Railway Act, 11
Ontario Railway and Municipal Board, creation, 10–11, 13, 193–4; hearings, conduct of, 13, 36; municipal debt, 12; municipal utilities, 11–12; planning, 17–19, 112; street railways, 11–12; OMB, succeeded by, 12
Ontario Railway and Municipal Board Act, 11
onus on parties, 199; double-onus test, 50, 94–5
opponent, meaning of, 8
ORMB. See Ontario Railway and Municipal Board

Palmer, J., 123
Parliament, Canada, 10, 11
Parliament, sovereignty, position of OMB, 194–5
parties to hearings, defined, 8, 211
Planning Act, 19, 31; appeal from local planning decisions, 4; 'be consistent with' provincial policy, 173; changes since 1959, 18; enactment in 1946, 18; 'have regard to' provincial policy, 145, 173; interim control by-laws, 91; matters of provincial interest, 148, 179–80; minor variances, 25, 98, 99, 100; notice and hearing requirements, 61–3, 69, 206; official plans, 74–5, 77, 81, 139–40; petitions to Lieutenant Governor in Council, 146; plans of subdivision, 24, 75; prematurity, 136–7; procedure, focus on, 18, 23–4, 81–2; provincial role in planning, 147–8; public interest, 30, 31, 45; severances, 24; statements of provincial policy, 172; White Paper on, 147; zoning by-laws, 18, 45, 74–5, 77
Planning Act, 1983, 61, 66, 67, 81–2, 91, 134, 145, 146, 147, 158, 180, 189

Planning Act Review Committee, 23, 26, 28, 105

planning community, 33–4

plans of subdivision, appeal or referral to OMB, 16, 30; as expressions of public interest, 29; purpose, 16

prematurity, 103, 136–44; application type, 142–3; decision data, 137–9; development controls, 141; official plans, 139–41; OMB policy, 103, 136–7, 139, 141–4; —, 1971–1978, 140; —, 1987–2000, 140–1; —, 1995–2000, 142; planning issues, consideration of, 142–3; planning procedures, 144; planning studies, 141–2; procedural elements, 139–43; substantive elements, 143

preponderant character test, 118–19

private interests: common law test, adoption by OMB, 39–40; expectations principle, 41–3, 119–21; good planning, 110–12; harm, credible perception of, 40–1; and interim control by-laws, 48–9, 95–7; majority v. minority rights test, 43–5; official plans, 48; OMB, evaluation by, 49–51; protection of, 36–7, 110–11, 119–20; public interest, balance with, 47–9, 135; public interest, distinguished from, 34–6; theory, 21; zoning by-laws, 48

Progressive Conservative government, Ontario, 13, 148, 173, 195, 196

property owners, involvement in hearings, 199; approval procedure adequacy, 61; commercial competition, 126; Food Land Guidelines, 167–8; interim control by-laws, 92; minor, meaning of, 98; neighbourhood character, 114

province, involvement in hearings: approval procedure adequacy, 61; council decision interference, 74; council decision making, 84–5; Food Land Guidelines, 167–8; neighbourhood character, 114–15; provincial policies, 152–5, 162, 174–5; social housing, 132

provincial policies, 23; Barrie annexation, 158, 161; 'be bound by,' 188; decision data, 150–5; evidence, treatment as, 189; good planning, conflict with, 109; 'have regard to,' 187, 188; ministry guidelines, 146–7, 149; municipal planning policies, conflict with, 157–8; official plans as, 149; OMB, application of, 150–5, 157, 185–6, 187; —, balance with own policies, 186–9; —, freedom from subordination to, 157; —, frequency of consideration by, 151–2, 161–2; —, general approach taken by, 155–60; —, internal discussion of, 155–6; —, public interest, identification with, 31–4; —, relationship with province, 189–90; planning process, integration into, 184–6; policy statements, 148, 150; province, involvement in hearings, 152–5, 162, 174–5; social housing, 135; sources of, 146–50; subordination to OMB policies, 6, 195. *See also* affordable housing; agricultural land protection; environmental protection policies; matters of provincial interest; regional planning policy; statements of provincial policy

General Index

Provincial Policy Statement, 32, 148, 150, 173, 177, 179
provincial social housing policy, 132, 134
public interest, 5; adverse impact test, subordination to, 45–9, 50–1; geographic area of 'public' defined, 34–5; good planning, identification with, 33–4, 111–12; group public interest theory, 28–9, 31, 80, 105, 204; interim control by-laws, 48–9, 95–7; matters in, 31, 32, 34; *minor*, meaning of, 102; municipal councils, expressed in decisions of, 29, 32; municipal interests, equation with, 29–31, 32, 34; neighbourhood character, 35–6, 120; official plans, equation with 29, 30, 32; OMB, role of, 4; Planning Act references, 45; planning process, integrity of, 100–1; plans of subdivision, 29, 30; private interests, balance with, 47–9, 135; —, distinguished from, 34–6; provincial policies, limited identification with, 31–3; social housing, 132, 134, 135; theory, 21,28; zoning by-laws, 29, 30

regional planning policy, 160–3, 187; OMB, infrequent consideration of, 161. *See also* Central Ontario Lakeshore Urban Complex; Design for Development; Toronto-Centred Region Plan
regulation, theories of, 21–2, 202, 204; capture theory, 51–2; independence of tribunals, 194–5
restricted area by-laws. *See* zoning by-laws

Saskatchewan, 205, 206, 207; Municipal Board, 191, 205
Scheffman, D.T., 149, 159–60
Select Committee of the Legislature on the Ontario Municipal Board, 23, 57, 145
Sewell Report, 190
severances, 16; adequacy of approval procedures, 68; appeal or referral to OMB, 16; purpose, 16
site plans, 17; adequacy of approval procedures, 68
social housing, 47, 103, 131–6; adverse impact and, 132, 134, 135; decision data, 132–3; fast-tracking applications, 135, 136; good planning and, 133, 135; housing types included, 131; OMB policy, 103; —, 1971–1978, 131–3; —, 1987–1994, 134–5; —, 1995–2000, 135; provincial policies and, 135; public interest in, 132, 134, 135, 200
Sossin, L., 7
South Peel Servicing Scheme, 148
statements of provincial policy, 172–9; balancing with other issues, 177–9; 'be consistent with,' 173; decision data, 174–5; as evidence, 175–6, 181, 189; 'have regard to,' 145, 173; official plans, equivalency with, 176–7; OMB, application by, 175–9. *See also* Comprehensive Set of Policy Statements; Flood Plain Planning; Land Use Planning for Housing; Mineral Aggregate Resources; Provincial Policy Statement; Wetlands
Statutory Powers Procedure Act, 63, 65, 206

Strategy for Ontario Farmland, 164, 166
subdivision control. *See* plans of subdivision
supporter, meaning of, 8

Toronto-Centred Region, 147
Toronto-Centred Region Plan, 33, 147, 160–1, 162, 185

upper tier municipality; approval of official plans, 29
Urban Development in Rural Areas, 147, 150, 163–5, 170, 187; OMB, consideration by, 164–5, 187; purpose of, 165

Wetlands, 172–3
White Paper on the Planning Act, 147

York-Durham Servicing Scheme, 148

zoning by-laws, 15; approval procedures, adequacy of, 68–9; council decisions, interference with, 72; purpose, 15; OMB appeal to, 15; —, role of, 24, 48, 74–5, 77; protection of residential uses, 112–13